DAS BUCH ZUM MUSEUM DER AUS- UND EINWANDERUNG

THE MUSEUM FOR EMIGRATION AND IMMIGRATION BOOK

edition
DAH

EDITORIAL

Liebe Leserinnen, liebe Leser,

das „Buch zum Museum der Aus- und Einwanderung" ist mehr als ein reiner Ausstellungskatalog, es ist ein lebendiges Geschichtsbuch mit reichhaltigen Informationen, einzigartigen Bildern und spannenden Geschichten. So spiegelt es das Konzept des Museums wider, in dem Neugierde und Emotionalität ebenso erlaubt sind wie die Freude daran, sich eine eigene Meinung über das hochkomplexe Thema Migration zu bilden.
In dieser dritten Auflage ist auch der 2012 eröffnete Ausstellungsteil zu 300 Jahren Einwanderungsgeschichte nach Deutschland enthalten. Im Museum werden nun beide Perspektiven gezeigt: die der deutschen Übersee-Auswanderer und die derjenigen Europäer, die eine neue Heimat in Deutschland gefunden haben. Aber eben auch jene Einwanderungsgeschichten, deren Enden noch offen sind, wie beispielsweise diejenigen der syrischen Kriegsflüchtlinge, die vor allem 2014 und 2015 in die Bundesrepublik kamen.
Ich wünsche allen Leserinnen und Lesern das Vergnügen und die Anregung bei der Lektüre, die wir jeden Tag im Deutschen Auswandererhaus erfahren, und freue mich, Sie (wieder) in unserem Museum begrüßen zu dürfen.

Dear Reader,

The "The museum for emigration and immigration book" is more than an exhibition catalogue; this publication is also a vibrant history book that provides a wealth of information, unique illustrations and exciting stories. It therefore reflects the concept of the museum, which combines awakening curiosity and sensitivity, as well as the gratification of forming one's own opinion about the highly complex topic of migration.
This third edition includes the section from the 2012 exhibition, which covers the history of 300 years of migration to Germany. The museum now shows both perspectives, as seen by the German emigrants, and by the Europeans who have found a new home in Germany. But it also reveals the migrant stories whose outcome remain unclear, for example the stories of the Syrian war refugees who came to the Federal Republic of Germany in 2014 and 2015.
I hope that this publication will give you the same enjoyment and motivation that we experience in the German Emigration Center every day, and look forward to welcoming you (again) in our museum.

Dr. Simone Eick
Direktorin / Director

Bremerhaven, März / March 2017

INHALT
CONTENTS

DIE GLEICHZEITIGKEIT VOM KOMMEN UND GEHEN
300 Jahre deutsche Migrationsgeschichte

THE SIMULTANEOUS FLOW OF COMING AND GOING
300 years of German migration history

SIMONE EICK

Das Deutsche Auswandererhaus zeigt in seiner Dauerausstellung 300 Jahre Geschichte der deutschen Auswanderung nach Übersee und der Einwanderung nach Deutschland. Die Darstellung beginnt mit zwei Wanderungsbewegungen, zum einen mit den französischen Glaubensflüchtlingen, den Hugenotten, die ab 1685 in deutsche Länder und Städte kamen, und zum anderen mit den deutschen Pietisten, die für ihre Glaubensfreiheit 1683 in die britische Kolonie Pennsylvania zogen und dort die erste deutsche Stadt in Nordamerika gründeten – Germantown, heute ein Stadtteil Philadelphias. Denn Deutschland war in den letzten dreihundert Jahren oft zeitgleich Ein- und Auswanderungsland. Heute wandern jährlich über 100.000 Deutsche aus; es sind Ärzte, die in die Schweiz, nach Skandinavien, nach Österreich ziehen, und Facharbeiter, die in die USA und nach Australien gehen. Es kehren junge gut ausgebildete Deutsch-Türken in das Land ihrer Eltern und Großeltern zurück. Und zeitgleich kommen die syrischen Bürgerkriegsflüchtlinge genauso wie die Arbeitssuchenden aus Rumänien und Spanien.

Natürlich bestand Mitte der 1680er Jahre kein einheitliches deutsches Staatsgebiet wie heute, es herrschte Kleinstaaterei statt europäische Freizügigkeit. So wie damals ein Sachse eine Einreiseerlaubnis in Form eines Passes brauchte, um nach Brandenburg reisen zu dürfen, müssen heute Nichteuropäer ein Visum vorlegen, um in die Bundesrepublik zu kommen. Trotz dieser mal mehr, mal weniger hohen juristischen Hürden herrscht seit Jahrhunderten ein Kommen und Gehen, herrscht die Gleichzeitigkeit von Aus- und Einwanderung. Migration in Deutschland ist also immer beides: Emi- und Immigration. Jede Geschichte für sich ist spannend und ereignisreich, wie die beiden folgenden Darstellungen zeigen.

In its permanent exhibition, the German Emigration Center covers the history of 300 years of German migration overseas and immigration to Germany. The exhibition begins with two migration movements, the French religious refugees, the Huguenots, who came to German states and cities since 1685, and the German Pietists, who, in 1683, moved to the British colony of Pennsylvania in search of religious freedom; here they established the first German township, "Germantown," which is now a district of Philadelphia. In the past 300 hundred years, Germany was always both – and often an immigration and an emigration country at the same time. Today, approximately 100,000 Germans emigrate every year, for instance doctors who go to Switzerland, Scandinavia and Austria, and highly-skilled workers who go to the United States and Australia. Young, well-educated German-Turks return to the country their parents and grandparents left behind when they came to Germany. Syrian civil war refugees are coming at the same time as jobseekers from Romania and Spain. It goes without saying that German territories in the mid-1680s were not united as today; a patchwork of small states prevailed rather than European liberality. In much the same way a Saxonian needed an entry permit in the form of a passport to travel to Brandenburg, today non-European nationals must produce a visa to enter the Federal Republic of Germany. Despite these legal hurdles – sometimes higher, sometimes lower – a coming and going has endured for hundreds of years. Migration in Germany is therefore always both: emigration and immigration. Each individual story is exciting and eventful, as the following narratives show.

AUSWANDERUNG
EMIGRATION

NACH ÜBERSEE
Auswanderung und Flucht aus Deutschland in den letzten drei Jahrhunderten

OVERSEAS
Emigration and Flight from Germany during the Last Three Centuries

SIMONE EICK

Bremerhaven, im Jahr 1929

An der Columbuskaje: Der Passagierdampfer „Bremen" steht kurz vor der Abfahrt. Bunte Luftschlangen wehen im Wind: Das eine Ende halten an der Reling lehnende Auswanderer, das andere Ende die auf der Kaje stehenden Verwandten und Freunde. Sobald das Schiff losfährt, werden sich die Papierschlangen straffen und irgendwann reißen. Lebewohl. Weiße Taschentücher flattern im Wind. So manche haben einen Knoten im Zipfel: Vergiss mich nicht. Eine Kapelle spielt: „Muss i denn, muss i denn, zum Städtele hinaus ..." Zeremonien des Abschieds. Etwas, an das man sich halten kann in diesem Augenblick voller Wehmut, Angst und Hoffnung. Da war er nun: der Augenblick, nach dem man sich so sehr gesehnt hatte. Der Beginn des Traumes vom Leben in der Neuen Welt.

Bremerhaven, in 1929

The Columbus wharf. The passenger steamship *Bremen* is ready for departure. Colorful streamers are blowing in the wind, one end held by emigrant passengers leaning against the railing, the other end held by family and friends standing on the wharf waving their loved ones off. As soon as the ship casts off, the streamers will tighten and eventually rip. Good-bye, farewell. White handkerchiefs, some with knots tied in them, fluttering in the breeze, reminding those on board not to forget those back home. And a band playing the well-known tune "Muss I denn, muss I denn, zum Städtele hinaus ..."

The farewell ceremonies. Something to hold onto during this wistful, fearful moment full of hope and melancholy. Suddenly, it had arrived, the moment those leaving had so longed for. The beginning of their dream of a new life in the New World.

MUSS I DENN, MUSS I DENN ZUM STÄDTELE HINAUS

Die „Europa" beim Ablegen von der Columbuskaje in Bremerhaven, um 1935.

The Columbus wharf. The *Europa* sets sail for America, about 1935.

Sammlung Deutsches Auswandererhaus, Schenkung Hanna Wolff

Deutsches Auswandererhaus, Photo: Tanja Fittkau

Die Neue Welt, das waren für Auswanderungswillige des 19. und 20. Jahrhunderts vor allem die Vereinigten Staaten von Amerika, Kanada, aber auch südamerikanische Staaten wie Brasilien und Argentinien sowie der Fünfte Kontinent, Australien. Allein zwischen 1821 und 1914 wanderten 44 Millionen Europäer in die Neue Welt aus, davon 5,5 Millionen Deutsche. Heute gibt es mindestens 40 Millionen US-Amerikaner, die deutsche Vorfahren haben, manche Angaben gehen sogar von 60 Millionen aus. In Argentinien leben eine Million Menschen mit deutschen Wurzeln, in Kanada 2,7 Millionen, in Brasilien fünf Millionen und in Australien etwa 800.000.

The New Worl – for those eager to emigrate during the nineteenth and twentieth centuries that invariably meant the United States of America and Canada, but also the South American countries of Brazil and Argentina, and the fifth continent, Australia. Forty-four million Europeans emigrated to the New World between 1821 and 1914 alone, of which 5.5 million were German. No less than 40 million U.S. citizens today are of German origin, some estimates even venture as high as 60 million. One million inhabitants of German descent live in Argentina, 2.7 million in Canada, five million in Brazil and an estimated 800,000 in Australia.

Sammelkarten für „Native Americans", die der deutsche Amerikaauswanderer Hans Collischan 1918 in sein Tagebuch klebte.

"American Indian" trading cards with images of Native Americans that Hans Collischan, a German who immigrated to America, pasted in his diary in 1918.

Warum verließen ihre Vorfahren Deutschland? Und wie war diese Massenauswanderung möglich? In der heutigen Zeit der Einwanderungsbeschränkungen erscheinen ihre Wanderungsmöglichkeiten paradiesisch – aber auch sie hatten ihren Preis: die Vertreibung und Vernichtung der Mehrheit der ursprünglichen Bevölkerung.

Die ersten Europäer in der Neuen Welt gehörten den großen Seefahrernationen an: Briten, Portugiesen, Spanier und Niederländer. Während Portugiesen und Spanier zunächst Südamerika besetzten, eroberten die Briten und Franzosen Nordamerika; auch Australien wurde britisch. Die Kolonialherren wüteten in der Neuen Welt: Die ursprüngliche Bevölkerung wurde ermordet oder versklavt, Reichtümer hochzivilisierter Gesellschaften, wie die der Inka und Maya in Mittel- und Südamerika, wurden geraubt. Lebten vermutlich in Mexiko um 1500 noch 25 Millionen Menschen, gab es um 1560, nach 60 Jahren spanischer Herrschaft, nur noch drei Millionen. Als die ersten größeren Gruppen deutscher Siedler Anfang des 19. Jahrhunderts nach Brasilien und Argentinien kamen, waren die ursprünglichen Kulturen fast zerstört. Die Vertreibung und Ausrottung der Ureinwohner auf dem Gebiet der USA hatten ihren Höhepunkt im 19. Jahrhundert und waren auch eine Folge der europäischen Masseneinwanderung. Auch die eingewanderten deutschen Bauern errichteten ihre Farmen auf ehemaligen indianischen Gebieten.

Gerade die deutschen Kleinbauern waren auf der Suche nach freiem Land in die USA gekommen, denn in Deutschland herrschte seit Ende des 18. Jahrhunderts akuter Landmangel. War das Land nach dem Dreißigjährigen Krieg (1618–1648) noch stark entvölkert, kam es innerhalb von 150 Jahren durch das Erbteilungsgesetz zu Landmangel. Verstärkt wurde der Effekt im 19. Jahrhundert noch durch das seit dem Ende des 18. Jahrhunderts herrschende Bevölkerungswachstum. 75 Prozent der Bauern besaßen Mitte des 19. Jahrhunderts nicht ausreichend Land, um davon leben zu können. Sie waren auf einen Nebenerwerb angewiesen: Durch die stetig wachsende Bevölkerung kämpften immer mehr Menschen um solch einen Arbeitsplatz, gleichzeitig wurden traditio-

What caused their ancestors to leave Germany? How was a mass emigration of this dimension even possible? In today's world of immigration restrictions the possibilities of one-time emigrants seem like heaven on earth, yet there was a high price to pay. The persecution or extermination of the native Americans.

The first Europeans to set foot in the New World came from seafaring nations – Great Britain, Portugal, Spain and the Netherlands. Whereas the Portuguese and Spanish first occupied and settled in South America, the British and French conquered and colonized North America; Australia, too, became a British possession. The colonial rulers wreaked havoc on the New World, slaying or enslaving the natives, and robbing the advanced Inca and Maya civilizations in Central and South America of their treasures. To think that Mexico, for example, numbering 25 million inhabitants in 1500, had dropped to a mere three million by 1560 after 60 years under Spanish rule, is rather hard to fathom. By the time the first large groups of German settlers arrived in Brazil and Argentina in the nineteenth century, the indigenous Indian population had nearly been wiped out. The persecution and extermination of Native Americans, which peaked in the nineteenth century, was none other than the direct result of mass European immigration to the United States. A large number of German farmers set up farms on land once inhabited by Indians.

Particularly the German farmers who immigrated to America were in search of farming land. Whereas after the Thirty Years' War (1618–1648) Germany was extremely sparsely populated, the Estate Distribution Law changed conditions considerably over the ensuing 150 years, creating an acute shortage of land. By the beginning of the nineteenth century the effects were compounded by the population growth which had set in with the outgoing eighteenth century. By the mid-nineteenth century, 75 percent of the farmers depended on side jobs as they were unable to make a living for themselves and their families off the land they owned. Not only were a growing number of people seeking work due to the steady population increase, but jobs were invariably becoming scarce or obsolete as industrialization spread and new

Sammlung Deutsches Auswandererhaus

Handbücher informierten Auswanderungswillige über Reisevorbereitungen, Lebensbedingungen und Geographie der Neuen Welt: „Der Führer nach Amerika", 1882; „Taschenbuch über die Vereinigten Staaten", 1923; „Katechismus der Auswanderung", 1881. / Those seriously considering emigration consulted manuals such as these for information on travel preparation, the economy and geography of the New World: *Der Führer nach Amerika* (The Guide to America), 1882; *Taschenbuch über die Vereinigten Staaten* (Pocketbook on the United States), 1923; *Katechismus der Auswanderung* (The Catechism of Emigration), 1881.

nelle Berufe, die sich als Nebenerwerb eigneten, durch die Industrialisierung überflüssig. So verschlang beispielsweise die rasant aufsteigende Textilindustrie nach und nach ganze Berufszweige: Leinenweber, Garnspinner, Schneider, Näherinnen und Stickerinnen. Die Spirale der Armut drehte sich für den unteren deutschen Mittelstand zwischen 1800 und 1850 immer schneller. Die Industrialisierung war in Deutschland zu diesem Zeitpunkt noch nicht so weit fortgeschritten, dass neue Berufszweige den von Armut bedrohten Menschen einen Ausweg geboten hätten. Typische deutsche Auswanderer Mitte des 19. Jahrhunderts waren Kleinbauern mit ihren Familien. Hinzu kamen Tagelöhner und Dienstmägde vom Lande und aus den Städten, die ebenfalls aufgrund des Bevölkerungswachstums von Arbeitslosigkeit bedroht waren. Die deutschen Auswanderer Mitte des 19. Jahrhunderts suchten Arbeit und freies Land. Die besten Chancen darauf hatten sie in den Vereinigten Staaten von Amerika. Der Rest der Neuen Welt bot schlechtere klimatische Bedingungen, weniger Jobs und eine größere Unsicherheit. Einige wagten es trotzdem nach Brasilien, Argentinien, Kanada und Australien auszuwandern.

Anders als in den USA gab es in Südamerika staatlich organisierte Kolonisationsprojekte, in denen den Siedlern freies Land, Steuerfreiheit und Befreiung vom Militär-

jobs were increasingly difficult to come by. Gradually, entire trades and crafts were swallowed up by newly flourishing industries. The textile industry for one did away with the linen weaving, spinning, tailor's, dressmaking and embroidery trades. The lower middle classes in Germany between 1800 and 1850 were caught up in a downward spiral of rapidly growing poverty. At that time, industrialization in Germany was not sufficiently advanced to offer people whose work in certain trades was threatened by redundancy, and hence poverty, new opportunities in emerging industries. Thus German emigrants during the mid-eighteenth century were typically peasants, their families working as day laborers, maids and farm girls who, as a result of the rising population figures, were confronted with joblessness and little hope for anything but a bleak future. Hence, eighteenth-century German emigrants were in dire search of work and free

dienst zugesagt wurden. Das war auch bitter nötig, denn die Siedlungsbedingungen in weiten Teilen Brasiliens und Argentiniens waren extrem hart. Angesprochen wurden die Auswanderungswilligen in Europa im Auftrag südamerikanischer Regierungen von Unternehmen und Reiseagenten, die wirtschaftlich von der Vermittlungszahl profitierten und oft skrupellos waren. Aber die Besiedlungsversuche unter für Europäer so ungewohnten klimatischen und geographischen Bedingungen endeten oft tragisch. Viele Menschen starben. Erfolgreich waren Siedlungsprojekte in Gebieten in der gemäßigten Zone, wie beispielsweise die deutsche Kolonie „São Leopoldo", gegründet 1824. Sie lag im Süden Brasiliens im Gebiet Rio Grande do Sul, wo bald weitere deutsche

land, both of which were available in great abundance in the United States of America. Nowhere else in the New World did the climatic conditions, the labor market and security equal the standards offered in America. Nevertheless, many emigrants ventured to Brazil, Argentina, Canada and Australia to try their luck.

In contrast to the United States, there were government-organized colonization projects in South America guaranteeing immigrant settlers open land, exemption from taxation and military service. All these benefits were sorely needed to attract settlers to the outback and extremely rough countryside prevailing in large areas of Brazil and Argentina. Companies and travel agents officially commissioned by South American governments approached potential emigrants in Europe, often profiting unscrupulously from the number of candidates they were able to acquire. For the Europeans, unaware and unfamiliar with the harsh climate and geographic conditions awaiting them in the new country, these attempts at land settlement invariably ended tragically. Countless immigrant settlers died, while those who settled in temperate zones, such as the German colony *São Leopoldo*, founded in 1824, were successful. This settlement in southern Brazil in the Rio Grande do Sul region was followed by various other German settlements. At the most, 101,800 Germans emigrated to Brazil and roughly 28,000 to Argentina between 1820 and 1900

Australia too recruited new settlers during the nineteenth century, as virtually no European found the idea of forging a new life in a British colony inhabited by deported convicts terribly enticing. In contrast to an estimated 30,000 convicts who lived on the fifth continent in 1828, there were a mere 5,000 voluntary settlers from European countries. By 1840 the situation had improved from the standpoint of the immigrants with 50,000 deported convicts compared to a total of 65,000 voluntary settlers. About this time a large

SÜD·AMERIKA

Aus: Eduard Pelz: „Katechismus der Auswanderung", Leipzig, 1881. / From: Eduard Pelz: *Katechismus der Auswanderung* (The Catechism of Emigration), Leipzig, 1881.

Siedlungen entstanden. Insgesamt wanderten zwischen 1820 und 1900 nur 101.800 Deutsche nach Brasilien und knapp 28.000 Deutsche nach Argentinien aus.

Auch Australien musste im 19. Jahrhundert um Siedler werben – wenige Europäer wollten in der britischen Sträflingskolonie ihr Glück versuchen: 1828 gab es knapp 30.000 Sträflinge, aber nur 5.000 freiwillige europäische Siedler auf dem Fünften Kontinent. 1840 sah die Lage aus der Sicht der Einwanderer schon angenehmer aus: 50.000 Deportierten standen 65.000 freiwillige Siedler gegenüber. Es ist auch der Zeitpunkt, zu dem eine größere Anzahl deutscher Einwanderer nach Australien kam; zwischen 1847 und 1914 gingen insgesamt 55.900 Deutsche nach Australien. Deutsche Siedlungen entstanden im Barossa-Tal in South Australia und in Queensland. 1868 wurde die Deportation von Sträflingen nach Australien durch die britische Regierung abgeschafft.

Kanada litt bis weit ins 20. Jahrhundert unter der größeren Attraktivität der USA: Allein von 1861 bis 1971 wanderten 7.750.000 Menschen von Kanada aus, die meisten von ihnen gingen in die USA. Die erste größere Gruppe deutscher Siedler gelangte zwischen 1750 und 1753 nach Kanada: Das britische Königshaus warb für seine Kolonie 2.300 Auswanderer, von denen 1.500 deutschsprachig waren. Sie stammten aus der Schweiz, Norddeutschland und der Pfalz und siedelten sich in Neuschottland an. Von 1851 bis 1910 wanderten 89.100 Deutsche nach Kanada ein.

Erst im 20. Jahrhundert kam es zu stärkeren Auswanderungswellen von Deutschen nach Südamerika, Australien und Kanada. „Nach Amerika!", dieser Ruf, der im 19. Jahrhundert von Süddeutschland ausgehend immer schneller durch ganz Deutschland hallte, meinte vor allem die Vereinigten Staaten von Amerika. Briefe von erfolgreich eingewanderten Verwandten forderten die in Deutschland zurückgebliebenen Verwandten, Freunde und Bekannten auf, es doch ebenfalls im Land der unbegrenzten Möglichkeiten zu versuchen. So setzte vor allem in der zweiten Hälfte des 19. Jahrhunderts eine starke Kettenwanderung ein.

number of Germans chose to emigrate to Australia. All told, between 1847 and 1914 a total of 55,900 Germans left their homeland for Australia. German colonies emerged in the Barossa Valley in South Australia and in Queensland. Finally, in 1868, the British government abolished the deportation of convicts to Australia.

In terms of attracting immigrants Canada took a back seat to the United States well into the twentieth century. In fact, 7,750,000 residents emigrated from Canada between 1861 and 1971, the majority immigrating across the border to the United States. The first sizeable group of Germans to settle in Canada is recorded between 1750 and 1753. At the time, the British monarchy recruited 2,300 emigrants for its colony, of which 1,500 happened to be German-speaking from Switzerland, Northern Germany and the Palatinate, and settling in Nova Scotia. From 1851 to 1910, a total of 89,100 Germans immigrated to Canada.

It was not until the twentieth century that large waves of emigrants left Germany for South America, Australia and Canada. The words "To America!," so often heard in nineteenth-century Southern Germany, now echoed throughout the country, referring to the United States of America. Letters from German immigrants to the U.S. regaling relatives, friends and acquaintances back home with their newly found lives and success encouraged increasing numbers of Germans to try their luck in the land of endless opportunity as well, culminating in a wave of chain-reaction emigration during the latter half of the nineteenth century.

Two principal aspects influenced the onset of mass German immigration to the United States in the eighteenth century, the search for individual religious freedom and the desire for men, even entire families, to be hired or contracted by large plantation owners for a specified period as indentured servants.
The first all-German settlement in the U.S.A. was Germantown, Pennsylvania, founded in 1683 by 13 families from Krefeld under the leadership of Franz Daniel Pastorius, a Mennonite seeking religious freedom for his religious com-

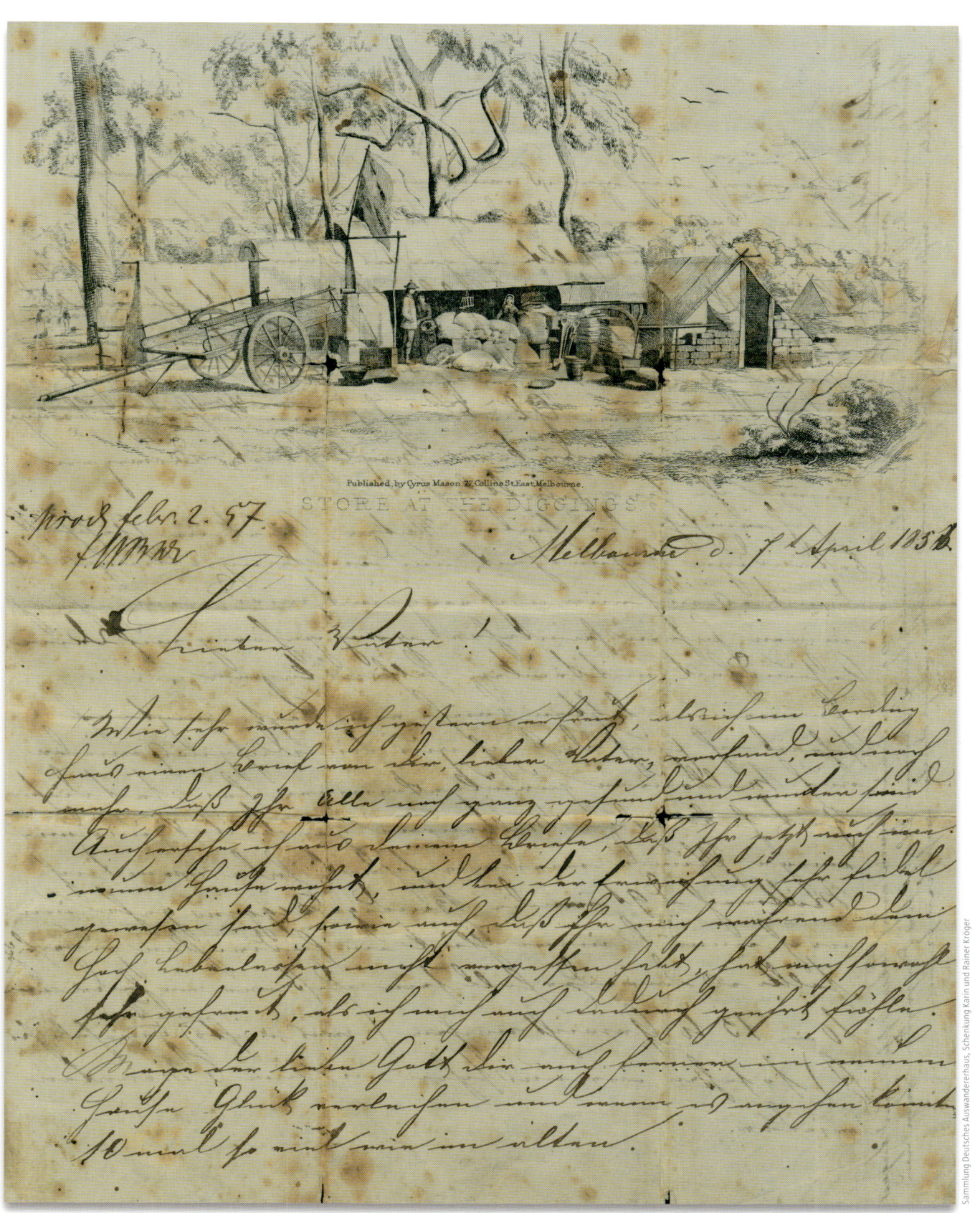

Brief aus Australien von Daniel Hoffheiser an seinen Vater in Deutschland, 1857. / Daniel Hoffheiser sent this letter from Australia to his father in Germany, 1857.

Sammlung Deutsches Auswandererhaus, Schenkung Karin und Rainer Kroger

Am Anfang der deutschen Masseneinwanderung in die USA standen im 18. Jahrhundert Menschen auf der Suche nach Religionsfreiheit und die „indentured servants", Männer, aber auch ganze Familien, die ihre Arbeitskraft auf Zeit an amerikanische Großgrundbesitzer verkauften.

Die erste geschlossene deutsche Siedlung in den USA war Germantown in Pennsylvania. Gegründet wurde sie 1683 von 13 Krefelder Familien unter ihrem Anführer Franz Daniel Pastorius, einem Mennoniten, der in den USA mit seiner Gemeinde freie Religionsausübung suchte. Eine weitere deutsche Religionsgemeinschaft ließ sich Ende des 18. Jahrhunderts in Pennsylvania nieder: Die „Amische", eine Glaubensgemeinschaft, die ursprünglich in Süddeutschland beheimatet war, hatten sich 1693 aufgrund ihrer strengeren Lebensvorstellungen von den Mennoniten abgespalten. Um 1700 wanderten größere Gruppen von ihnen nach Nordamerika aus und ließen sich in Pennsylvania nieder. Die „Amish people" leben auch heute noch in den USA als geschlossene religiöse Gemeinschaft, in der die meisten Mitglieder jeglichen Komfort ablehnen, keinen Strom und keine Autos nutzen und sich dem Militärdienst verweigern.

Eine Mehrheit deutscher Einwanderer in den USA stellten im 18. Jahrhundert die „indentured servants": In Deutschland mittellos lebend, ohne Geld für die Schiffspassage, verkauften sie ihre Arbeitskraft ebenso wie die ihrer Familienmitglieder für vier oder mehr Jahre an amerikanische Großgrundbesitzer. Diese bezahlten die Überfahrt und übernahmen Kost und Logis für die Dauer des Dienstverhältnisses. Am Ende erhielten die Arbeiter meist noch etwas Geld und ein eigenes Stück Land von ihrem Dienstherren. In die Selbstständigkeit entlassen, hatten sie die gleichen Rechte und Pflichten wie alle Bürger der britischen Kolonien in Nordamerika. Als 1776 nordamerikanische Kolonien ihre Unabhängigkeit von Großbritannien erklärten und sich Vereinigte Staaten von Amerika nannten, lebten etwa 300.000 Deutsche dort.

Napoleon hatte Europa zwischen 1792 und 1815 mit seinen Freiheitskriegen überzogen, aber er verbreitete auch die Ideen von „Freiheit, Gleichheit und Brüderlichkeit". Die Gedanken der Aufklärung, die zuvor nur Politiker und Intel-

munity in the U.S. The *Amish*, a strict Mennonite sect that separated from the Mennonite community in 1693 and originally came from Southern Germany, were another German religious group to settle in Pennsylvania in the late eighteenth century. Large numbers of *Amish* immigrated to the U.S. around 1700, all settling in Pennsylvania. The *Amish* people continue to live today as a closed religious community. They are noted for their simplicity of life, rejecting virtually all comforts including electricity and automobiles, and refusing to do military service.

Indentured servants constituted the majority of German immigrants to the U.S. in the eighteenth century. These people, destitute in Germany, had no means of paying for their passage to America, hence selling themselves and their families as laborers to land owners in the United States for a period of four or more years. The land owners in turn paid their passage and provided the indentured servants living quarters and food for the tenure of their service. When the contracted period was over, most employers gave the laborers money and a piece of land to work. Thus released into a life of independence, these men and women had the same rights and duties as any citizen of the North American British colonies. An estimated 300,000 Germans lived in the United States of America at the time the colonies obtained their independence from Great Britain in 1776.

Although Napoleon had waged wars of liberation all over Europe from 1792 to 1815, he also disseminated the concept of "freedom, equality and brotherhood." The reasoning behind the intellectual movement of the Age of Enlightenment, until now the sole domain of thinkers, politicians and writers, suddenly became accessible to everyone. The politician and philosopher Friedrich Gentz speaks of the revolution in 1790 as "the first practical triumph of philosophy, the hope and consolation for many of the ills which previously weighed so heavily on mankind. Should this revolution abate, these very ills would be past remedy tenfold." With the defeat of Napoleon in 1815, the governments of the German states largely revoked the reforms carried out in the regions formerly occupied by the French. Henceforth German farmers continued to suffer from the tax burdens and were frequently forced to

Sammlung Deutsches Auswandererhaus

Links: Weizenspeicher in Wichita, Sedgwick County, Kansas. Aus: Adolf Ott: „Der Führer nach Amerika", Basel, 1882. Rechts: Familie Breit vor ihrer Farm im brasilianischen Santa Cruz do Sul, um 1925. / Left: Grain silo in Wichita (Sedgwick County), Kansas. Taken from Adolf Ott: *Der Führer nach Amerika* (The Guide to America), Basle, 1882. Right: The Breit family outside their barn in Santa Cruz do Sul, Brazil, about 1925.

lektuelle verfolgt hatten, berührten nun alle. Der Politiker und Philosoph Friedrich Gentz schrieb über die Revolution 1790: „Sie ist der erste praktische Triumph der Philosophie. (…) Sie ist die Hoffnung und der Trost für so viel alte Übel, unter denen die Menschheit seufzt. Sollte diese Revolution zurückgehen, so würden alle diese Übel zehnmal unheilbar." [1] Nachdem Napoleon 1815 besiegt war, nahmen die deutschen Regierungen Reformen, die in den zuvor französisch besetzten deutschen Gebieten eingeführt worden waren, wieder weitestgehend zurück. Die deutschen Bauern litten weiterhin unter ihren Abgabenlasten. Dort, wo sie abgelöst werden konnten, mussten die Bauern oft Schulden aufnehmen, um die Ablösung bezahlen zu können. Die Unfreiheit und die Nichtbeteiligung an der Politik blieben für alle Untertanen weiterhin bestehen. 1848 kam es zur Revolution, aber die demokratischen Kräfte in Deutschland scheiterten. Anführer der Revolution wurden steckbrieflich gesucht und flohen ins Ausland. Bekanntestes Beispiel ist Carl Schurz. Der Anführer des badischen Aufstandes flüchtete zunächst nach Frankreich, dann nach Großbritannien und schließlich in die USA. Dort ging er in die Politik. 1868 wurde er Senator des US-Bundesstaates Missouri und von 1877 bis 1881

borrow money in order to pay off tax debts. People continued to live in bondage and were excluded from politics. Finally in 1848 the people rose in revolt, but the forces of democracy did not prevail. The leaders of the revolution were on the wanted list and fled the country. Carl Schurz is a prominent example of that time. The leader of the Baden revolt first escaped to France, then to Great Britain, landing ultimately in the United States where he went into politics. In 1868 he was elected senator of Missouri and was Secretary of the Interior from 1877 to 1881. The percentage of 1848 revolutionaries who emigrated to the U.S. was small in numbers, but the failure of the 1848 revolution was for many final proof that Germany was not charting a course of change, hence creating additional motivation to seek a new way of life in the U.S.A.

Economic reasons were the driving force behind the majority of German emigrants to the United States in the nineteenth

„Secretary of the Interior". Zahlenmäßig war der Anteil der 1848er Revolutionäre an der deutschen Amerikaauswanderung gering, aber das Scheitern der Revolution war für viele Menschen der endgültige Beweis, dass sich in Deutschland wenig ändern würde. So stellte das Scheitern der demokratischen Bewegung 1848 für viele Menschen eine zusätzliche Motivation dar, in die demokratischen USA auszuwandern.

Bei der Mehrheit der Deutschen, die im 19. Jahrhundert in die USA auswanderten, überwogen wirtschaftliche Motive. Die Bauern lockte das freie Land oder zumindest die Möglichkeit, nach einigen Jahren als Lohnarbeiter eine Farm erwerben zu können. Um 1850 war die Gründung einer Farm eine einfache Angelegenheit: Nachdem sichergestellt war, dass auf dem gewünschten Stück Land kein anderer siedelte, steckte man es für sich ab und besaß damit einen „claim", einen Rechtsanspruch. Nach vier Jahren musste man für das Land bezahlen: 1 Acre (0,4 Hektar) kostete 1,25 Dollar. Viele begannen mit 40 Acres (16 Hektar), für die sie 50 Dollar zahlten. Kleinbauern, die in Deutschland unter fünf Hektar Land besessen hatten, konnten nach 15 Jahren harter Arbeit in den USA eine Farm besitzen, die 160 Acres, also 64 Hektar, groß war. Solche Erfolgsgeschichten veranlassten in Deutschland gebliebene Verwandte und Freunde ebenfalls auszuwandern. Es entstanden zahlreiche deutsche Gemeinden, in denen es deutsche Schulen, Kirchen und Vereine gab und in denen Deutsch gesprochen wurde. Gleichzeitig feierten die Bewohner amerikanische Feste wie „Halloween" oder den „Columbus Day" am 12. Oktober, an dem die Entdeckung Amerikas durch Christoph Columbus zelebriert wird. Es waren typische Deutsch-Amerikaner; sie gehörten zu den klassischen „Hyphen-Americans" (Bindestrich-Amerikanern).

Ende des 19. Jahrhunderts, als es in den von Deutschen bevorzugten Siedlungsgebieten wie dem Mittleren Westen, Texas und Kansas kaum noch freies Land gab, wurden Farmen teurer. So zogen viele Deutsche zunächst als Lohnarbeiter in boomende Städte wie New York oder Chicago. Chicago beispielsweise hatte 1830 erst 50 Einwohner, 1880 lebten dort bereits über eine halbe Million Menschen. Nach einigen Jah-

century. Peasants and farmers were attracted by the promise of land availability or at least the chance to buy farmland after earning wages for a number of years as a hired hand. Setting up a farm was an easy task in and around 1850. Once determined that a desired piece of land had not been staked out by anybody else, one was entitled to put a claim on it. Four years later, payment of the land was required: one acre (0.4 ha) cost one dollar and twenty-five cents. Most land claims started at 40 acres (16 ha), adding up to a total of fifty dollars. Small farmers who had owned a scant five hectares back home in Germany, now owned 160 acre (64 ha) farms after 15 years of hard work. It comes as no surprise that success stories of this type encouraged relatives and friends to follow in their fellow emigrants' footsteps. Various German communities came into being and with them German schools, churches and clubs. This did not prevent people from celebrating American holidays such as *Halloween or Columbus Day* (October 12, the day commemorating Christopher Columbus' discovery of America). They were typical German-Americans, so-called *hyphen-Americans*.

As by the late nineteenth century there was only very little unclaimed land left in the Middle West, Texas and Kansas, the regions most favored by Germans, farms went up in price. German immigrants began moving to major cities such as Chicago and New York where they took jobs as laborers. Chicago, for example, which in 1830 counted no more than a scant 50 inhabitants, had evolved into a bustling city of over one half million inhabitants, by 1880. After years of scrimping and saving, a large number of German immigrants was finally able to buy a farm.

During the nine-year period spanning 1880 to 1889, some 1,362,500 Germans emigrated, with 200,000 people leaving Germany in each of the two peak years 1881 and 1882 due to a severe economic crisis. The German Empire, booming economically for two years following its formation, suddenly collapsed. Businesses and companies went broke, unemployment soared. It wasn't until 1887 that the German economy began to slowly and steadily recover, ushering in an era of full employment.

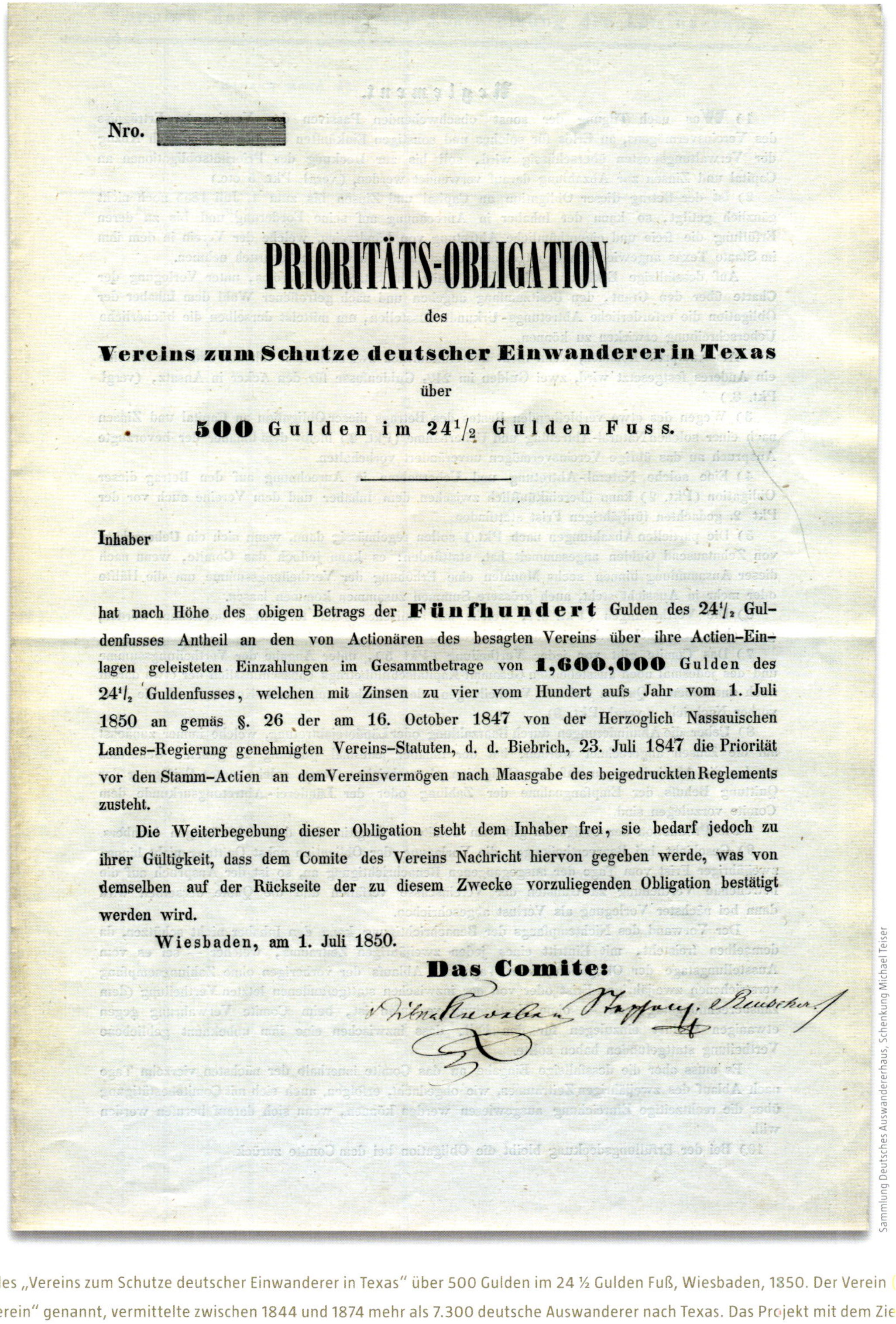

Nro. ▓▓▓▓▓▓▓

PRIORITÄTS-OBLIGATION

des

Vereins zum Schutze deutscher Einwanderer in Texas

über

500 Gulden im 24½ Gulden Fuss.

Inhaber

hat nach Höhe des obigen Betrags der **Fünfhundert** Gulden des 24½ Guldenfusses Antheil an den von Actionären des besagten Vereins über ihre Actien–Einlagen geleisteten Einzahlungen im Gesammtbetrage von **1,600,000** Gulden des 24½ Guldenfusses, welchen mit Zinsen zu vier vom Hundert aufs Jahr vom 1. Juli 1850 an gemäs §. 26 der am 16. October 1847 von der Herzoglich Nassauischen Landes-Regierung genehmigten Vereins-Statuten, d. d. Biebrich, 23. Juli 1847 die Priorität vor den Stamm-Actien an dem Vereinsvermögen nach Maasgabe des beigedruckten Reglements zusteht.

Die Weiterbegebung dieser Obligation steht dem Inhaber frei, sie bedarf jedoch zu ihrer Gültigkeit, dass dem Comite des Vereins Nachricht hiervon gegeben werde, was von demselben auf der Rückseite der zu diesem Zwecke vorzulegenden Obligation bestätigt werden wird.

Wiesbaden, am 1. Juli 1850.

Das Comite:

Priorität-Obligation des „Vereins zum Schutze deutscher Einwanderer in Texas" über 500 Gulden im 24 ½ Gulden Fuß, Wiesbaden, 1850. Der Verein (1842–1848), auch „Mainzer Adelsverein" genannt, vermittelte zwischen 1844 und 1874 mehr als 7.300 deutsche Auswanderer nach Texas. Das Projekt mit dem Ziel der Gründung einer deutschen Kolonie in Texas endete für den Verein in einem finanziellen Debakel, versprochene große Landzuweisungen an Auswanderungswillige blieben aus.
Priority obligations from the *Verein zum Schutze deutscher Einwanderer in Texas* (Association for the Protection of German Immigrants to Texas) worth 500 guilders in 24 ½ guild feet, Wiesbaden, 1850. The registered association, also known as the *Mainzer Adelsverein* (Mainz Association of Nobility), acted as an agent for more than 7,300 German immigrants to Texas between 1844 and 1874. The project originally aimed at setting up a German colony in Texas, however, eventually defaulted and large land grants promised to German emigrants never materialized.

ren des Sparens war es dann für viele deutsche Einwanderer möglich eine Farm zu erwerben.

Allein zwischen 1880 und 1889 wanderten 1.362.500 Deutsche aus. Höhepunkte waren die Jahre 1881 und 1882, in denen jeweils über 200.000 Menschen gingen. Ursache für diese starke Auswanderungsbewegung war eine schwere Wirtschaftskrise: Nachdem die deutsche Wirtschaft nach der Gründung des Deutschen Kaiserreiches 1871 für zwei Jahre geboomt hatte, brach sie danach umso stärker ein. Unternehmenspleiten und Arbeitslosigkeit waren die Folge. Erst ab 1887 erholte sich die deutsche Wirtschaft wieder dauerhaft und es begann in Deutschland eine Zeit der Vollbeschäftigung.

Anhand dieses Zeitraumes lassen sich klassische Muster von Auswanderungswellen aufzeigen, die sich in der Migrationsgeschichte wiederholen: Selten kommt es zu Massenauswanderungen zu Beginn einer Wirtschaftskrise. Einige Jahre lang hoffen die Menschen auf Verbesserung, auf einen Job, auf eine bessere Zukunft im Heimatland. Nach fünf wirtschaftlich schlechten Jahren beginnen die Auswandererzahlen zu steigen. Eine solche Situation ist auch im heutigen Deutschland zu beobachten: Infolge der Wirtschaftskrisen in den 2000er Jahren bestanden gleich bleibend hohe Auswandererzahlen um 150.000 pro Jahr. Das waren die höchsten Zahlen seit Bestehen der Bundesrepublik Deutschland. Aufgrund der besseren Arbeitsmarktsituation der europäischen Nachbarländer und der strikten Einwanderungsgesetze in den klassischen Einwanderungsländern wie USA, Kanada und Australien gingen die meisten deutschen Auswanderer 2000 bis 2008 in europäische Nachbarländer. Die Finanzkrise von 2008/2009 senkte die Chancen deutscher Auswanderungswilliger, im Ausland Aufnahme zu finden. Die Wahl Donald Trumps zum 45. Präsidenten der USA im November 2016 wird die Zahl der Rückkehrer erneut erhöhen.

Wer im 19. und frühen 20. Jahrhundert den Plan zur Auswanderung gefasst hatte, kaufte bei einem Auswandereragenten eine Schiffspassage und machte sich auf den Weg an die Küste. Standen zunächst für deutsche Auswanderer

This period in time is a perfect example of how migratory movements occur. Seldom, if ever, does emigration result at the outset of an economic crisis. People are confident things will improve, they hope to find a job, a better future in their mother country. If an economy falters over a period of five years emigration figures tend to rise. We are witnessing the same situation in Germany today. As a result of the economic crises in the 2000s the emigration figure was consistently high with approximately 150,000 German nationals emigrating every year. These figures were the highest since the foundation of the Federal Republic of Germany. Most have chosen neighboring European countries to emigrate to, as the job market is invariably better in those countries and immigration restrictions not as tight as in the classic immigration countries U.S.A., Canada and Australia. For Germans the financial crisis of 2008/2009 reduced chances of acceptance in other European countries or the U.S.A. The election of Donald Trump as the 45th president of the United States of America in november 2016 will again increase the number of returning foreigners.

When in the nineteenth and early twentieth centuries the decision to emigrate had been made, a passage was purchased through an emigration agent and the journey to the designated seaport began. While at first German emigrants headed for the seaports of Le Havre (France), Rotterdam (Netherlands) and Liverpool (England), the first German port of emigration was Bremerhaven, developing in the 1830s.

Hamburg was rather late in discovering the lucrative business of emigration. In fact, it wasn't until the 1840s that the city began to establish itself as a port of embarkation. In 1847, the *Hamburg-Amerikanische Packetfahrt-Actien-Gesellschaft* (Hapag) shipping line was formed, initially operating sailing ships, followed by regular steamship service between Hamburg and the United States in the 1880s. As of 1889, Hapag ships no longer sailed from Hamburg, but largely from the North Sea port of Cuxhaven. Altogether 5.5 million people sailed to America on ships under the Hamburg flag. Unfortunately, exact figures as to the percentage of passengers who were emigrants, businessmen or tourists do not exist.

55

vor allem das französische Le Havre, das niederländische Rotterdam und das britische Liverpool als Einschiffungshafen zur Verfügung, stellte ab den 1830er Jahren Bremerhaven den ersten deutschen Auswandererhafen. Bremerhaven und Hamburg wurden die größten deutschen Auswandererhäfen.

Hamburg entdeckte relativ spät das lukrative Geschäft mit den Auswanderern: Erst in den 1840er Jahren begann sich die Stadt als Einschiffungshafen zu etablieren. 1847 wurde die „Hamburg-Amerikanische Packetfahrt-Actien-Gesellschaft" (Hapag) gegründet, die zunächst mit Segelschiffen, ab den 1880er Jahren auch mit Dampfschiffen einen regelmäßigen Verkehr zwischen Hamburg und den USA einrichtete. Ab 1889 fuhren die Schiffe der Hapag größtenteils nicht mehr von Hamburg, sondern von Cuxhaven ab. Insgesamt reisten auf Schiffen unter Hamburger Flagge 5,5 Millionen Menschen: Leider liegen noch keine exakten Zahlen darüber vor, wie viele von diesen Passagieren Auswanderer und wie viele Geschäftsleute und Touristen waren.

Auswanderer der III. Klasse besteigen an der Columbuskaje in Bremerhaven ein Schiff. Als Passagiere des Zwischendecks mussten sie ihr Gepäck selber tragen, Ende 1920er. Emigrants in steerage board the ship docked at the Columbus wharf in Bremerhaven, about 1920. Steerage passengers had to carry their own baggage on board.

The mouth of the Weser River, December 1847

The sailing ship *Bremen* cast off from Bremerhaven an hour ago and has set sail for the North Sea. One hundred and sixty-nine passengers are on board, among them the Laufkoetter family. Auguste and Clemens Laufkoetter with their six children Emilie (11), Johann (9), Hermine (7), Louise (4), Fritz (3) and Pauline (1). The ship's destination is New Orleans. At worst, the crossing can take up to 15 weeks or longer. The Laufkoetters share a bunk measuring about 2.25 m in breadth and 1.70 m in length – a total of 3.8 sq. m. in space for the entire family to eat, sleep, live during the entire ocean crossing. The food is drab and unhealthy, the family's diet consists of zwieback, pulses, porridge, bacon

Wesermündung, im Dezember des Jahres 1847

Das Segelschiff „Bremen" hat Bremerhaven vor einer Stunde verlassen und nimmt Kurs auf die Nordsee. An Bord befinden sich 169 Passagiere, unter ihnen auch die Familie Laufkötter. Auguste und Clemens Laufkötter mit ihren sechs Kindern Emilie (11), Johann (9), Hermine (7), Louise (4), Fritz (3) und Pauline (1). Ziel der Reise ist New Orleans. Schlimmstenfalls dauert die Fahrt 15 Wochen oder noch länger. Die Familie Laufkötter teilt sich eine Koje, die etwa 2,25 Meter breit und 1,70 Meter lang ist: 3,8 Quadratmeter, auf denen sie schlafen, essen, leben muss – über Wochen. Das Essen ist eintönig und ungesund: Zwieback, Hülsenfrüchte, Getreidebrei, Speck und brackiges Wasser. Bei

and brackish water. In good weather conditions passengers are allowed to go up on deck once a day; in stormy conditions the hatch stays closed. Many of the passengers are seasick and fatal diseases, such as typhoid fever and dysentery, spread easily in the stale air between decks. Two to three percent of the passengers die on ships from Bremen in the nineteenth century, a low death rate by comparison to the English and Irish ships. The Laufkoetters are lucky. They arrive safe and sound in New Orleans on Feburary 11, 1848. Their trail is lost in the New World.

Bremerhaven was established as a seaport by the Hanseatic city of Bremen in 1827, with the first harbor basin, the so-called *Alter Hafen*, or old port, opened after a three-year

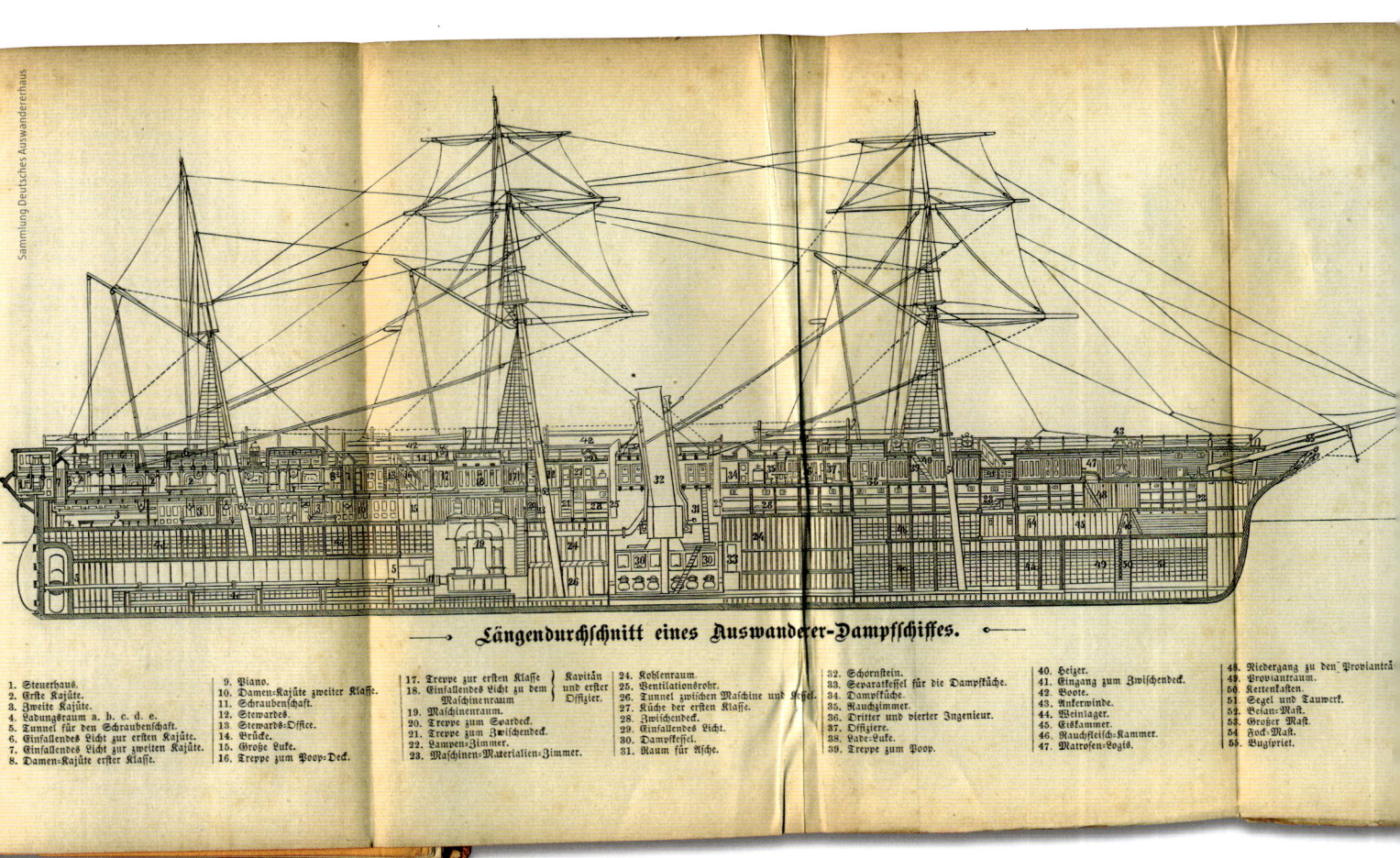

Längsschnitt eines Auswandererdampfschiffes. Aus: Eduard Pelz: „Katechismus der Auswanderung", Leipzig, 1881. Bis in die 1870er Jahre überquerten die meisten Auswanderer den Atlantik auf Segelschiffen. Zwölf Wochen und mehr konnte die Überfahrt dauern. Mit Einführung der Dampfschiffe verringerte sich die Reisedauer nach Amerika zunehmend auf acht bis 15 Tage. / Longitudinal section of a steamship carrying emigrants. Taken from Eduard Pelz: *Katechismus der Auswanderung* (The Catechism of Emigration), Leipzig, 1881. Up through 1870, the majority of emigrants made the long ocean journey to America on sailing ships with the crossing lasting up to 12 weeks or more. With the advent of the steamship the length of the journey dropped to eight, at the most 15 days.

gutem Wetter dürfen die Auswanderer einmal pro Tag an Deck, bei Sturm bleibt die Luke geschlossen. Die Seekrankheit plagt viele Menschen, lebensgefährliche Krankheiten wie Typhus und Ruhr verbreiten sich rasend schnell im engen Zwischendeck. Mitte des 19. Jahrhunderts sterben auf Bremer Schiffen zwei bis drei Prozent der Passagiere. Im Vergleich mit den englischen und irischen Schiffen ist das eine niedrige Sterbeziffer. Die Familie Laufkötter hat Glück: Sie kommt am 11. Februar 1848 heil in New Orleans an. Danach verliert sich ihre Spur in der Neuen Welt.

Bremerhaven wurde 1827 als Seehafen von der Hansestadt Bremen gegründet. Das erste Hafenbecken, heute der „Alte Hafen', wurde 1830 nach dreijähriger Bauzeit eröffnet. Ursprünglich als Handelshafen geplant, wurde Bremerhaven schnell zum Auswandererhafen. Die Bremer Kaufleute, deren Segelschiffe Waren wie Tabak, Baumwolle, Tee und Petroleum aus der Neuen Welt nach Europa brachten, konnten auf dem Hinweg mit der Auslastung der Schiffe durch den Transport von Auswanderern sehr gute Gewinne erzielen. Durch die Bremer „Verordnung wegen der Auswanderer mit hiesigen oder fremden Schiffen" von 1832 wird Bremerhaven zum modernen Auswandererhafen: Mindeststandards müssen auf den Schiffen, die unter Bremer Flagge fahren eingehalten werden. Die Schiffe gelten so unter den Auswanderungswilligen als sicher. Als 1849 das Auswandererhaus, in dem bis zu 2.000 Auswanderer zu günstigen Preisen und unter guten hygienischen Bedingungen logieren können, in Bremerhaven eingerichtet wird, steigt die Stadt zum beliebtesten Auswandererhafen für Deutsche auf.

Als 1857 der „Norddeutsche Lloyd" gegründet wurde, gab es die erste regelmäßige Dampfschiffsverbindung zwischen Deutschland und den USA. Heimathafen des „Norddeutschen Lloyd" war Bremerhaven, die Schiffe fuhren unter Bremer Flagge. Die Reederei stieg Ende des 19. Jahrhunderts zur weltweit größten Passagierdampfschifffahrtsgesellschaft auf. Ihre Schiffsrouten gingen nach Nord- und Südamerika, nach Asien und nach Australien. Millionen Menschen fuhren auf Schiffen des „Norddeutschen Lloyd" in die Neue Welt.

construction period in 1830. Originally planned as a port of trade, Bremerhaven quickly developed into a port of emigration. Bremen merchants whose ships transported goods from the New World such as tobacco, cotton, tea and mineral oil back to Europe, profited of course handsomely by transporting emigrant passengers from Europe to the New World when they would otherwise return empty. The Bremen Decree of 1832 actually contributed to making Bremerhaven a modern port of emigration by ensuring that minimal standards were maintained on all ships sailing under the Bremen flag. Among emigrants, the ships had a reputation of being safe. When the Emigration House, a boarding house of sorts offering reasonable room and board and good sanitary conditions with a capacity of up to 2,000, opened in Bremerhaven in 1849, the port town advanced to become the Germans' leading port of emigration.

Regular steamship service between Germany and the United States went into operation with the founding of *North German Lloyd* in 1857. The line's home port was Bremerhaven and ships sailed under the Bremen flag. By the end of the nineteenth century, the shipping line had grown to become the world's largest passenger steamship company with routes to North and South America, Asia and Australia. Millions of Germans and East Europeans emigrated to the New World on board ships operated by *North German Lloyd*. A total of 7.2 million people emigrated to the New World by way of Bremerhaven between 1830 and 1974. Almost half this number – 3.4 million – were from Eastern Europe and were primarily Polish, Russian, Czech, Slovak, Hungarian or Rumanian. The first major emigration wave from Eastern Europe set in during the 1880s and ended with World War I. The next major wave of emigrants arrived at this port of embarkation during the 1920s. East Europeans and Germans emigrating as a result of the Great Depression shortly after World War I came together on board the ships. In the aftermath of the First World War and the Great Depression, Germans, too, for the first time in three decades, left the country in overwhelming numbers. The dream of America was unattainable for many. The *Quota Act* of 1921 limited annual European immigration to three percent of the number of a

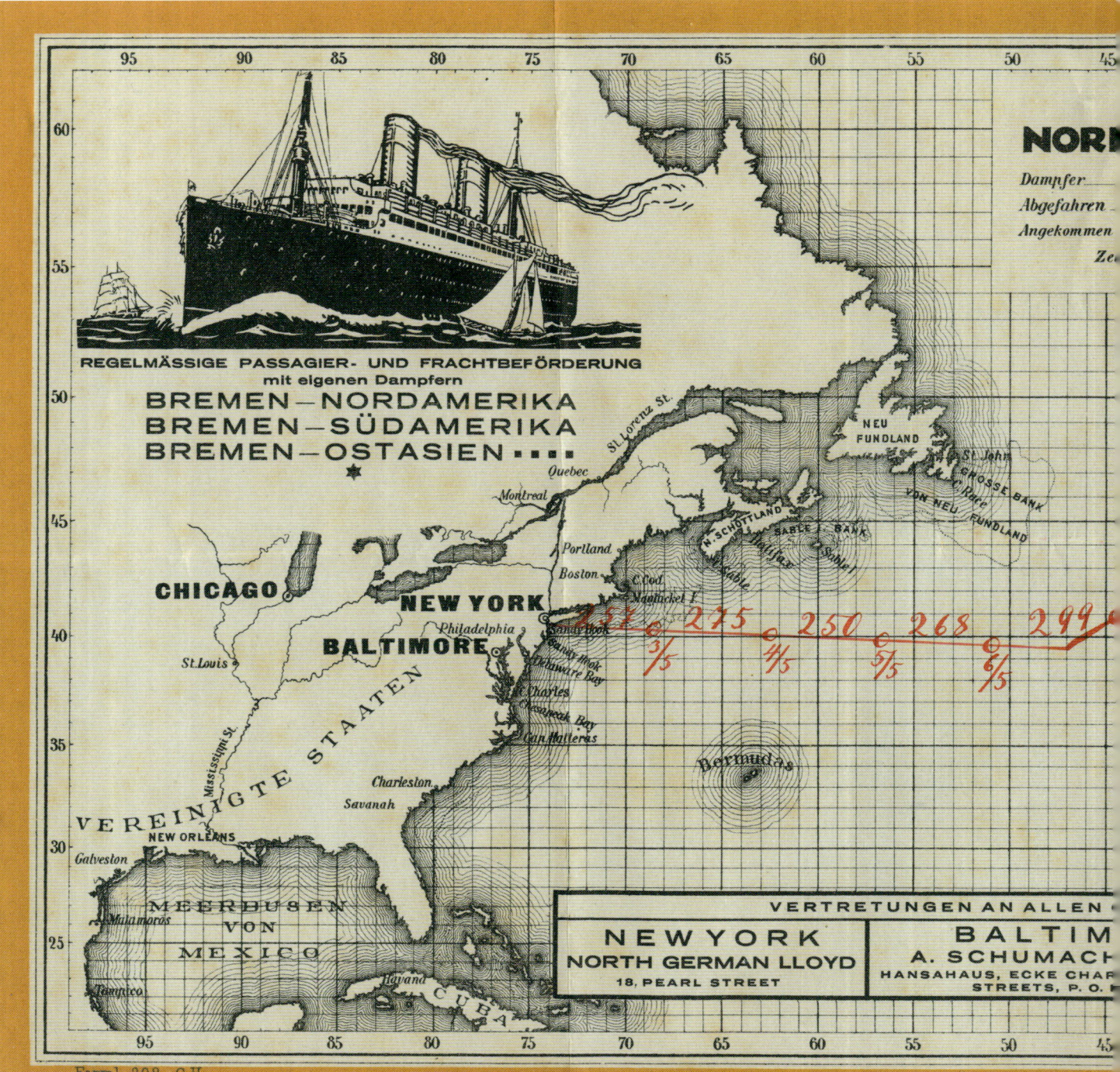

REGELMÄSSIGE PASSAGIER- UND FRACHTBEFÖRDERUNG
mit eigenen Dampfern

BREMEN—NORDAMERIKA
BREMEN—SÜDAMERIKA
BREMEN—OSTASIEN····

VERTRETUNGEN AN ALLEN

NEW YORK
NORTH GERMAN LLOYD
18, PEARL STREET

BALTIM
A. SCHUMACH
HANSAHAUS, ECKE CHAR
STREETS, P. O.

Forml. 208. G.H.

G.H

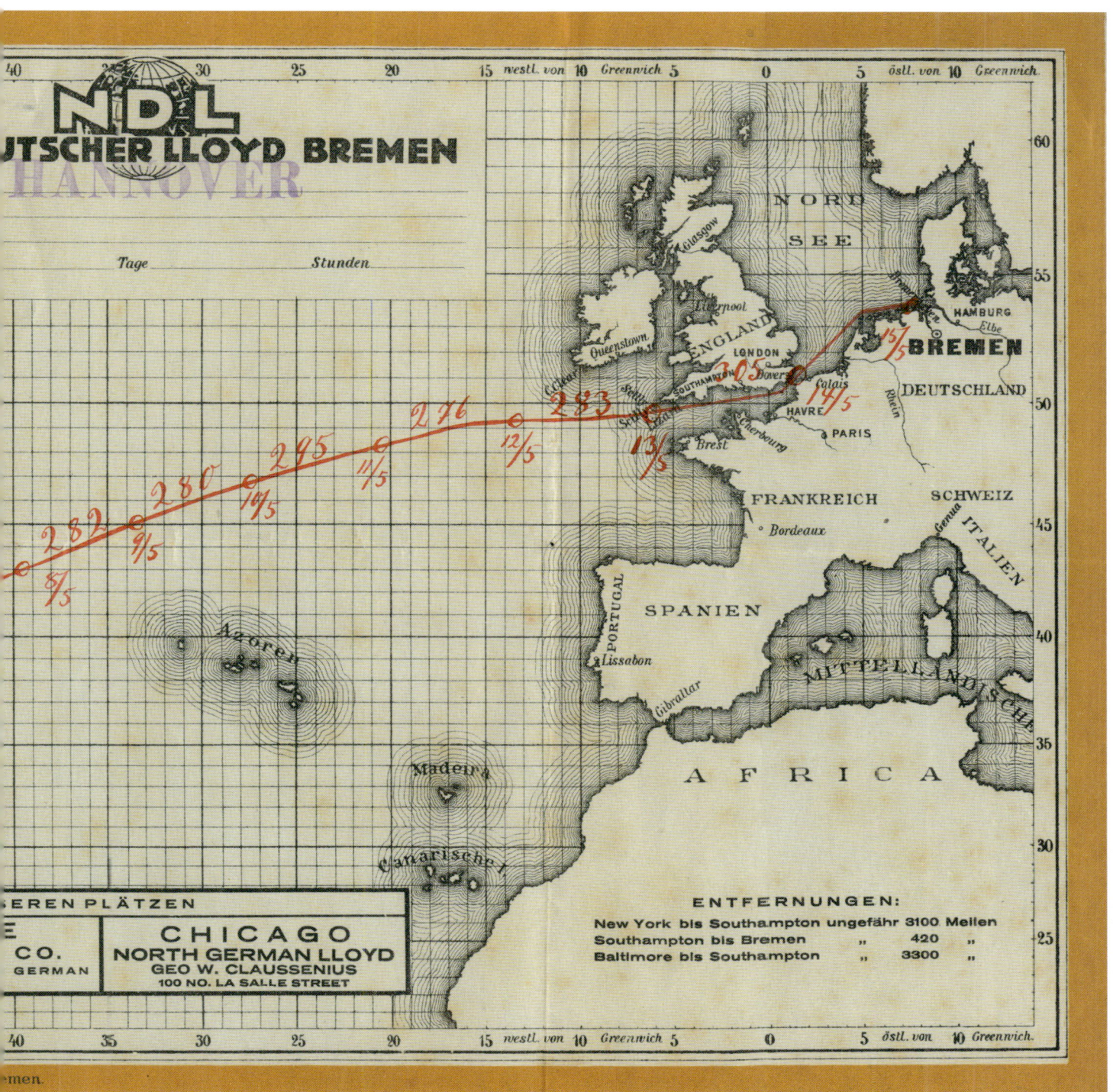

Von einem Passagier eingezeichnete Fahrtstrecke des NDL-Dampfers „Hannover" auf dem Weg von New York nach Bremerhaven mit den täglich zurückgelegten Seemeilen, 02.–15.05.1923. / A passenger has drawn the route of the NGL steamer *Hannover* from New York to Bremerhaven and the number of nautical miles covered each day, 2–15 May 1923.

Über Bremerhaven wanderten zwischen 1830 und 1974 insgesamt 7,2 Millionen Menschen aus. Von ihnen stammten 3,4 Millionen aus Osteuropa: Es waren vor allem Polen, Russen, Tschechen, Slowaken, Ungarn und Rumänen, die Deutschland als Transitland nutzten. Die erste große Auswanderungswelle aus Osteuropa setzte Anfang der 1880er Jahre ein und endete mit dem Ersten Weltkrieg. Eine weitere große Welle osteuropäischer Auswanderer schiffte sich Anfang der 1920er Jahre in Bremerhaven ein. Sie vermischten sich auf den Schiffen mit den Deutschen, die aufgrund der Depression nach dem Ersten Weltkrieg und der Wirtschaftskrise zum ersten Mal seit drei Jahrzehnten wieder massenhaft auswanderten. Für viele Europäer wurde der Traum Amerika unerreichbar. Durch die Quotenregelung bei der Einreise, die für die USA seit dem „Quota Act" von 1921 galt, konnte nur eine bestimmte Anzahl Menschen einer Nationalität einreisen. Glück hatte, wer einen Bürgen in den USA hatte: Verwandte oder Freunde, die gegenüber dem Staat schworen, dass sie im Falle von Arbeitslosigkeit oder Geldnot helfen würden, damit der Einwanderer dem amerikanischen Staat nicht zur Last fallen würde. Durch die seit dem frühen 19. Jahrhundert anhaltende Kettenwanderung besaßen sehr viele Deutsche Verwandte, Bekannte oder Freunde in Amerika und so konnten viele trotz der Einreisebeschränkungen einwandern.

Die Gründe für die starke osteuropäische Auswanderung ab 1880 waren vor allem wirtschaftlicher Natur. So wanderten viele beispielsweise aus dem wirtschaftlich von der zaristischen Regierung absichtlich klein gehaltenen Galizien aus, weil sie für sich und ihre Kinder dort keine Zukunft sahen. Auch politische Gründe spielten eine Rolle: Die gescheiterte Revolution von 1905 und die erfolgreiche Novemberrevolution 1918 führten zur Flucht zahlreicher Menschen. Abgefahren sind auch zehntausende von osteuropäischen Juden von Bremerhaven: Sie flohen vor den ab 1881 einsetzenden Pogromen in Russland und in den von Russland besetzten Teilen Polens. Die Pogrome dauerten bis 1913 an.

In der Zeit des Nationalsozialismus (1933–1945) gab es mehr Flüchtlinge als Auswanderer, die das Deutsche Reich verlie-

nationality group already living in the United States as of 1910. Immigrants who had sponsors vouching for them were lucky indeed—a relative or friend who took an official oath stating that in the event the incoming immigrant was rendered jobless or hard-pressed for money, the sponsor would support that person so as not to burden the U.S. Government. Due to sustained immigration to the United States beginning in the early 1900s many Germans had relatives, friends or acquaintances in America and hence were able to enter the country despite tight immigration restrictions.

The reason for the high number of East European emigrants as of 1880 is to be found in the foundering economy of those countries. Many, for example, left Galicia, a region economically suppressed by the Czarist regime, as they realized there was no future for them or their children in their homeland. Political motives also played a vital role. The revolution of 1905, which had been crushed, and the success of the November Revolution of 1918 forced countless people to flee. Tens of thousands of Jews also fled East Europe by way of Bremerhaven, escaping the pogroms which set in in Russia and in Russian-occupied Poland as of 1881. The pogroms continued up through 1913.

During National Socialism (1933–1945) refugees fleeing the German Reich outnumbered emigrants. Reich President Paul von Hindenburg's appointment of Adolf Hitler, leader of the *National Socialist German Workers' Party* or Nazi Party, as Reich Chancellor of Germany, unleashed the beginning of the Nazi dictatorship, costing the lives of millions all over Europe through late 1945.

February 28, 1933, one day after the Reichstag fire, the deliberate burning down of Germany's parliament building, the new Nazi government used the situation to ban and suppress the German Communist Party by issuing an *Ordinance for the Protection of People and State* which remained in force until 1945 and deprived all citizens of their basic rights. Anybody could now be arrested on suspicion only, imprisoned without trial, without any recourse or right to legal remedy whatsoever. This naturally gave the Nazi Party a

ßen. Am 30. Januar 1933 ernannte Reichspräsident Paul von Hindenburg Adolf Hitler, den Führer der „Nationalsozialistischen Deutschen Arbeiterpartei" (NSDAP), zum Reichskanzler. Es war der Beginn der nationalsozialistischen Diktatur, die bis zu ihrem Ende 1945 Millionen von Menschen in ganz Europa das Leben kostete.

Am 28. Februar 1933, einen Tag nach dem Brand des Reichstages, beschloss der Reichstag unter Federführung der Nationalsozialisten die „Verordnung zum Schutz von Volk und Staat' („Reichstagsbrandverordnung"), die bis 1945 gültig blieb. In dieser Verordnung wurden die Grundrechte der Bürger aufgehoben. Jeder Bürger konnte nun auf bloßen Verdacht hin verhaftet, ohne Urteil in Gefangenschaft gehalten werden und hatte keinerlei Anspruch auf Rechtsmittel. Damit hatten die Nationalsozialisten freie Handhabe gegenüber allen Menschen, die sie aufgrund ihrer „Rasse" oder Überzeugung verfolgten. Mit den „Nürnberger Gesetzen"

Columbuskaje in Bremerhaven: Zurück Bleibende verabschieden ein ablegendes Schiff, 1920er. / The Columbus wharf in Bremerhaven: Those staying behind bid farewell to a ship casting off, 1920s.

free hand to treat people however they pleased, persecuting people on the basis of race or belief. The *Nuremberg Laws*, two racial laws promulgated in Nuremberg on September 15, 1935 during a Nazi Party rally, deprived those not of "German or related blood" of German citizenship and made marriage or extra-marital relations illegal between non-Jews and Jews. German Jews were segregated economically and politically. Robbed of all legal security, Germans of Jewish faith and all those proclaimed Jewish on the basis of the *Nuremberg Laws*, realized that the only chance of survival lay in escape. In addition to persecuting Jewish Germans, the Nazis also persecuted non-Jewish democrats, communists,

vom 15. September 1935 wurden allen Juden die Vollbürgerrechte entzogen, sie wurden wirtschaftlich ausgegrenzt und ihrer politischen Rechte beraubt. Glaubensjuden und alle, die durch die „Nürnberger Gesetze" zu Juden erklärt wurden, besaßen nun endgültig keinerlei Rechtssicherheit mehr. Flucht war für viele Menschen die einzige Überlebenschance. Unter der Verfolgung durch die Nationalsozialisten litten vor allem jüdische Bürger sowie nichtjüdische Demokraten, Kommunisten, Schriftsteller und Künstler. Viele gingen zunächst in europäische Nachbarländer, später dann nach Übersee. Die strikten Einwanderungsbestimmungen oder -beschränkungen ließen für viele ihre Flucht zur Odyssee durch mehrere Staaten werden.

writers and artists. Many escaped to neighboring European countries, only to flee overseas at a later time. The tight immigration regulations and restrictions often turned these journeys into a never-ending odyssey through many states. According to the statistical yearbooks of the German Reich for the years 1933 to 1939, a total of 117,014 people emigrated from Germany. Interestingly, the reports of the *Central Committee* or the *Reich Representative Committee of German Jews* record that at least 234,000 Jews fled Germany during the same period of time. This figure is restricted to Germans of Jewish faith or those considered Jewish by virtue of the *Nuremberg Laws*. In other words, the statistical yearbooks of the German Reich withheld the number of Jewish fugitives.

Der deutsche Reisepass von Moses Kirchheimer. Im Pass befinden sich zwei lebensentscheidende Stempel: ein „J" für „Jude" der deutschen Polizeibehörde und ein Einreisevisum des US-Konsulates in Hamburg für die USA, 1939. / Moses Kirchheimer's German passport. It contains two life-changing stamps: a "J" for "Jew" issued by the German police, and an entry permit for the United States issued by the U.S. Consulate in Hamburg, 1939.

Laut den Statistischen Jahrbüchern des Deutschen Reiches emigrierten zwischen 1933 und 1939 insgesamt 117.014 Menschen aus Deutschland. In den Arbeitsberichten des „Zentralausschusses" bzw. der „Reichsvertretung der Deutschen Juden" sind jedoch im gleichen Zeitraum mindestens 234.000 Juden als Flüchtlinge aus Deutschland verzeichnet. Es handelte sich um Glaubensjuden und um Menschen, die nach den „Nürnberger Gesetzen" von 1935 zu Juden ernannt worden waren. In den Statistischen Jahrbüchern des Deutschen Reiches wurden demnach die jüdischen Flüchtlinge unterschlagen.

Vor allem nach der von den Nationalsozialisten benannten „Reichskristallnacht" am 9. November 1938 begann die Weltöffentlichkeit auf die lebensbedrohliche Situation der deutschen Juden aufmerksam zu werden. Die britische Regierung reagierte umgehend: Knapp drei Wochen nach der Pogromnacht begannen die ersten Kindertransporte von Deutschland nach Großbritannien. Mit Kriegsbeginn am 1. September 1939 mussten sie eingestellt werden. Insgesamt konnten etwa 10.000 meist jüdische Kinder gerettet werden. Offiziell wurde im Oktober 1941 ein Auswanderungsverbot im Deutschen Reich erlassen, de facto machte der Ausbruch des Zweiten Weltkrieges die Ausreise für Juden und Nichtjuden unmöglich. Trotzdem gelang zwischen 1939 und 1941 insgesamt 23.000 deutschen Juden die Flucht vor der nationalsozialistischen Vernichtungspolitik.

1945, nach dem Ende des Zweiten Weltkrieges, lebten in ganz Europa nach Schätzungen sieben bis neun Millionen Displaced Persons (DPs): Heimatlose, Entwurzelte, Wanderer wider Willen. Es waren jüdische und nichtjüdische überlebende KZ-Häftlinge, ehemalige Zwangsarbeiter, Fremdarbeiter; auch Kriegsgefangene zählten dazu. Viele von ihnen stammten aus Osteuropa. Zwischen 1945 und 1947 fanden umfassende Repatriierungsmaßnahmen der Alliierten statt und etwa sieben Millionen Heimatlose wurden in ihre ehemaligen Heimatländer zurückgeschickt. Im August 1947 befanden sich noch 1.214.500 Displaced Persons in den Westzonen Deutschlands und Österreichs, davon allein 747.000 in der US-amerikanischen Zone.

Particularly after what the Nazis termed the "Reichskristallnacht" on November 9, 1938, a massive nationwide pogrom in Germany and Austria directed at Jewish citizens and portending the events of the Holocaust, the world gradually became aware of the life-threatening situation of the Jews. The British government was the first to react. Less than three weeks after the nationwide pogrom a program was set up to transport children out of Germany to Great Britain. When the war broke out on September 1, 1939 they had to be stopped. All told, 10,000 mostly Jewish children were saved. In October 1941, an official decree was issued prohibiting citizens to emigrate from the German Reich, but with the outbreak of the war emigration had de facto become impossible for Jews and non-Jews alike. Nevertheless, 23,000 German Jews managed to escape extermination at the hands of Nazi Germany between 1939 and 1941.

By the end of World War II in 1945, an estimated seven to nine million DPs – Displaced Persons who were homeless, uprooted, banished, wanderers against their will – lived throughout Europe. They included Jewish and non-Jewish concentration camp survivors, former forced laborers and foreign workers, many of whom originally came from East Europe. Among them were also prisoners of war. For two years after the war, the Allied forces carried out major repatriation efforts so that by 1947 an estimated seven million DPs had returned to their former native countries. In August 1947, there were still 1,214,500 Displaced Persons in the western zones of Germany and Austria, of which 747,000 alone were in the American zone.

Transporting Displaced Persons back to Soviet Russia often proved very dangerous as the Soviet regime thought of them not as victims, but as spies from the capitalist West, invariably sending them to labor camps in Siberia. This knowledge and the shocking report by President Truman's agent for the *Intergovernmental Committee on Refugees*, Earl G. Harrison, caused the U.S. and Great Britain to alter their DP policy. Harrison's report to the president noted that, "Evidently we are not treating the Jews any differently than the Nazis did, the only difference being that we don't exterminate them." The displaced Jews referred to themselves

Gerade der Rücktransport in die UdSSR hatte sich als gefährlich erwiesen, denn die sowjetische Regierung betrachtete die Displaced Persons nicht als Opfer, sondern oft auch als Spione des kapitalistischen Westens, und schickte sie in die Lager nach Sibirien. Diese Erfahrung und der erschütternde Bericht des vom amerikanischen Präsidenten Harry S. Truman eingesetzten Beauftragten des „Intergovernmental Committee on Refugees", Earl G. Harrison, veranlassten die USA und Großbritannien zum Umschwenken in ihrer DP-Politik. Harrison hatte unter anderem dem Präsidenten berichtet: „Wir behandeln die Juden allem Anschein nach nicht anders als die Nazis, nur dass wir sie nicht vernichten."[2]

Die jüdischen Displaced Persons nannten sich selbst „She'erith Hapletah": der überlebende Rest. Oft lebten sie noch jahrelang in den zu DP-Camps umfunktionierten ehemaligen Konzentrationslagern. Unmittelbar nach der Befreiung der Lager hatte es unter den jüdischen Überlebenden einen starken Idealismus und Hoffnung auf die Zukunft gegeben: „Die Toten befahlen zu leben" (Ze'ev Mankowitz)[3]. Aber die mangelnde internationale Solidarität und die sich über Jahre hinziehende Unentschlossenheit vor allem der US-amerikanischen und britischen Regierungen, wie mit den jüdischen Displaced Persons umzugehen sei, führte zu Resignation. Während sich Großbritannien gegen eine starke jüdische Einwanderung nach Palästina sperrte, wollten die USA bis 1948 eine große Einwanderung in ihr Land nicht zulassen. Letztendlich konnten bis 1952 100.000 jüdische Überlebende mit ihren Kindern nach Nordamerika und 250.000 nach Palästina ausreisen.

Bremerhaven wurde zwischen 1946 und 1952 zum „Port of Embarkation": Knapp 800.000 jüdische und nichtjüdische Displaced Persons bestiegen hier zwischen 1946 und 1952 die Schiffe, die sie in ein neues Leben bringen sollten.

In den Jahrzehnten nach dem Zweiten Weltkrieg war Deutschland von starken Aus- und Einwanderungswellen geprägt. Allein zwischen 1945 und 1950 kamen knapp 7,9 Millionen Flüchtlinge aus den ehemaligen deutschen Ostgebieten in das Gebiet der 1949 gegründeten Bundesrepublik. Ihre Integration in die Dörfer und Städte zog sich

as *She'erith Hapletah*—the Holocaust survivors—many of whom lived for years in the former concentration camps. Immediately following the liberation of the concentration camps strong idealism and hope for the future had sprung up among the Jewish survivors. To quote Ze'ev Mankovitz: "The dead commanded that we live."[3] Yet the lack of international solidarity and the protracted indecision on the part of the U.S. and British governments as to how to best deal with Jewish DPs, led to resignation on their part. Whereas Great Britain on the one hand was against widespread Jewish immigration to Palestine, the U.S. on the other hand was against widespread Jewish immigration to the U.S.A., until 1948. Eventually, 100,000 Jewish Holocaust survivors were permitted to enter North America with their children and 250,000 allowed to travel to Palestine.

Bremerhaven evolved into a port of embarkation between 1946 and 1952 with an estimated 800,000 Jewish and non-Jewish DPs boarding ships destined to take them to a new life.

In the decades following the Second World War, Germany was characterized by waves of migratory movement. Between 1945 and 1950 alone, some 7.9 million refugees from regions in Eastern Europe formerly inhabited by ethnic Germans immigrated to the 1949 newly formed Federal Republic of Germany. Their integration in the towns and cities took years. The last refugee camp in Germany for Displaced Persons wasn't dissolved until the early 1970s.

In addition to the Displaced Persons waiting to leave the country, a large number of Germans also wished to leave war-torn Germany. However, up until the formation of the Federal Republic of Germany in 1949 immigration restrictions for Germans in the classic countries of immigration, such as the U.S., Canada and Australia were very tight. Only spouses and children of foreign nationals and officially recognized victims of Nazi persecution were allowed to immigrate. Thousands of *war brides* – the wives of British and U.S. soldiers – left from Bremerhaven for the New World.

By 1949 the Western Allied Forces had begun to loosen immigration restrictions for Germans which resulted in a large wave of German emigration during the 1950s. While between

SHIP TO FREEDOM!

BREMERHAVEN PORT OF EMBARKATION

Abfahrt des ersten „Displaced Persons"-Transportes von Bremerhaven nach New York, 1948. / Departure of the first "Displaced Persons" transport from Bremerhaven to New York in 1948.

Jahrzehnte hin. Das letzte Vetriebenenlager in der Bundesrepublik wurde erst Anfang der 1970er Jahre aufgelöst. Neben den auf ihre Ausreise wartenden Displaced Persons gab es viele Deutsche, die in der Nachkriegszeit das zerstörte Land verlassen wollten. Allerdings gab es bis zur Gründung der Bundesrepublik Deutschland 1949 für Deutsche stark reglementierte Einreisemöglichkeiten in die klassischen Einwanderungsländer wie die USA, Kanada und Australien: Auswandern durften nur Ehepartner und Kinder von ausländischen Staatsangehörigen und offiziell anerkannte Verfolgte der nationalsozialistischen Regierung. Tausende der „War Brides" – Ehefrauen britischer oder US-amerikanischer Soldaten – reisten von Bremerhaven in die Neue Welt.
1949 begannen die westlichen Alliierten die Einreisebeschränkungen für Deutsche zu lockern und zu Beginn der 1950er Jahre kam es zu einer starken deutschen Auswanderung: Zwischen 1946 und 1961 wanderten insgesamt 779.700 Deutsche aus. Gleichzeitig begann mit dem 1955 zwischen

1946 and 1961 a total of 779,700 Germans left the country, Italian guest workers began to migrate to Germany in response to the German-Italian recruitment contract of 1955, continuing until recruitment was stopped in 1973. In the interest of reuniting families, relatives of guest workers are still migrating to Germany today. The next major migratory movement to Germany took place towards the end of the 1980s with the immigration of *Aussiedler* and *Spätaussiedler* (German resettlers from Eastern and Southern Europe), most specifically from the Soviet Union, Poland and Romania. To date, altogether more than four million *Aussiedler* and *Spätaussiedler* have immigrated to Germany.

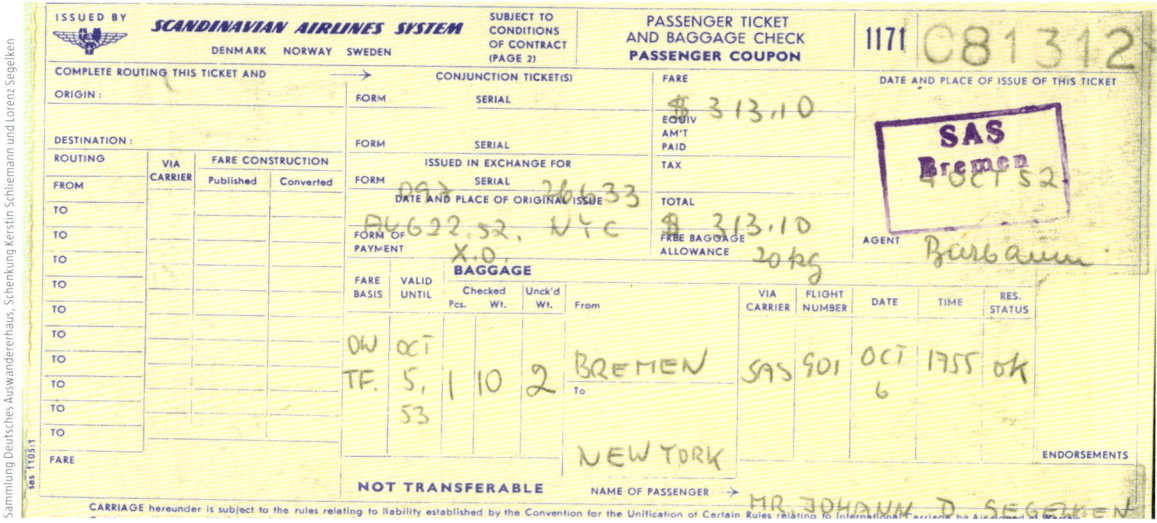

Sammlung Deutsches Auswandererhaus, Schenkung Kerstin Schliemann und Lorenz Segelken

Italien und Deutschland abgeschlossenen Anwerbevertrag für italienische Arbeiter die Einwanderung europäischer Arbeitsmigranten nach Deutschland, die bis zum „Anwerbestopp" 1973 andauerte. Durch Familienzusammenführungen wandern bis heute Verwandte der Arbeitsmigranten nach Deutschland ein. Die nächst größere Einwanderungsbewegung setzte Ende der 1980er Jahre in der Bundesrepublik ein, als die Aussiedlerzuwanderung vor allem aus der UdSSR, Polen und Rumänien begann. Insgesamt sind bis heute über vier Millionen Aussiedler und Spätaussiedler nach Deutschland eingewandert.

Das Flugzeug löst das Schiff als Transportmittel für Auswanderer langsam ab. Flugticket des Amerikaauswanderers Johann Diedrich Segelken von Bremen nach New York, 1952. / Airplanes slowly replaced ships as a means of transport for emigrants. Airline ticket belonging to Johann Diedrich Segelken, a German who emigrated from Bremen to New York in 1952.

Germany today is a country of migration. Three hundred years of German migratory history prove one thing: hardly a decade went by in which migration was not a topic of focus in Germany.

Sammlung Deutsches Auswandererhaus, Schenkung Inge Magrs

Ehepaar Stinshoff auf dem Weg nach Kanada, 1956. / Mr. and Mrs. Stinshoff on their way to Canada, 1956.

Deutschland ist heute Ein- und Auswanderungsland. Der Rückblick auf 300 Jahre deutsche Geschichte von Auswanderung und Flucht zeigt eines: Es gab kaum ein Jahrzehnt, in dem Migration kein Thema in Deutschland war.

Bremerhaven, 17. Mai 1974
Um 18 Uhr legt die „Britanis" mit mehr als 350 Auswanderern an Bord von der Columbuskaje in Richtung Australien ab. Die „Nordsee-Zeitung" brachte am Morgen eine kleine Meldung über das Ereignis. Was zu diesem Zeitpunkt niemand wusste: Die „Britanis" war das letzte Auswandererschiff, das Bremerhaven in Richtung Neue Welt verließ. 140 Jahre lang war Bremerhaven die Stadt des Abschieds.

Bremerhaven, 24. September 2005
Gegen 12 Uhr mittags betritt der Deutsch-Australier Klaus Schwarz das Deutsche Auswandererhaus. Er war einer der Auswanderer auf der „Britanis". Der Kreis schließt sich.

Notiz aus der „Nordsee-Zeitung" vom 17.05.1974.
Notice in the *Nordsee-Zeitung*, dated May 17, 1974.

Bremerhaven, May 17, 1974
With over 350 emigrant passengers on board, the *Britanis* cast off from the Columbus wharf at 6:00 P.M., headed for Australia. The local daily newspaper *Nordsee-Zeitung* featured a brief article on the event. What no one at the time realized was that the *Britanis* was to be the last emigrant ship to leave Bremerhaven for the New World. For a period of 140 years, Bremerhaven had been the city of farewells.

Bremerhaven, September 24, 2005
Klaus Schwarz, German-Australian, and among the emigrants on board the *Britanis,* enters the German Emigration Center around noon. History comes full circle.

Mit Auswanderern nach Australien

Im Liniendienst aus Australien läuft heute um 14 Uhr die „Britanis" (24351 BRT) die Columbuskaje an. Das Passagierschiff hat in Rotterdam bereits 200 Auswanderer an Bord genommen sowie 50 Agenten von Reisebüros, die eine Rundreise über Bremerhaven nach England unternehmen. Wenn die „Britanis" heute um 18 Uhr mit weiteren 153 Auswanderern aus Deutschland wieder Bremerhaven verläßt, nimmt sie Kurs auf Southampton, um dann mit vollem Schiff den fünften Kontinent anzulaufen.

Archiv Nordsee-Zeitung

Quellen und Literatur / Sources and References

*Aus den mit Hochziffern gekennzeichneten Werken stammen
die im Text verwendeten Zitate. / The literature preceded by a number
was used for the quotations in this catalogue.*

[1] Wittichen, Friedrich Carl / Salzer, Ernst (Hrsg.): Briefe von und an Friedrich Gentz, München, 1909, S. 178.

[2] The Harrison Report; zitiert nach Dinnerstein, Leonard: Britische und amerikanische DP-Politik; in: Fritz Bauer Institut (Hrsg.): Überlebt und unterwegs. Jüdische Displaced Persons im Nachkriegsdeutschland. Jahrbuch zur Geschichte und Wirkung des Holocaust, Frankfurt am Main / New York, 1997, S. 109–117, S. 111.

[3] Mankowitz, Ze'ev, zit. n. Peck, Abraham J.: „Unsere Augen haben die Ewigkeit gesehen". Erinnerung und Identität der She'erith Hapletah; in: Fritz Bauer Institut (Hrsg.), wie Anmerkung 2, S. 27–49, S. 35.

Zahlen und Prozentangaben entstammen folgenden Werken:
Figures and percentages are from the following sources:

Arbeitsberichte des Zentralausschusses der deutschen Juden für Hilfe und Aufbau bei der Reichsvertretung der deutschen Juden für die Jahre 1933–1941.

Chicago Historical Society (bearb. von): Population Figures by Single Years of the City of Chicago, 1988.

Craig, Gordon A.: *Germany 1866–1945*, Oxford, 1980.

Hoerder, Dirk / Knauf, Diethelm (Hrsg.): Aufbruch in die Fremde. Europäische Auswanderung nach Übersee, Bremen, 1992.

Howard, Robert P.: *Illinois. A History of the Prairie State*, Grand Rapids, 1972.

Nerger-Focke, Karin: Die deutsche Amerikaauswanderung nach 1945, Stuttgart, 1995.

Ritter, Gerhard A. / Tenfelde, Klaus: Arbeiter im Deutschen Kaiserreich 1871 bis 1914, Bonn, 1992.

Statistisches Bundesamt Deutschland: Wanderungsstatistik. Wanderungen über die Grenzen Deutschlands 1950–2004, Wiesbaden, 2005.

Statistisches Reichsamt (Hrsg.): Statistik des Deutschen Reiches, Berlin, Jahrgänge 1933–1941.

Wehler, Hans-Ulrich: Deutsche Gesellschaftsgeschichte, Bd. 1: Vom Feudalismus des Alten Reiches bis zur Defensiven Modernisierung der Reformära 1700–1815, München, 1996.

Wehler, Hans-Ulrich: Deutsche Gesellschaftsgeschichte. Bd. 2: Von der Reformära bis zur industriellen und politischen „Deutschen Doppelrevolution" 1815–1845/49, München, 1995.

EINWANDERUNG
IMMIGRATION

NACH DEUTSCHLAND
Ein Land, ständig in Bewegung

TO GERMANY
A country on the move

SIMONE EICK, TANJA FITTKAU, KARIN HESS, JÖRG RÜSEWALD

EPOCHE DER „GLAUBENSFLÜCHTLINGE" 1683 – 1789

Glaubensfreiheit ist eine Errungenschaft der Moderne. Im Mittelalter und in der frühen Neuzeit werden Juden und auch Protestanten in Teilen Europas verfolgt. Einige Mitglieder deutscher protestantischer Glaubensgemeinschaften wandern deshalb nach Amerika aus. So gründet eine Gruppe von Pietisten 1683 „Germantown", heute ein Stadtteil Philadelphias. In Europa schützen einige wenige Länder die Glaubensflüchtlinge, dazu gehören auch deutsche Staaten und Städte.

Juden

1492 stellt das „Alhambra-Edikt" die spanischen Juden vor die Wahl: Entweder sie treten zum Christentum über oder sie müssen ins Exil gehen. Um Zwangstaufen und Pogromen zu entkommen, flüchten viele in den Süden des heutigen Deutschlands.

Auch in Altona bei Hamburg werden unterschiedliche Glaubensrichtungen toleriert. Ende des 16. Jahrhunderts erhalten von der iberischen Halbinsel geflohene Juden hier das Wohnrecht. Offiziell werden sie jedoch als Katholiken geführt. Um 1780 zählt die Jüdische Gemeinde Altona 1.911 Gemeindemitglieder.

Im Jahr 1671 gibt der brandenburgische Große Kurfürst Friedrich Wilhelm 50 wohlhabenden jüdischen Familien aus Wien das Privileg, sich in seinem Reich niederzulassen. 70 Jahre später bietet Friedrich der Große religiösen Minderheiten wie Protestanten und Juden das Recht in Brandenburg-Preußen zu bleiben. Ganz im Sinne seines geflügelten Ausspruches: „Jeder soll nach seiner Façon selig

ERA OF THE "RELIGIOUS REFUGEES," 1683 – 1789

Freedom of worship is an achievement of modernism. In medieval and early modern times Jews and Protestants are persecuted in some parts of Europe. Some members of Protestant German congregations immigrate to America, and in 1683, a group of Pietists establish a township called "Germantown" – today it is a district of Philadelphia. Few European countries and cities are willing to shelter the religious refugees – these include German states and cities.

Jews

The Alhambra Decree (also known as the Edict of Expulsion), an edict issued on March 31, 1492, orders the expulsion of the Jews unless they convert to Christianity. Thousands of Jews seek to escape coerced conversion and the pogroms by fleeing to what is today the South of Germany. The city of Altona near Hamburg is one of the cities that welcomes and tolerates people of various faiths. In the latter 16th century Jews fleeing the Iberian Peninsula are offered the right of abode here, however, they are officially registered as Catholics. The Jewish community in Altona counts 1,911 congregants by around 1780.

Frederick William, Elector of Brandenburg, extends the privilege of settling in his electorate to 50 affluent Jewish families from Vienna in the year 1671. Seventy years later, Frederick the Great extends the right to settle in Brandenburg-Prussia to religious minorities such as Protestants and Jews, true to his own belief that each man should be happy in his own way. And Frederick the Great prof-

werden." Er profitiert von den Einwanderern durch höhere Steuereinnahmen. Erst mit der Gründung des Deutschen Kaiserreichs 1871 erhalten Juden die gesetzliche Gleichstellung in ganz Deutschland.

Hugenotten

Am 18. Oktober 1685 stellt der „Sonnenkönig" Ludwig XIV. im katholischen Frankreich die protestantischen Hugenotten vor die Wahl: Entweder sie treten zum Katholizismus über oder es drohen ihnen Verfolgung, Haft und Tod. Rund 150.000 Hugenotten fliehen heimlich aus Frankreich.

Viele protestantische Herrscher in Europa nehmen ihre Glaubensbrüder auf. So auch der Große Kurfürst Friedrich Wilhelm von Brandenburg. Er sichert den Hugenotten am 29. Oktober 1685 mit dem „Edikt von Potsdam" neben der Religionsfreiheit auch die Steuerfreiheit sowie freies Bauland und Baumaterialien zu. Nicht nur aus Mitleid macht der Große Kurfürst seinen Glaubensbrüdern dieses großzügige Angebot: Brandenburg leidet noch immer unter den Folgen des Dreißigjährigen Krieges. Der europäische Glaubenskampf von Katholiken und Protestanten hat zwischen 1618 und 1648 auch hier viele Opfer gefordert. Mit den rund 20.000 Hugenotten, die nun nach Brandenburg kommen, erhöht sich nicht nur die Zahl der Untertanen Brandenburgs, sie kurbeln auch die Wirtschaft an. Friedrich Wilhelms Nachfolger nehmen weitere Glaubensflüchtlinge in Preußen auf.

its from the immigrants through higher tax revenues. It is not until the founding of the German Empire in 1871 that Jews actually receive equality under public law throughout Germany.

Huguenots

On October 18, 1685, Louis XIV, the "Sun King," forces the Protestant Huguenots in Catholic France to choose between converting to Catholicism or risking persecution, imprisonment, even death. Close to 150,000 Huguenots manage to escape France secretly.

Many Protestant rulers in Europe accept their fellow Christians, among them Frederick William, Elector of Brandenburg. In addition to freedom of worship the Edict of Potsdam, issued on October 29, 1685, also ensures exemption from taxes, free building land and building material for the Huguenots. This Great Elector's generous offer does not stem solely from compassion for his fellow Christians. Indeed, Brandenburg is still suffering from the consequences of the Thirty Years' War. The religious wars between Catholics and Protestants in Europe between 1618 and 1648 claimed many victims. Not only do the 20,000 Huguenots settling in Brandenburg raise the number of royal subjects, they also stimulate the economy. Frederick Williams successors follow in his footsteps, settling further religious refugees in Prussia.

Empfang der Hugenotten durch den Großen Kurfürsten im Potsdamer Stadtschloss, 1685. / The Elector of Brandenburg welcoming the arriving Huguenots in the Potsdam City Palace in 1685.

Auf dem sogenannten Auswandererbahnhof Ruhleben bei Berlin bestiegen viele Osteuropäer ihre Züge in die Auswandererhäfen Hamburg und Bremerhaven, um 1900. / Many Eastern Europeans boarded the trains that would take them to the emigration ports in Hamburg and Bremerhaven at the so-called "Auswandererbahnhof Ruhleben," near Berlin, about 1900.

EPOCHE DER DEUTSCHEN „MASSENWANDERUNG" 1789 – 1913

Im 19. Jahrhundert sind die Menschen in Deutschland sehr mobil: Nicht nur wandern 5,5 Millionen Deutsche nach Übersee aus, auch über 50 Millionen Menschen ziehen als Binnenwanderer für einen Arbeitsplatz um. Als Soldaten oder Wanderarbeiter legen Deutsche tausende Kilometer zurück.

Ende des 19. Jahrhunderts ist Deutschland Transitland für Millionen Osteuropäer, die mit Zügen über Berlin in die Auswandererhäfen Bremerhaven und Cuxhaven reisen und von dort nach Übersee fahren. Allein von Bremerhaven sind es rund 3,4 Millionen, darunter hunderttausende Juden, die vor den Pogromen im zaristischen Russland fliehen.

Soldaten

Mit der Französischen Revolution beginnt 1789 in Europa ein neues Zeitalter: „Freiheit, Gleichheit und Brüderlichkeit" ist ihr Schlachtruf, der bald durch ganz Europa hallt. Die Forderungen der Revolutionäre, die den alten Ständestaat abschaffen wollen, stellen die Monarchien Europas in Frage. Ab 1792 brechen zahlreiche Kriege aus. Millionen

ERA OF GERMAN "MASS MIGRATION," 1789 – 1913

People in Germany are very mobile in the course of the 19th century. In addition to the 5.5 million Germans who decide to immigrate overseas, as many as 50 million people move within Germany in search of employment. German soldiers and migrant workers also cover distances of thousands of miles.

At the end of the 19th century, Germany became a transit country for millions of Eastern Europeans. Traveling by train via Berlin to the emigration ports in Bremerhaven and Cuxhaven, they embarked on their journey overseas. Approximately 3.4 million emigrants left from Bremerhaven, including hundreds of thousands of Jews fleeing the pogroms in czarist Russia.

Soldiers

The French Revolution in 1789 marks the dawning of a new age in Europe. The rallying cry, "Liberty, Equality and Fraternity," rings throughout Europe. The revolutionists demand abolition of a state with three estates, thus challenging the monarchies in all the countries of Europe. Beginning in 1792, numerous wars break out. Millions of young men march across Europe, the majority leaving their

junge Männer marschieren jahrelang quer durch Europa. Die meisten von ihnen verlassen zum ersten und einzigen Mal ihren Heimatort und können nach Kriegsende davon berichten. Viele jedoch sterben: allein zwischen 1803 und 1815 mindestens 2,5 Millionen Soldaten. Am Ende verliert Frankreich und die Demokratisierung Deutschlands verzögert sich um weitere 100 Jahre.

Wanderarbeiter

In Deutschland leben seit dem ausgehenden Mittelalter immer mehr Kleinbauern, die ihre Familien von ihren viel zu kleinen Ländereien nicht ernähren können. Sie brauchen Nebenjobs. So werden die Männer zu Wanderarbeitern, die ihr Geld für einige Monate in den Nachbarländern verdienen. Seit dem ausgehenden 17. Jahrhundert verkaufen die sogenannten Tödden aus dem nördlichen Münsterland

hometown for the first and only time in their lives. Those returning home after the war is over report what they have seen and experienced. But millions have died, at least 2.5 million between 1803 and 1815 alone. In the end, France is defeated and the process of democratization in Germany is delayed by a hundred years.

Migrant Workers

In Germany, since the late Middle Ages there is a growing population of peasants and their families who are unable to subsist on the meager yield of their limited acreage. In search for additional work the men migrate to neighboring countries for several months each year to earn money there. As of the late 17th century the Tödden from the northern Münsterland region sell cloth in the Netherlands. Many families even own a business there. When the rise of cheap industrial products in the mid-19th century destroys traveling trade many of the traveling merchants sink into poverty. Tödden families who are better off, for example, the Hettlages or Brenninkmeijer of C&A, establish department stores in many cities for industrial textile goods.

Ruhr Poles

As industrialization develops in Germany in the mid-19th century the number of jobs in mining grows, too. Earning good wages, day laborers and peasants move to the industrial areas with their families. Tens of thousands of Polish families from the eastern territories of Prussia move to the Ruhr Area. By 1914, the number has risen to more than 400,000. The majority of the "Ruhr Poles" work in the mining industry. Frequently labeled as scabs and wage squeezers by their German colleagues the police also monitor the many Ruhr Poles involved in the trade and other unions. Even today, a large number of the Ruhr Poles' descendants live in North Rhine-Westphalia as the numerous Polish surnames disclose.

Sammlung Deutsches Auswandererhaus; Schenkung Karl-Heinz Käller

Patent für Cornelius Käller, mit dem es dem Westfalen in der niederländischen Stadt Leeuwarden erlaubt war, Handel zu treiben, 1875. / Patent for Cornelius Käller, permitting the native Westphalian to trade in the Dutch town of Leeuwarden, 1875.

beispielsweise Stoffe in den Niederlanden. Viele Familien besitzen dort sogar ein Geschäft. Als der Wanderhandel ab Mitte des 19. Jahrhunderts mit dem Aufkommen billiger Industrieprodukte jedoch zugrunde geht, verarmen viele von ihnen. Reichere Tödden-Familien, wie die Hettlages oder C&A Brenninkmeijers, gründen Kaufhäuser für industrielle Textilwaren in zahlreichen Städten.

Ruhrpolen

Mit Beginn der deutschen Industrialisierung Mitte des 19. Jahrhunderts entstehen immer mehr Arbeitsplätze im Bergbau. Tagelöhner und Kleinbauern finden hier ein gutes Einkommen und ziehen mit ihren Familien in die Industriegebiete. So gehen zehntausende polnische Familien aus den östlichen preußischen Provinzen ins Ruhrgebiet. Im Jahr 1914 leben bereits über 400.000 Polen dort. Die meisten der „Ruhrpolen" arbeiten im Bergbau. Oft werden sie von ihren deutschen Kollegen als Streikbrecher und Lohndrücker abgestempelt und wegen ihrer Gewerkschafts- und Vereinsarbeit polizeilich überwacht. Noch heute leben viele Nachfahren der Ruhrpolen in Nordrhein-Westfalen, wovon die zahlreichen polnischen Nachnamen erzählen.

EPOCHE DER „KRIEGSBEDINGTEN WANDERUNGEN" 1914 – 1932

Es ist der 1. August 1914: Deutschland löst den Ersten Weltkrieg aus. 15 Millionen Menschen sterben, 60 Millionen Soldaten stehen bis Kriegsende 1918 unter Waffen. Ausländische Zwangsarbeiter müssen in der deutschen Industrie und Landwirtschaft schuften. Nach Kriegsende verlassen über eine Million Deutsche Gebiete, die Deutschland an Frankreich und Polen abtreten muss. Im Januar 1919 wird mit der Weimarer Republik der erste demokratische deutsche Staat gegründet. In den Anfangsjahren prägen Wirtschaftskrise und Inflation, Arbeitslosigkeit und Hunger den Alltag der Menschen. Viele junge Menschen wandern in die USA aus. Deutschland ist weiterhin Transitland für Osteuropäer. Nach einer kurzen Zeit der wirtschaftlichen Erholung bricht 1929 die Weltwirtschaftskrise über Deutschland herein. Ende 1932 ist jeder dritte Deutsche arbeitslos.

THE ERA OF "MIGRATION CAUSED BY WAR," 1914 – 1932

Germany starts World War I on August 1, 1914. A total of 15 million people are killed, and by the end of the war in 1918, 60 million soldiers have served in the ranks. Foreign forced laborers are assigned as workers in German industry and agriculture. After the war, over one million Germans must leave the territories that Germany has surrendered to France and Poland. In January 1919, the founding of the Weimar Republic establishes the first democratic German state. In its first years, the effects of a financial crisis and inflation, as well as unemployment and hunger have a major impact on everyday life. Many young people immigrate to the United States. Germany continues to be a transit country for Eastern Europeans. After a brief period of economic recovery, the Great Depression hits Germany in 1929. By the end of 1932, one in three Germans is unemployed.

Forced Laborers during the First World War

The German economy is lacking the men who have been drafted into military service. There is a shortage of food supplies. Military supplies for the war machine are grinding to a halt. German women and foreign prisoners of war are supposed to bridge the gap. At least 1.9 million prisoners of war are recruited as forced laborers in addition to hundreds of thousands of civilians from the occupied territories. To a great extent, they are discriminated and abused by the Germans. Nevertheless, several thousand Polish and Russian forced laborers remain in Germany after the war therefore becoming immigrants.

German Immigrants from the Ceded Territories

The country must pay reparations, yield territories. New states come into being, the borders change. To the West, Alsace-Lorraine, annexed by the Germans in 1871, passes back to France. Subsequently, some 150,000 German residents are expelled. For the most part they settle in Baden, Hessen-Nassau, Württemberg, the Palatinate and the Saar region, which is administrated by the League of Nations. Assimilating the Germans from Alsace-Lorraine poses no problems.

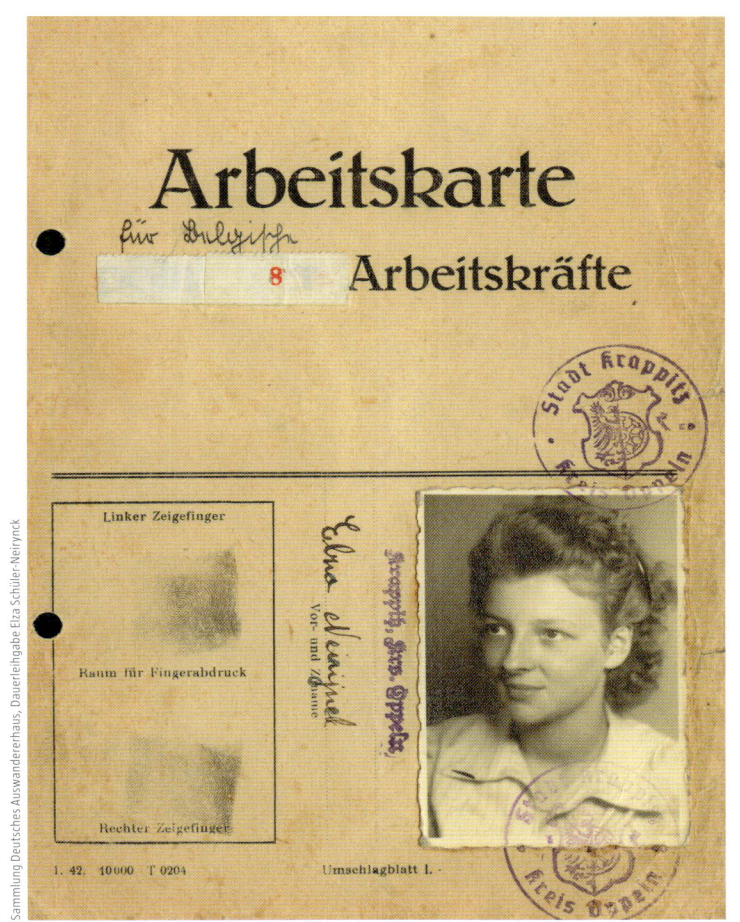
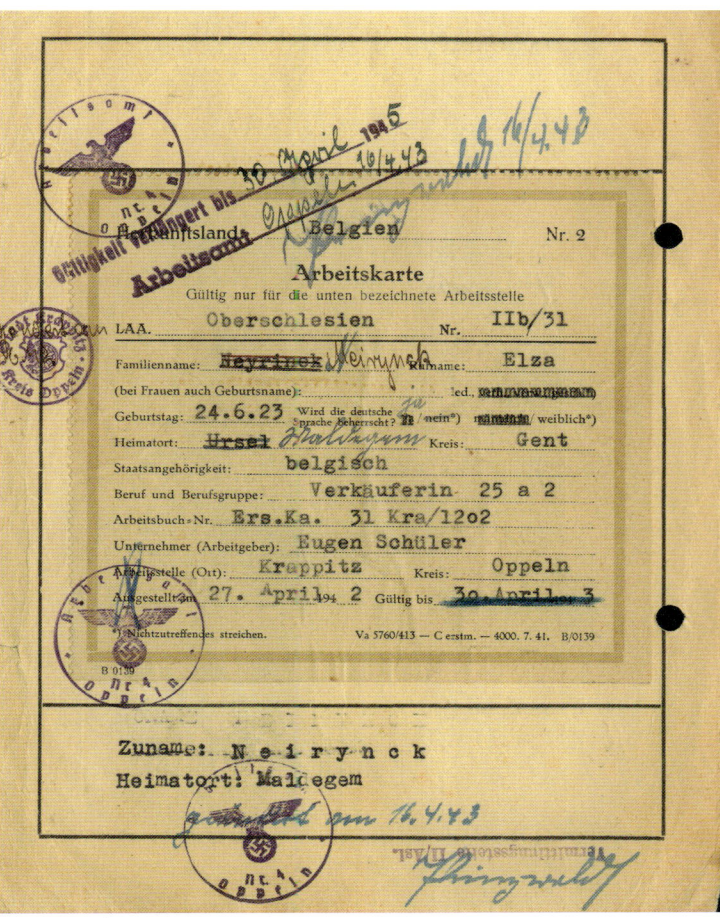

Arbeitskarte für die Belgierin Elza Neirynck. Sie wurde 1942 aus dem von den Deutschen besetzten Belgien ins Deutsche Reich zwangsdeportiert, 1943. / Work card issued to Elza Neirynck, a Belgian citizen. She was forcibly deported to the German Reich in 1942, during the German occupation of Belgium, 1943.

Zwangsarbeiter im Ersten Weltkrieg

Der deutschen Wirtschaft fehlen die zum Kriegsdienst eingezogenen Männer. Lebensmittel werden knapp und der Nachschub für die Kriegsmaschinerie gerät ins Stocken. Deutsche Frauen und ausländische Kriegsgefangene sollen die Lücken schließen. Mindestens 1,9 Millionen Kriegsgefangene werden zu Zwangsarbeitern. Hinzu kommen hunderttausende Zivilisten aus den besetzten Gebieten, die man ebenfalls zur Zwangsarbeit nötigt. Meist werden sie von den Deutschen diskriminiert und misshandelt. Trotzdem bleiben einige tausend polnische und russische Zwangsarbeiter auch nach Kriegsende in Deutschland und werden zu Einwanderern.

Poland proclaims a republic on November 11, 1918. Now the Weimar Republic must cede all territories whose population consists of a Polish majority. This includes large parts of the Prussian provinces Pozna, Western Prussia and East Upper Silesia. Close to 850,000 Germans from these regions immigrate to the Weimar Republic by 1925. Until now, the majority has worked in farming. The resettlement also forces them to rethink as they discover there is no work for them on German farms.

Deutsche Einwanderer aus den abgetretenen Gebieten

Hohe Reparationszahlungen müssen von Deutschland geleistet, Territorien abgegeben werden. Neue Staaten entstehen in Europa, die Grenzen verändern sich. Im Westen wird das von den Deutschen im Jahr 1871 annektierte Elsass-Lothringen an Frankreich zurückgegeben. Etwa 150.000 der dort ansässigen Deutschen werden anschließend aus Frankreich ausgewiesen. Sie lassen sich zumeist in Baden, Hessen-Nassau, Württemberg, der Pfalz und im Saargebiet nieder, das vom Völkerbund verwaltet wird. Die Aufnahme der Deutschen aus Elsass-Lothringen läuft zumeist unproblematisch ab.

In Polen wird am 11. November 1918 die Republik ausgerufen. Nun muss die Weimarer Republik alle Gebiete abtreten, in denen mehrheitlich Polen leben. Dazu zählen große Teile der ehemaligen preußischen Provinzen Posen, Westpreußen und Ostoberschlesien. Etwa 850.000 Deutsche aus diesen Regionen wandern bis 1925 in die Weimarer Republik ein: Sie müssen umdenken. Die meisten von ihnen waren bisher in der Landwirtschaft tätig, doch auf den deutschen Höfen gibt es keine Arbeit für sie.

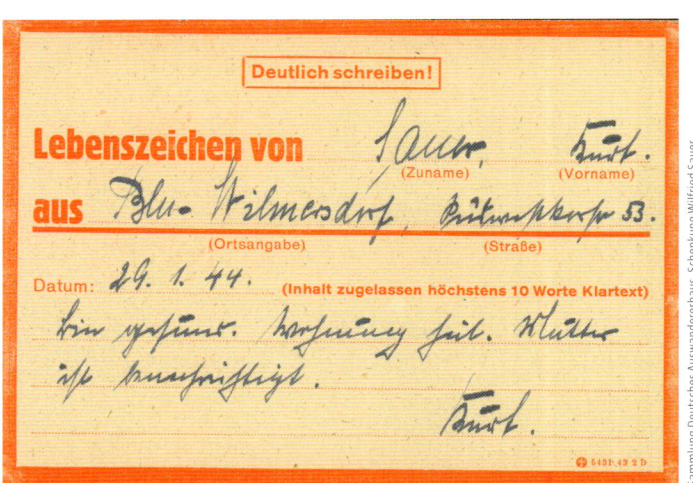

Nach jedem schweren Bombenangriff auf Berlin schickt Kurt Sauer eine so genannte Bombenkarte an seine in die Provinz Pommern evakuierte Familie, um sein Überleben mitzuteilen, 1944. / After every heavy air raid on Berlin, Kurt Sauer sends a so-called "bomb card" informing his family, who had been evacuated to the province of Pomerania, that he has survived, 1944.

EPOCHE DER KRIEGSBEDINGTEN ZWANGSWANDERUNG 1933 – 1954

Die grausamen Folgen der nationalsozialistischen Diktatur spürt Europa bis heute. Mehr als zehn Millionen Menschen werden ermordet – die Mehrheit sind Juden. Rund 13 Millionen müssen allein im Deutschen Reich Zwangsarbeit leisten. 12,5 Millionen Deutsche müssen ihre Heimat für immer verlassen. In den frühen 1950er Jahren wandern hunderttausende Deutsche vor allem in die USA, nach Kanada und Australien aus.

Zwangsarbeiter im Zweiten Weltkrieg

Mit der Wahl Adolf Hitlers zum deutschen Reichskanzler am 30. Januar 1933 wandelt sich die Weimarer Republik zur nationalsozialistischen Diktatur. In den nächsten zwölf Jahren werden sechs Millionen europäische Juden und hunderttausende Sinti und Roma, Homosexuelle und Behinderte verfolgt, in Konzentrationslager eingesperrt und ermordet.

ERA OF FORCED MIGRATION CAUSED BY WAR, 1933 – 1954

Europe still feels the dreadful impact of the National Socialist dictatorship today. During the period of this dictatorship more than 10 million people were murdered. In the German Reich alone around 13 million are committed to forced labor. An additional 12.5 million Germans are forced to leave their home country forever. In the early 1950s, hundreds of thousands of Germans immigrate to the United States, Canada and Australia.

Forced Laborers during the Second Worl War

With the election of Adolf Hitler as German Reich Chancellor on January 30, 1933 the Weimar Republic is transformed into a National Socialist dictatorship. In the course of the next 12 years six million European Jews and hundreds of thousands of Sinti and Roma, homosexuals and disabled persons will be persecuted, imprisoned in concentration camps and exterminated. The Second World War is ignited

Am 1. September 1939 beginnt mit dem deutschen Einmarsch in Polen der Zweite Weltkrieg. Rund 13 Millionen Kriegsgefangene, Insassen der Konzentrationslager und Zivilisten aus besiegten Ländern wie Polen, Frankreich und den Beneluxstaaten werden als Zwangsarbeiter nach Deutschland verschleppt.

Displaced Persons

Nach Kriegsende leben in Europa zehn Millionen Menschen, die von den Nationalsozialisten verschleppt oder vertrieben wurden. Die Alliierten bezeichnen sie als „Displaced Persons". Die Russen unter ihnen werden in ihre Heimat zurückgeschickt, obwohl sie dort zur Zwangsarbeit verurteilt oder sogar erschossen werden, da Stalin ihnen unterstellt, sie hätten sich mit dem Feind verschworen. Die meisten jüdischen Displaced Persons wandern bis 1950 in die USA oder nach Israel aus. Die Westeuropäer kehren in ihre jeweiligen Länder zurück. 150.000 ehemalige „Displaced Persons" bleiben in Deutschland. Viele werden später in die Bundesrepublik eingebürgert.

Umsiedler, Flüchtlinge und Vertriebene

Die Nationalsozialisten zählen auch die Nachfahren früherer deutscher Einwanderer in Osteuropa zum deutschen Volk. Nicht wenige leiden dort seit dem Ersten Weltkrieg unter Diskriminierungen durch die Russen, Rumänen und Tschechen. So jubeln tausende Sudetendeutsche Hitler zu, als er 1938 das tschechische Land annektiert. In Rumänien stimmen die meisten dort lebenden Bessarabiendeutschen ihrer Umsiedlung mit Begeisterung zu. Mehr als eine Million dieser „Volksdeutschen" aus Osteuropa werden unter dem Motto „Heim ins Reich" zwischen 1939 und 1943 nach Deutschland geholt.
Gegen Ende des Zweiten Weltkriegs fliehen Millionen Deutsche aus Ostpreußen, Schlesien und Pommern vor der anrückenden Roten Armee. Ihre alte Heimat sehen die meisten von ihnen nie wieder. Die Ostgebiete fallen nach Kriegsende an Polen und Russland. Wer nicht geflohen ist, wird nach der deutschen Kapitulation am 7. Mai 1945 vertrieben. Polen, Tschechen und Russen rächen sich für die grausamen deut-

by Germany's invasion of Poland on September 1, 1939. Close to 13 million prisoners of war concentration camp prisoners and civilians from the defeated countries Poland, France and the Benelux countries will be carted off to Germany to work as forced laborers.

Displaced Persons

After the war, 10 million persons, displaced by the National Socialists, live in Europe. The Allied Forces refer to them as "displaced persons." Displaced Russians are sent back to their country even though they will surely be convicted to forced labor or possibly even shot as Stalin maintains that they have conspired with the enemy. Most of the Jewish displaced persons emigrate either to the United States or Israel by 1950. Western Europeans return to their native countries. 150,000 former displaced persons remain in Germany, many of whom will later become naturalized German citizens.

Repatriates, Refugees and Displaced Persons

The National Socialists consider the descendants of earlier German immigrants in Eastern Europe part of the German nation. Many of them have suffered discrimination at the hands of the Russians, Romanians and Czechs since the First World War. Consequently, thousands of Sudeten Germans cheer Hitler when he annexes Czechoslovakia in 1938. And in Romania the majority of the Bessarabia Germans enthusiastically agree to be resettled. Over one million "Volksdeutsche" – ethnic Germans – from Eastern Europe are resettled in Germany as part of the Heim ins Reich (Back to the Reich) program between 1939 and 1945.
Towards the end of the Second World War millions of Germans flee East Prussia, Silesia and Pomerania in February 1945 to escape the advancing Red Army. Most of them will never see their homes again. After the war the eastern territories pass over to Poland and Russia. Those who do not flee are expelled after Germany capitulates on May 7, 1945. The Polish, Czechs and Russians seek revenge for the atrocities during the years of German occupation. Germany assimilates close to 12.5 million refugees and displaced persons by 1950.

schen Besatzungsjahre. Bis 1950 werden rund 12,5 Millionen Flüchtlinge und Vertriebene in Deutschland aufgenommen.

EPOCHE DER ARBEITSWANDERER UND SPÄTAUSSIEDLER 1955 – 1989

Bis 1989 kommen in die Bundesrepublik Deutschland vor allem europäische Arbeitswanderer und die „Spätaussiedler". In die DDR hingegen wandern in erster Linie sogenannte Vertragsarbeiter aus den verbündeten afrikanischen und asiatischen Ländern ein. Die Zahl der deutschen Überseeauswanderer sinkt stark ab.

Arbeitswanderer: „Gastarbeiter"

Zwischen 1950 und 1973 erlebt die Bundesrepublik ein fulminantes „Wirtschaftswunder" – auch dank der Südeuropäer, die man zur Hilfe holt. Ab 1955 können Einheimische den hohen Bedarf an Arbeitskräften nicht mehr decken. Die Bundesrepublik beginnt Arbeiter aus Italien anzuwerben. Bis 1964 folgen Verträge mit Spanien, Griechenland, Portugal, der Türkei und weiteren Ländern. Zudem besetzen bis zum Mauerbau im Jahr 1961 2,7 Millionen deutsche Zuwanderer aus der DDR viele der freien Stellen. Insgesamt kommen von 1955 bis 1973 14 Millionen „Gastarbeiter" in die Bundesrepublik, von denen jedoch fast zwölf Millionen in ihre Heimatländer zurückkehren. Bereits Ende der 1960er Jahre will die Bundesregierung die weitere Zuwanderung von Arbeitsmigranten einschränken. Die Ölkrise wird am 23. November 1973 zum Anlass genommen, einen Anwerbestopp zu verkünden. Da der Familiennachzug weiterhin erlaubt ist, kommen in den folgenden Jahren vor allem türkische Frauen und Kinder in die Bundesrepublik.

In der DDR beginnt eine Zuwanderung in größerem Umfang erst Anfang der 1980er Jahre. Der Staat schließt Verträge mit anderen sozialistischen Ländern wie Kuba, Mosambik und Vietnam ab, um Arbeiter anzuwerben. Nach dem Fall der Mauer im Jahr 1989 werden viele der 190.000 ausländischen Arbeiter von ihren Regierungen zurückgeholt oder aus der DDR abgeschoben. Einige jedoch bleiben und kämpfen jahrelang um einen gesicherten Aufenthalt im vereinten Deutschland.

ERA OF WORK MIGRANTS AND GERMAN REPATRIATES, 1955 – 1989

Up until 1989 predominantly European migrant workers and repatriates of German origin arrive in the Federal Republic of Germany whereas it is primarily "contract workers" from allied African and Asian countries who enter the German Democratic Republic. Only small numbers of Germans emigrate overseas.

Migrant Workers: "guest workers"

Between 1950 and 1973 Federal Germany experiences a veritable "economic miracle," thanks also to workers recruited from southern Europe. Beginning in 1955, the high demand for manpower cannot be filled by the German workforce alone. Federal Germany begins recruiting manpower from Italy. Contracts with Spain, Greece, Portugal, Turkey and other countries follow up through 1964. Also, about 2.7 million immigrants from East Germany fill job vacancies until the Berlin Wall is built in 1961. A total of 14 million migrant workers enter the Federal Republic of Germany between 1955 and 1973, however, about 12 million return to their native countries. As early as the late 1960s the federal government decides to limit further immigration of migrant workers. The oil crisis of November 23, 1973 serves as an ideal occasion for announcing the recruitment stop. Family unification for immigrants living in Germany is not restricted, so that in the years to follow mainly Turkish women and children enter the Federal Republic of Germany.

Immigration on a large scale does not take place in the GDR until the early 1980s when the state signs contracts with other socialist countries, among them Cuba, Mozambique and Vietnam, to recruit manpower. After the fall of the wall in 1989 many of the 190,000 foreign workers are called back by their countries or deported by the GDR. Some stay and struggle to obtain documented alien status in reunified Germany.

Repatriates of German Origin

During the Second World War the Soviet Union deports all German-speaking inhabitants living in the Volga Region to Kazakhstan. Due to the war guilt of the Germans the federal government feels responsible for the fate of these

Eine lange Tradition haben italienische Eismacher in Deutschland: Schon im Kaiserreich verkauften sie hier „Speiseeis", wie auch Primo Olivier aus Südtirol, um 1909.
The tradition of Italian ice cream makers goes far back in Germany: "iced cream" was already sold here in the German Empire, for instance by Primo Olivier from South Tirol, around 1909.

Die Spätaussiedler

Im Zweiten Weltkrieg werden in der Sowjetunion alle deutschsprachigen Bewohner der Wolga-Region nach Kasachstan deportiert. Wegen der deutschen Kriegsschuld fühlt sich die Bundesregierung für das Schicksal dieser Menschen verantwortlich. Sie sichert den sogenannten Spätaussiedlern 1953 Anspruch auf die deutsche Staatsbürgerschaft zu. 1987 leben 1,4 Millionen Spätaussiedler in der Bundesrepublik. Mit dem Zerfall der Sowjetunion 1991 setzt eine neue Einwanderungswelle ein und die Zahl der Spätaussiedler steigt bis 1996 auf 2,6 Millionen.

people, therefore guaranteeing repatriates of German origin in 1953 the right to German citizenship. In 1987, 1.4 million repatriates of German origin live in the Federal Republic of Germany. With the new wave of immigration resulting from the collapse of the Soviet Union in 1971 that number rises to 2.6 million by 1996.

EPOCHE DER GESELLSCHAFTLICHEN ANERKENNUNG DES EINWANDERUNGSLANDES DEUTSCHLAND: SPÄTAUSSIEDLER, BÜRGERKRIEGSFLÜCHTLINGE UND FREMDENFEINDLICHKEIT 1990 BIS HEUTE

Zwischen 1990 und 2010 kommen vor allem russische Spätaussiedler und jugoslawische Bürgerkriegsflüchtlinge nach Deutschland. Zum ersten Mal seit Ende des Zweiten Weltkriegs finden in dieser Zeit wieder Pogrome in Deutschland statt. Gleichzeitig beginnt die „Integrationsdebatte", die besonders durch die hohen Flüchtlingsankünfte 2015 zu tiefen Rissen in

ERA OF THE SOCIAL ACKNOWLEDGEMENT OF GERMANY AS AN IMMIGRATION COUNTRY – GERMAN REPATRIATES, CIVIL WAR REFUGEES AND XENOPHOBIA, 1990 UNTIL TODAY

Between 1990 and 2010 it is predominantly Russian repatriates of German origin and Yugoslav civil war refugees who arrive in Germany. For the first time since the end of the Second World War Germany is once again the scene of pogroms. At the same time, the so-called "integration debate" begins. The influx of refugees arriving in 2015, has led to deep rifts in German

der deutschen Gesellschaft führt: An der Frage, wie viel Menschen Deutschland aufnehmen kann und will, scheiden sich die Geister. Die Anzahl der Wähler rechtsgerichteter, deutschnationaler Parteien wie der AfD nehmen stark zu. In einigen Jahren wandern über 100 000 Deutsche für einige Zeit oder immer nach Übersee, in die skandinavischen Länder, nach Österreich und in die Schweiz aus.

Die Spätaussiedler aus Osteuropa

Mit dem Zusammenbruch der kommunistischen Staaten Osteuropas setzt 1989 eine neue Einwanderungswelle von Spätaussiedlern in die Bundesrepublik ein. Die Greueltaten der Deutschen in zwei Weltkriegen werden den Nachfahren deutscher Einwanderer in den osteuropäischen Ländern nicht verziehen. Die deutschsprachige Minderheit leidet unter der anhaltenden Diskriminierung. Gleichzeitig lockt der Wohlstand im Westen. Seit 1953 erhalten Spätaussiedler in der Bundesrepublik die deutsche Staatsbürgerschaft. Ab 1997 müssen sie vor ihrer Einreise nachweisen, dass sie die deutsche Sprache beherrschen. In der Folge sinken die Einwandererzahlen. Insgesamt reisen zwischen 1990 und 2010 etwa 2,5 Millionen Spätaussiedler nach Deutschland ein.

Die Bürgerkriegsflüchtlinge aus dem ehemaligen Jugoslawien

1991 brechen im Vielvölkerstaat Jugoslawien mehrere Kriege aus. Es sind die gewalttätigsten Auseinandersetzungen in Europa seit dem Zweiten Weltkrieg. Slowenien, Kroatien, Bosnien-Herzegowina und die anderen Teilrepubliken streben die Unabhängigkeit an. Serbien kämpft mit der verbliebenen Volksarmee bis 1999 gegen seine Nachbarn. Mehr als 100.000 Menschen sterben. Rund 7,5 Millionen Menschen fliehen innerhalb des Landes oder ins Ausland.

Pogrome und rechtsradikale Gewalt in Deutschland

Knapp 50 Jahre nach Ende des Zweiten Weltkriegs haben einige Deutsche die Kriegsschuld Deutschlands und den Völkermord an Juden, Sinti und Roma vergessen. Für ihre eigene Perspektivlosigkeit nach der Wiedervereinigung 1989 versuchen sie, Einwanderer verantwortlich zu machen.

society. Opinions tend to differ sharply about the number of people Germany can and will accept. There is a strong increase in voters for right-wing populist parties such as the AfD. In some years over 100 000 German emigrate for some years or forever overseas, to Scandinavia, Austria and Switzerland.

Repatriates of German Origin from Eastern Europe

The collapse of the Communist states of Eastern Europe in 1989 initiates a new wave of immigration with ethnic German immigrants coming to the Federal Republic of Germany. The Eastern European countries where the descendants of German immigrants live cannot forgive the Germans for the atrocities they committed during the two world wars. The German-speaking minority suffers constant discrimination. At the same time the prosperity of Western Europe is very enticing. As of 1953, the federal German government issues German citizenship to repatriates of German origin but from 1997 on, entrance to Germany depends on their fluent command of the German language. As a result, the number of immigrants drops. Altogether, between 1990 and 2010 about 2.5 million ethnic German immigrants arrive in Germany.

Civil War Refugees from Former Yugoslavia

In 1991, several wars break out in multi-ethnic Yugoslavia, the most violent conflicts Europe has witnessed since the Second World War. Slovenia, Croatia, Bosnia-Herzegovina and the other constituent republics are struggling for independence. Serbia, together with what is left of the People's Army, fights against its neighbors until 1999. Over 100,000 people die. Close to 7.5 million flee to other parts of the country or abroad.

Pogroms and Right-Wing Violence in Germany

Evidently, just 50 years after the end of the Second World War some Germans have forgotten the country's war guilt and the genocide committed against the Jews, Sinti and Roma. After the reunification of East and West Germany in 1989 they try to shift the blame for their own lack of prospects onto the immigrants. Hoyerswerda in Saxony is the scene of the first pogrom aimed at asylum-seekers and immi-

Das erste Pogrom richtet sich 1991 gegen Asylsuchende und Einwanderer im sächsischen Hoyerswerda. Im selben Jahr wird ein Brandanschlag im Nordrhein-Westfälischen Hünxe verübt, ein Jahr später ein weiterer in Rostock-Lichtenhagen. Drei Menschen sterben, als Rechtsradikale die Häuser türkischer Familien in Mölln und Solingen anzünden. Knapp 1.500 rechtsextreme Gewalttaten registriert das Bundeskriminalamt 1991. Bis ins Jahr 2000 steigt die Zahl weiter an. 1999 beginnt eine rechtsradikale Terrorzelle aus Sachsen – vom Verfassungsschutz über Jahre unbemerkt –, tödliche Attentate auf mindestens zehn Einwanderer zu verüben. Ende 2011 fliegt die Zelle auf, das gut funktionierende Netzwerk der Rechtsradikalen in Ost- und Westdeutschland wird nach und nach aufgedeckt. Bundeskanzlerin Angelika Merkel spricht von einer „Schande für Deutschland".

In den Anfangsjahren des 21. Jahrhunderts beginnt in Deutschland die sogenannte „Integrationsdebatte". Deutsche, Deutsche mit ausländischen Wurzeln und Ausländer sind unzufrieden damit, wie sich ihr Zusammenleben gestaltet. Man wirft sich gegenseitige Intoleranz vor. Aber endlich wird in Deutschland darüber diskutiert, wie eine gemeinsame Gesellschaft aussehen könnte.

Die Bürgerkriegsflüchtlinge 2014–2016

Der syrische Bürgerkrieg und der Krieg des IS (Islamischer Staat) zwingen seit 2014 Millionen Menschen zur Flucht. Hunderttausende versuchen, ins sichere Europa – vor allem nach Schweden und Deutschland – zu gelangen. Zwei Routen

grants in 1991. There is an arson attack in Hünxe the same year and another occurs in Rostock-Lichtenhagen a year later. Three people die when right-wing extremists set fire to the homes of Turkish families in Mölln and Solingen. The Federal Criminal Police Office registers almost 1,500 acts of violence by right-wing extremists in 1991, a figure that continues to rise until the year 2000.

Unnoticed by the Federal Office for the Protection of the Constitution, in 1999, a right-wing terror cell in the federal state of Saxony begins assassinating immigrants, at least 10 altogether. Finally, in late 2011 the terror cell and the efficient network of right-wing extremists in East and West Germany are exposed. Federal Chancellor Angela Merkel refers to it as a "disgrace to Germany."

In the early days of the 21st century the so-called "integration debate" picks up momentum in Germany. Germans, Germans with foreign roots, and foreigners are dissatisfied with the way they live together. Everybody blames everybody else for mutual intolerance. But finally, Germany is discussing how and what a joint society should look like.

The civil war refugees 2014–2016

Since 2014, the civil war in Syria and the ISIS (so-called Islamic State) war have forced millions of people to flee. Hundreds of thousands attempt to reach safe havens in Europe, Sweden and Germany, in particular. They use two routes: the so-called Balkan route to Turkey, and from there via Bulgaria, Hungary and Austria to Germany and Swe-

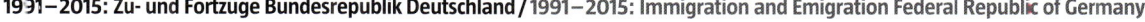

1991–2015: Zu- und Fortzüge Bundesrepublik Deutschland / 1991–2015: Immigration and Emigration Federal Republic of Germany

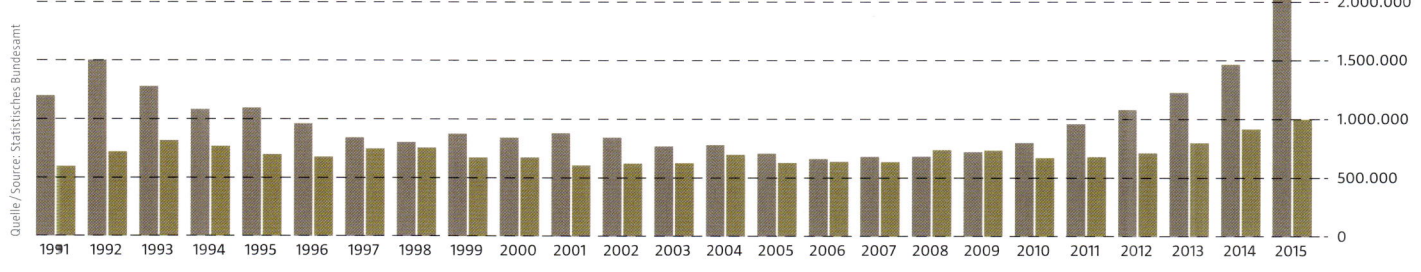

Quelle / Source: Statistisches Bundesamt

■ Zuzüge in die Bundesrepublik Deutschland / Immigrants Immigrants to the Federal Republic of Germany
■ Fortzüge aus der Bundesrepublik Deutschland / Emigrants from the Federal Republic of Germany

nutzen sie dafür: die sogenannte Balkanroute in die Türkei, über Bulgarien, Ungarn und Österreich nach Deutschland und Schweden. Und die lebensgefährliche Route über das Mittelmeer nach Griechenland und Italien. Wo auch immer sie europäischen Boden betreten: Rechtlich handelt es sich um eine illegale Einreise, die meist durch „Schlepper" organisiert wird. Am 4. September 2015 öffnen Österreich und Deutschland ihre Grenzen für in Ungarn festsitzende Flüchtlinge. Hunderttausende beantragen Asyl in der Bundesrepublik. Die Grenzen der darauffolgenden hitzigen gesellschaftlichen Debatte verlaufen zwischen „Willkommenskultur", „Obergrenze für Zuwanderung" und „Abschottung". Während Flüchtlinge größere Akzeptanz erfahren, wird den Arbeitsmigranten, die sich unter die Flüchtlinge mischen, oft der Zugang zu den deutschen Sozialsystemen nicht zugestanden. Im März 2016 werden die Grenzen der Länder, durch die die „Balkanroute" verläuft, geschlossen. Der sogenannte Flüchtlingsdeal, den die EU wenig später mit der Türkei schließt, verhindert vor allem die Mittelmeerüberquerung nach Griechenland. Seitdem nimmt die Zahl der hoch lebensgefährlichen Überfahrten von Libyen nach Europa wieder zu. Tödliche Terroranschläge, die auch von sich unter die Flüchtlinge mischenden Terroristen in einigen europäischen Städten verübt werden, rücken Sicherheitsfragen in den Fokus.

den. And the perilous route across the Mediterranean to Greece and Italy. Yet, wherever they set foot on European soil, it is officially an illegal entry, which is often organized by so-called *people smugglers*. On September 4, 2015, Austria and Germany open their borders to refugees stranded in Hungary. Hundreds of thousands apply for asylum in the Federal Republic of Germany. The divide of the heated social debates that followed run between "welcoming culture," "upper immigration limit" and "isolation." While refugees experience more acceptance, economic migrants who mix with the refugees are often not conceded the right to access the German social system. In March 2016, the Balkan countries close their borders to stem the flow of migrants. The so-called *refugee deal,* an agreement the European Union and Turkey reached shortly after, prevents the Mediterranean crossing to Greece. Since then the number of people attempting the perilous sea crossing from Libya to Europe has increased. Deadly terror attacks carried out in several European cities by terrorists who have infiltrated the refugee flow, raise the issue of security matters.

BIOGRAPHIEN (AUSWAHL)
BIOGRAPHYS (SELECTION)

AUSWANDERER UND EINWANDERER
EMIGRANTS AND IMMIGRANTS

CHRISTOPH BONGERT, SIMONE EICK, TANJA FITTKAU, JULIAN HERBIG,
KARIN HESS, JÖRG RÜSEWALD, KATRIN QUIRIN

Im Deutschen Auswandererhaus können Besucher teilhaben am Leben eines anderen: Während des Rundgangs begleitet man zunächst einen Auswanderer nach Übersee und im Anschluss begibt man sich auf Spurensuche nach einer Familie, die nach Deutschland eingewandert oder geflüchtet ist oder dorthin vertrieben wurde.

Viele Besucher finden so Anknüpfungspunkte an die eigene Familiengeschichte: sei es, weil sie ausgewanderte Vorfahren haben, sei es, weil die Großeltern deutsche Flüchtlinge oder Vertriebene waren oder sei es, weil sie als „Gastarbeiter" in die Bundesrepublik kamen.

So wie diejenigen, die nach 1949 eingewandert sind und nun in offiziellen Statistiken als „Bevölkerung mit Migra-

At the German Emigration Center, visitors can share in someone else's life. On their tour of the museum, visitors accompany an emigrant on their journey overseas. This is followed by searching for traces of a family that has immigrated to Germany, fled or been expelled from their home country. Many visitors find links to their own family history. Either because they are descendants of emigrants, or because their grandparents were German refugees or expellees, or came to the Federal Republic of Germany as guest workers.

Such as the individuals who immigrated after 1949, and are now registered in the official statistics as "population with migrant background": at the end of 2015, they accounted

Bà nội và gia đình tại Hà Nội 04-01-1981

DDR-Vertragsarbeiterin Mai Phuong Kollath (hinten stehend, 1. v. r.) mit ihrer Familie, 1981.
GDR contract worker, Mai Phuong Kollath (standing at the back, 1st from the right) with her family, 1981.

Sammlung Deutsches Auswandererhaus, Dauerleihgabe Mai Phuong Kollath

USA-Auswanderin Hermine Levien an Bord der „Bremen" (angekreuzt), 1930.
Hermine Levien (marked) on board the "Bremen" on her way to the United States,

Sammlung Deutsches Auswandererhaus, Schenkung Christel Schmidt

tionshintergrund" erfasst werden: Das waren Ende 2015 insgesamt 20,5 Prozent der deutschen Gesamtbevölkerung; etwa 16,5 Millionen von 80,6 Millionen. Hinzu kommen jene, die in dieser Statistik nicht erfasst sind: die Nachfahren der 12,5 Millionen deutschen Flüchtlinge und Vertriebenen, die zwischen 1945 und 1949 kamen. Oder auch diejenigen, in deren Familien die Migration schon mehrere Generationen zurückliegt, die diesen Teil der Familiengeschichte aber noch erinnern; dazu zählen vor allem die Nachfahren der Hugenotten und der „Ruhrpolen". Fast jeder in Deutschland kann also eine Migrationsgeschichte erzählen.

for 20.5 percent of the German population; about 16.5 million of the 80.6 million. There are also those who are not included in these statistics: the descendants of the 12.5 million German refugees and expellees who came between 1945 and 1949. Or the families whose migration history goes back several generations and who are still aware of this part of their family history. These include, in particular, the descendants of the Huguenots and the "Ruhrpolen" (Poles who migrated to the Ruhr district). Therefore, almost everyone in Germany has a migration story of their own.

Bessarabiendeutsche Melitta Klein (3. v. l.) mit ihrer Familie, 1979.
Bessarabia German Melitta Klein (3rd from left) with her family, 1979.

Sammlung Deutsches Auswandererhaus, Schenkung Melitta Klein

Familie des Ruhrpolen Wilhelm Somplatzki, 1932.
"Ruhrpole" (Pole who migrated to the Ruhr area) Wilhelm Somplatzki with his family, about 1930.

Sammlung Deutsches Auswandererhaus, Dauerleihgabe Herbert Somplatzki

Nachfahren des Hawaii-Auswanderers Paul Lemke, 2004.
Descendants of Paul Lemke who immigrated to Hawaii, 2004.

Sammlung Deutsches Auswandererhaus, Schenkung Renate Jaeckel

Sammlung Deutsches Auswandererhaus, Schenkung Barbara Kissling

Australien-Auswanderin Barbara Kissling mit ihren zwei Kindern, 1960.
Australia emigrant, Barbara Kissling with her two children, 1960.

AUSWANDERER
EMIGRANT

Paul Lemke

20.11.1851 – 11.02.1908
Auswanderung 1886 von Bremerhaven
Emigration 1886 from Bremerhaven

Bereits als Geselle zieht es den Schneider Paul Lemke bis
nach London. Mit 23 Jahren wagt er 1886 den Sprung nach
Amerika. Von dort kehrt er noch einmal für einige Jahre in
seine Heimat Brandenburg zurück, um wenig später wieder in die Neue Welt aufzubrechen: diesmal mit dem Ziel
Hawaii. Das Glück will es, dass der König von Hawaii ein
Faible für preußisches Militärzeremoniell hat. Seine Kapelle
wird bereits von einem preußischen Kapellmeister gelei-
tet, nun will er sie auch in preußischen Uniformen sehen.
Die Wahl fällt auf Paul Lemke, der so 1881 zum königlichen
Hofschneider von Hawaii ernannt wird. Nun fehlt ihm nur
noch eine Frau. Er fährt nach Hause und hält erfolgreich um
die Hand seiner Cousine Agnes Graumann an. Gemeinsam
gehen sie 1886 nach Honolulu.

The tailor Paul Lemke journeyed as far as London after completing his apprenticeship. At twenty-three he ventured to
America. Later he returned home to Brandenburg for several years, but departed yet again for the New World; this
time his destination was Hawaii. As luck would have it, the
King of Hawaii was fond of Prussian military ceremonies.
His music-band already had a Prussian "Kapellmeister," but
the King wanted them to appear in Prussian uniforms. So
in 1881, Paul Lemke was named Royal Court Tailor of Hawaii. Now, all he needed was a wife. He traveled home and
successfully asked for his cousin Agnes Graumann's hand
in marriage. They returned to Honolulu together in 1886.

Weihnachtsgrüße an Paul Lemkes Familie in Deutschland, 1905. Als Hofschneider näht Paul Lemke
auch die Uniformen der „Royal Hawaiian Band" – natürlich nach preußischem Vorbild.
Christmas greetings to Paul Lemke's family in Germany, 1905. In his function as Court Tailor, Paul
Lemke also sewed the uniforms of the "Royal Hawaiian Band", naturally according to Prussian models.

Sammlung Deutsches Auswandererhaus, Schenkung Renate Jaeckel

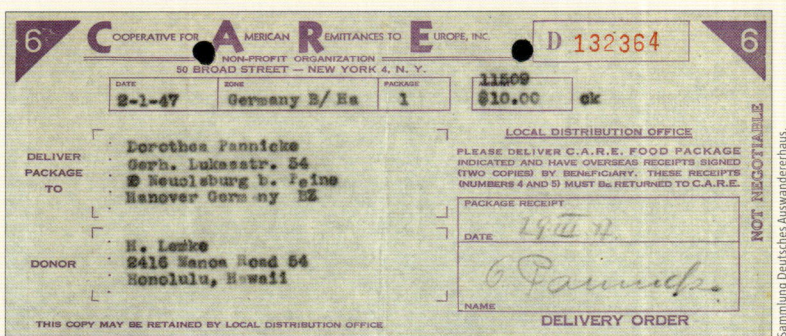

Sammlung Deutsches Auswandererhaus, Schenkung Renate Jaeckel

Die Lemkes in Hawaii halten stets den Kontakt nach Deutschland aufrecht: So unterstützen sie ihre
deutschen Verwandten nach dem Zweiten Weltkrieg mit CARE-Paketen. / The Lemke's in Hawaii keep
in touch with their family in Germany. Following World War II, they helped their German relatives by
sending them CARE packages.

Sammlung Deutsches Auswandererhaus, Schenkung Renate Jaeckel

Agnes und Herman Lemke (mit
Hut und Blumengirlanden) mit
ihren Kindern und Enkelkindern:
„Aloha" zum Neuen Jahr 1960.
Agnes and Herman Lemke (with
hat and garland of flowers) with
their children and grandchildren:
"Aloha" to the New Year 1960.

EINWANDERER
IMMIGRANT

Philippé Connor

1660 – 1758
Einwanderung nach 1710 nach Berlin
Immigration after 1710 to Berlin

Religiöse Überzeugung bewegt Philippé Connor, seine Heimat Frankreich zu verlassen. Der Kammmacher ist überzeugter Protestant – ein Hugenotte –, doch die Ausübung seines Glaubens ist schon seit 1685 durch den katholischen „Sonnenkönig" Ludwig XIV. verboten. So kann Connor seinem Glauben nur im Untergrund nachgehen. Nach der Geburt seines Sohnes wird ihm dieses Leben in Heimlichkeit und ständiger Angst vor Entdeckung zunehmend unerträglich, und so flieht er nach 1710 mit seiner Frau Anna und seinem Sohn aus Frankreich nach Berlin. Der Große Kurfürst von Brandenburg hatte seinen verfolgten Glaubensbrüdern bereits 1685 mit dem „Edikt von Potsdam" sichere Aufnahme und Zuflucht zugesagt, und sein Nachfolger Friedrich I. führt diese Politik fort. Connors Familie lebt heute in achter Generation in Berlin.

Religious beliefs moved Philippé Connor to leave his home in France. The combmaker was a staunch Protestant, a Huguenot. However, in 1685, during the reign of the Catholic "Sun King," Louis XIV, Protestants were not allowed to practice their faith openly. As a result, Connor was forced to worship in secret. Following the birth of his son, he decided to put an end to this clandestine life and the constant fear of discovery. In 1710, he fled together with his wife, Anna, and his son from France to Berlin. With the 1685 "Edict of Potsdam," the Great Elector of Brandenburg welcomed his fellow-believers and promised them safety and refuge; his successor, Frederick the Great, continued this policy. The eighth generation of Connor's family are currently living in Berlin.

Jeannette Connor mit ihren Eltern. Hier steht die 5. und 6. Generation von Nachfahren Philippé Connors um 1900 im eigenen Garten in Berlin. / Jeannette Connor with her parents. The fifth and sixth generation of Philippé Connor's descendants, standing in their garden in Berlin, about 1900.

Sammlung Deutsches Auswandererhaus, Schenkung Petra Behringer

Jeannette Connor wird 1890, wenige Wochen nach ihrer Geburt, der Tradition entsprechend im Französischen Kloster in Berlin getauft. Dieses filigrane Taufgeschenk bekommt sie von ihrem Großvater und Taufpaten zur Erinnerung geschenkt. Der Glaube und die Französische Kirche spielen auch bei den heute noch lebenden Nachfahren von Philippé eine sehr wichtige Rolle. / In accordance with family traditions, Jeannette Connor was only a few weeks old at the time of her baptism in the French Cloister in Berlin in 1890. Her grandfather and Godfather gave her this commemorative, filigree baptism gift. Faith and the French Church continued to play an important role in the lives of Philippé's descendants.

Sammlung Deutsches Auswandererhaus, Schenkung Petra Behringer; Photo: Stefan Volk

Aufnahmeländer der bis zum Jahr 1700 geflohenen Hugenotten (ca. 150.000) /
Host countries of the approximately 150,000 Huguenots who had fled by 1700

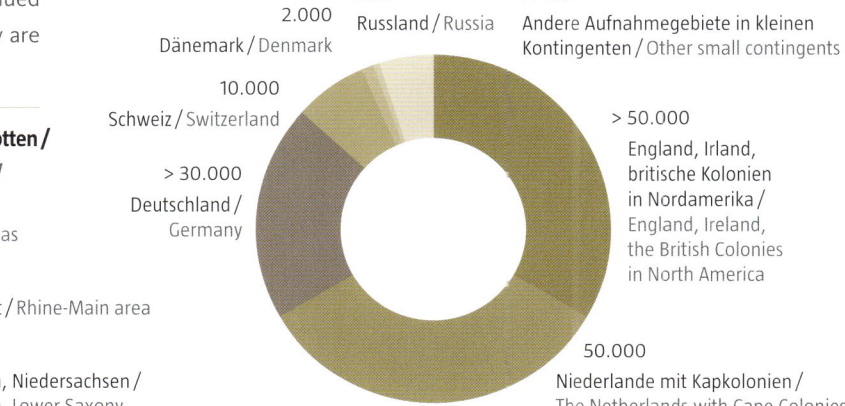

2.000
Dänemark / Denmark

600
Russland / Russia

7.400
Andere Aufnahmegebiete in kleinen Kontingenten / Other small contingents

10.000
Schweiz / Switzerland

> 30.000
Deutschland / Germany

> 50.000
England, Irland, britische Kolonien in Nordamerika / England, Ireland, the British Colonies in North America

50.000
Niederlande mit Kapkolonien / The Netherlands with Cape Colonies

Regionale Verteilung nach Deutschland geflohener Hugenotten /
Regional distribution of Huguenots who fled to Germany

7%
Franken / Franconia

8%
Andere / Other areas

9%
Hessen-Kassel / Hesse-Kassel

6%
Rhein-Main-Gebiet / Rhine-Main area

67%
Brandenburg-Preußen / Brandenburg-Prussia

3%
Hamburg, Bremen, Niedersachsen / Hamburg, Bremen, Lower Saxony

Ludwig und Ilse Tesch

1862–1946 / 1928–2010
Auswanderung 1863 von Hamburg / 1949 von Neapel
Emigration 1863 from Hamburg / 1949 from Napoli

Ludwig Tesch ist 14 Monate alt, als sich dessen Eltern, Groß-eltern und weitere Familienmitglieder 1863 entschließen, das karge Leben in der preußischen Uckermark zugunsten des bis dahin fast unbekannten australischen Queensland aufzugeben. Im Alter von 30 Jahren geht der Familienvater mit seiner Frau und den Kindern in den kaum erschlossenen Norden von Brisbane, wo er mitten im subtropischen Regen-wald eine Sägemühle errichtet. 1946 stirbt er hoch betagt. Drei Jahre nach Ludwigs Tod kommt die wanderlustige Ilse Prechtel nach Australien. Ende der 1940er Jahre hat es die 21-Jährige nicht mehr in ihrer bayerischen Heimat gehalten. 1958 zieht die Abenteurerin nach Brisbane, wo sie Ludwig Teschs Enkel Colin begegnet und ihn heiratet. Als ihr Sohn Peter 2009 australischer Botschafter in Deutschland wird, schließt sich der Kreis einer mehrere Generationen um-spannenden deutsch-australischen Familiengeschichte.

Ludwig Tesch was 14 months old in 1863 when his parents, grandparents and relatives decided, to leave behind their bleak lives in the Prussian Uckermark in favor of the vir-tually unknown Queensland in Australia. At the age of thirty, Ludwig Tesch, together with his wife and children, moved to the undeveloped area north of Brisbane, where he opened a lumber mill in the middle of the rainforest. He died, well advanced in years, in 1946.
Enterprising and adventurous, Ilse Prechtel came to Aus-tralia three years after Ludwig Tesch's death. There was nothing to keep the 21 year-old in her Bavarian hometown at the end of the 1940s. In 1958, Ilse moved to Brisbane where she met Ludwig's grandson, Colin Tesch. The mar-riage took place nearly one hundred years after the Tesch family set foot on Australian soil. When, in 2009, their son Peter became the Australian ambassador to Germany, the story of a family that comprises several generations came full circle.

Ludwig Tesch vor Thorneycroft Langholztransporter, 1922
Ludwig Tesch in front of a Thorneycroft logging truck, 1922

Picture Sunshine Coast, Sunshine Coast Libraries

Picture Sunshine Coast, Sunshine Coast Libraries

1935 baut Ludwig Tesch einen Apparat zur Herstellung von Angelschnuren. Dieser Wachsblock dient dazu, die Schnur einzuschmieren und wasserfest zu machen.
In 1935 Ludwig Tesch built a machine that produced fishing lines. This block of wax was used to lubricate the line and waterproof it.

Sammlung Deutsches Auswandererhaus, Schenkung Matthew und Peter Tesch

Ilse Prechtel in den 1950er Jahren. Nach ihrer Ankunft am anderen Ende der Welt lebte sie zunächst in Darwin, von wo aus sie per Motorrad, Dop-peldecker oder Auto zu ihren zahlrei-chen Reisen quer über den Fünften Kontinent aufbrach. / Ilse Prechtel in the 1950s. On her arrival at the other end of the world she initially lived in Darwin; from here she set off, by motorcycle, double-decker plane or car, on her numerous trips across the fifth continent.

Sammlung Deutsches Auswandererhaus, Schenkung Matthew und Peter Tesch

EINWANDERERIN
IMMIGRANT

Şerife Seyitler

01.01.1928 – 26.03.2015
Einwanderung 1969 nach Bremerhaven
Immigration 1969 to Bremerhaven

1969 trifft Şerife Seyitler eine folgenreiche Entscheidung: Sie ist 40 Jahre alt, als sie sich entschließt, in Deutschland Geld für ihre Familie zu verdienen. Seit 1961 werden türkische Arbeitskräfte für den deutschen Arbeitsmarkt angeworben. Ihre beiden ältesten Töchter arbeiten bereits seit sechs Jahren in Bremerhaven. Ihre übrigen sechs Kinder muss sie zunächst in der Türkei zurücklassen. In ihrem Heimatland hört sie, dass es in Deutschland kein Wasser gibt und alles mit Bier erledigt wird: Kochen, Waschen, Trinken. Entsprechend erleichtert ist sie, als sie nach ihrer Ankunft in München vom Zug aus doch Flüsse und Gewässer sieht. Sie arbeitet bis 1986 bei der Firma „Nordsee" in Bremerhaven. Bis 1980 hatte sie auch ihren Ehemann und die anderen Kinder in die Seestadt nachgeholt.

Şerife Seyitler made a momentous decision in 1969. At the age of forty, she decided to go to Germany, to earn money for her family. In 1961, the German labor market began searching for turkish workers. Her two eldest daughters had already been employed in Bremerhaven for six years. Şerife initially left her other six children in Turkey. In her native country, she had heard rumors that there was no water in Germany and that they used beer for everything, including cooking, washing and drinking. So, following her arrival, she was relieved to see rivers and stretches of water on the train ride from Munich to Bremerhaven. By 1980, her husband and other children had joined her in the seaport. She worked for the "Nordsee" company in Bremerhaven until 1986.

Fünf von Şerifes Seytlers Kindern sind in Deutschland geblieben und leben heute hier mit ihren eigenen Kindern und Enkeln. Zwei Söhne sind mit ihren Familien in die Türkei zurückgegangen. Die Aufnahme entstand am 8. Oktober 2011 in der Wohnung von Şerife Seytler und zeigt drei Generationen: Şerifes Seytler, Tochter Aygül und Enkelin Zübeyde. / Five of Şerife Seytler's children remained in Germany. Today, they live here with their children and grandchildren. Two of her sons returned to Turkey with their families. This picture was taken in Şerife Seytlers's apartment on October 8, 2011. Three generations are present: her granddaughter, Zübeyde, is next to Şerifes Seytlers's daughter, Aygül.

Sammlung Deutsches Auswandererhaus, Schenkung Zübeyde East

Im Alter von 14 Jahren bestickt Şerife Seytler in ihrem damaligen Heimatort Maraş ihr eigenes Aussteuerkissen. Als Andenken nimmt sie es mit nach Deutschland. 2011 schenkt sie es dem Deutschen Auswandererhaus.
Şerife Seytler embroidered her dowry pillow in her hometown of Maraş, when she was fourteen. She took it to Germany as a keepsake. In 2011, she donated it to the German Emigration Center.

Sammlung Deutsches Auswandererhaus, Schenkung Aygül Bağcı, Photo: Stefan Volk

Ausländische Erwerbstätige und deren Familienangehörige / Foreign Employees and Family Members

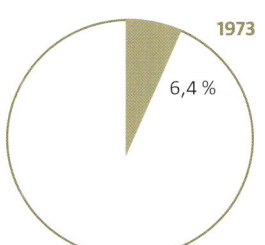

6,4 %

1973 Anteil an der Gesamtbevölkerung in der Bundesrepublik Deutschland / Share of the total population in the Federal Republic of Germany

Vom Ende der 1950er Jahre bis zum „Anwerbestopp ausländischer Arbeitnehmer" 1973 kommen rund 14 Millionen ausländische Arbeitnehmer – und deren Angehörige – in die Bundesrepublik Deutschland. Rund elf Millionen kehren wieder zurück. Bilaterale Verträge regeln die Anwerbung von Arbeitskräften aus Italien (1955), Spanien (1960), Griechenland (1960), Türkei (1961), Marokko (1963), Portugal (1964), Tunesien (1965) und Jugoslawien (1968). / Between the end of the 1950s and the "recruitment ban for foreign workers" in 1973, approximately 14 million foreign workers and their families come to the Federal Republic of Germany. Approximately 11 million later returned to their home countries. Bilateral treaties regulate the recruitment of workers from Italy (1955), Spain (1960), Greece (1960), Turkey (1961), Morocco (1963), Portugal (1964), Tunisia (1965) and Yugoslavia (1968).

Erich Koch-Weser

26.02.1875 – 19.10.1944

Flucht 1933 von Bremerhaven

Flight 1933 from Bremerhaven

Der Anwalt und Politiker Erich Koch-Weser ist überzeugter Demokrat. Mit der antijüdischen Gesetzgebung ab 1933 entziehen die Nationalsozialisten dem 1875 in Bremerhaven geborenen Innenminister, Vizekanzler und Justizminister der Weimarer Republik die Zulassung als Rechtsanwalt und Notar, weil seine Mutter jüdisch ist. Zwar wird dies nach dem Protest des Reichspräsidenten von Hindenburg rückgängig gemacht, doch Erich Koch-Weser ist gewarnt. Nach dem Verbot seines Buches „Und dennoch aufwärts" droht ihm zudem politische Verfolgung. Zehn Monate nach dem Machtantritt Hitlers flieht Erich Koch-Weser mit seiner zweiten Frau Irma und ihren beiden Söhnen ins Exil nach Brasilien. Sein ältester Sohn Geert aus erster Ehe folgt dem Vater wenige Wochen später.

Born in Bremerhaven in 1875, the lawyer and politician Erich Koch-Weser was a staunch democrat. He served as Federal Minister of the Interior, Vice-Chancellor and Minister of Justice of the Weimar Republic. Following the anti-Semitic legislations passed in 1933, he was banned from practicing law and his profession as a notary because of his mother's Jewish background. After the intervention by Paul von Hindenburg, the German President, the restrictions were revoked; however, Koch-Weser was forewarned. Since his book "Und dennoch aufwärts" had been banned, he also risked political persecution. Koch-Weser fled into exile to Brazil with his second wife, Irma, and her two sons ten months after Hitler's accession to power. His eldest son, Geert, from his first marriage followed him just a few weeks later.

Die Familie Koch-Weser 1942 unterwegs: Erich (zu Pferde, li.), Irma (in der Kutsche, li.) und ihre beiden Söhne Eta (Erich jr.; in der Kutsche, re.) und Jan. / The Koch-Weser family on tour in 1942: Erich (on horseback, le.), Irma (in the coach, le.) and their two sons Eta (Erich jr.; in the coach, ri.) und Jan.

Sammlung Deutsches Auswandererhaus, Schenkung Elisabeth Lincke

Dieser Mehlsack wird von Carl von Blanquet in die brasilianische Kolonie „Rolândia" geschickt. Er ist der Bruder von Irma Koch-Weser, geborene von Blanquet, der zweiten Frau Erich Koch-Wesers. / The sack of flour is sent by Carl von Blanquet to the settlement "Rolândia". He is the brother of Irma Koch-Weser, née Blanquet.

Das in Brasilien entstandene Emblem der Fazenda Veseroda birgt sowohl die Initialen der Familie Koch-Weser als auch die der neuen Heimat: K – W – V. The emblem of the Fazenda Veseroda in Brazil is made up of the initials of the Koch-Weser family and the new home: K – W – V.

Sammlung Deutsches Auswandererhaus, Schenkung Elisabeth Lincke; Photo: Stefan Volk

Deutsche Auswanderung nach Brasilien 1871–1908 / German Immigrants to Brasil 1871–1908

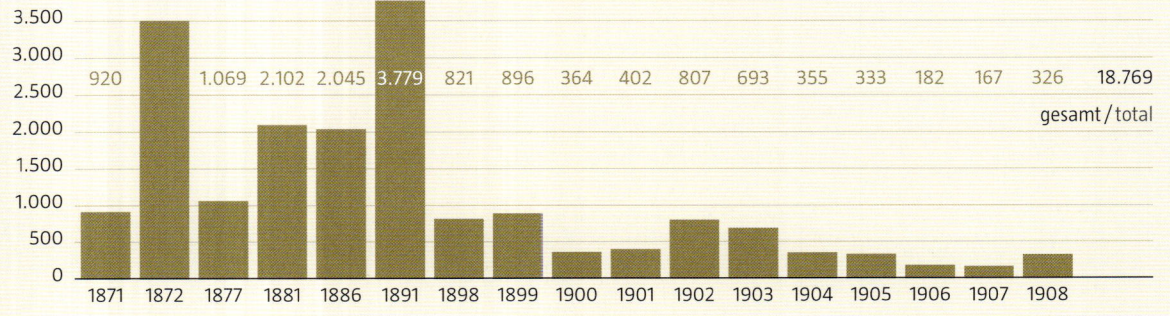

	1871	1872	1877	1881	1886	1891	1898	1899	1900	1901	1902	1903	1904	1905	1906	1907	1908	gesamt / total
	920		1.069	2.102	2.045	3.779	821	896	364	402	807	693	355	333	182	167	326	18.769

Die Koch-Wesers emigrieren nach Brasilien, in das vor allem seit den 1870er Jahren Deutsche gezogen sind. / The Koch-Wesers moved to Brasil, which did have a constant German emigration since the 1870s.

Quelle / Source: Marschalck, Peter: Deutsche Bevölkerungsgeschichte im 19. und 20. Jahrhundert, Frankfurt a. M., 1984

Recep Keskin

01.01.1949

Einwanderung 1967 nach Karlsruhe

Immigration 1967 to Karlsruhe

Als 18-Jähriger verlässt Recep Keskin, der aus einem kleinen Dorf im Westen der Türkei stammt, seine Heimat und kommt 1967 mit einem Stipendium für Hotelfachschulabsolventen nach Deutschland. An einer Abendschule holt er das Fachabitur nach und beschließt 1971 nach einer kurzen Rückkehr in die Türkei in Deutschland zu studieren. In den 1980er Jahren beginnt seine Karriere als Unternehmer und Honorarprofessor für Bauingenieurwesen. Viele Jahre gehörte ihm die Firma „Betonfertigteilwerk Mark GmbH" in Gevelsberg am Rande des Ruhrgebiets mit mehr als 150 Mitarbeitern. Er ist heute im Ruhestand. Recep Keskin sieht sich als Vermittler und Brückenbauer zwischen der Türkei und Deutschland.

In 1967, the eighteen-year old Recep Keskin left his small, native village in the western region of Turkey and came to Germany with a hotel management scholarship. He successfully completed his technical diploma at night school and in 1971, after a short visit to Turkey, he decided to again return to Germany to study. In the 1980s, he began his career as a contractor and honorary professor of civil engineering. For many Years he owned the "Betonfertigteilwerk Mark GmbH" in Gevelsberg. Located on the edge of the Ruhr region, the company employs approximately 150 people. He is retired today. Recep Keskin considers himself a mediator and builder of bridges between Turkey and Germany.

Im Anschluss an seine Ausbildung zum Hotelfachmann erhält Recep Keskin 1967 eines der wenigen Stipendien für einen Auslandsaufenthalt in Deutschland. Nach einem Sprachkurs in Heidelberg arbeitet er für ein Jahr im „Steigenberger Hotel" in Karlsruhe. Das Diplom über die „berufliche Fortbildung in der Bundesrepublik" erhält Keskin im Februar 1970 vom Bundesministerium für wirtschaftliche Zusammenarbeit. / After completing his training as a hotel manager in Turkey, Recep Keskin was offered one of the few scholarships available for a stay abroad in Germany in 1967. On completing a language course in Heidelberg, he worked for the "Steigenberger Hotel" in Karlsruhe for one year. In February 1970, he received this diploma from the Federal Ministry for Economic Cooperation and Development confirming his "further vocational training in the Federal Republic of Germany."

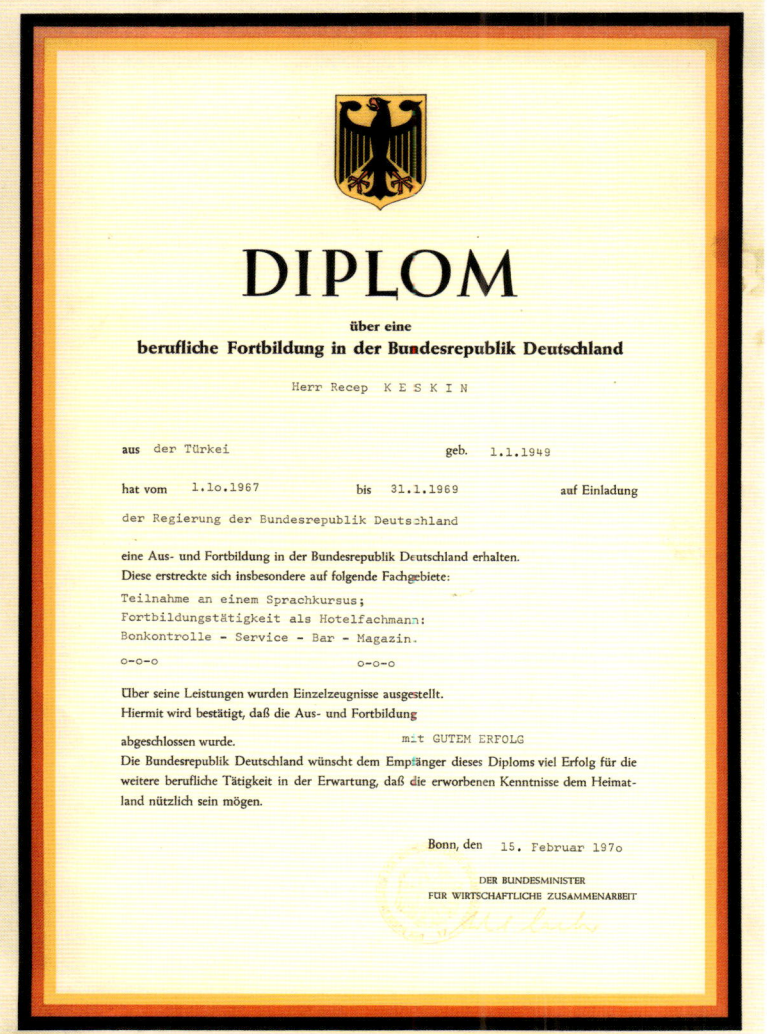

Sammlung Deutsches Auswandererhaus, Dauerleihgabe Recep Keskin

Sammlung Deutsches Auswandererhaus, Dauerleihgabe Recep Keskin

Im Jahr 2000 erhält Recep Keskin den Staatsorden Ersten Grades der Republik Türkei für sein soziales Engagement nach den verheerenden Erdbeben in Izmit (Türkei) 1999. Der Orden und eine Urkunde werden von dem damaligen Staatspräsidenten Süleyman Demirel verliehen. In 2000, Recep Keskin received the Order of the Turkish Republic for his social commitment following the devastating earthquakes in 1999 in Izmit, Turkey. The medal and the certificate were presented by the former Turkish president Süleyman Demirel.

AUSWANDERIN
EMIGRANT

Martha Hüner

01.07.1906 – 03.07.1987
Auswanderung 1923 von Bremerhaven
Emigration 1923 from Bremerhaven

Martha Hüner ist Dienstmädchen und sehnt sich in der Zeit der Weltwirtschaftskrise 1923 nach Sicherheit und neuen Chancen. Ihre in den USA lebenden Tanten versprechen der 17-Jährigen gute Berufsaussichten, bürgen für sie und bezahlen die Reise. Die junge Frau heiratet wenig später den deutschen Bäcker Willy Seegers und arbeitet in der gemeinsamen Bäckerei, bis nach dem Ausbruch des Zweiten Weltkrieges 1939 keiner mehr bei Deutschen kaufen möchte und sie geschlossen werden muss. Nach dem Tod ihres Mannes verdient Martha ihren Unterhalt als Hausdame. Nach einer schweren Krankheit holt ihre Schwester Hanna sie 1987 zurück nach Bremerhaven, wo sie die letzten Monate ihres Lebens verbringt.

Martha Hüner was a servant and in 1923, during the depression era she was looking for better opportunities and security. Her aunts lived in the United States and promised good job prospects. They vouched for her and paid for her crossing. Shortly after arriving, the young woman marries. Her husband Willy Seegers, is a German baker. They worked together in their bakery shop until the outbreak of World War II in 1939 forced them to close because nobody wanted to buy from Germans. After her husband's death Martha earned her living as a housekeeper. Martha became severely ill and her sister Hanna arranged for her to return to Bremerhaven in 1987, where she spent the last months of her life.

Der Vater von Martha Hüner meint, dass seine Tochter in Amerika nur einen Cowboy heiraten könne. So gibt er ihr 1923 diese Pferdebürste mit auf den Weg in die USA, die sie ihr Leben lang begleiten soll. Die Bürste ist nicht nur ein origineller Talisman – sie ist auch eine Erinnerung an den großväterlichen Bauernhof. / Martha Hüner's father was convinced that his daughter would marry a cowboy in America. So in 1923 when she emigrated, he gave her this horse brush to take along to the United States. The brush remained with her all of her life. The brush is not only a keepsake, it is also a memento of her grandfather's farm.

Sammlung Deutsches Auswandererhaus, Schenkung Hanna Wolff

Hanna Wolff: Martha. Geschichte einer Auswanderung, Carl Schünemann Verlag 2016

Martha Hüners Schwester Hanna, die zum Zeitpunkt ihrer Auswanderung noch kein Jahr alt ist, verfasst 2005 diese Biografie über ihre Schwester. / When Martha Hüner emigrated, her sister Hanna was just under a year-old. In 2005, she wrote this biography of her sister.

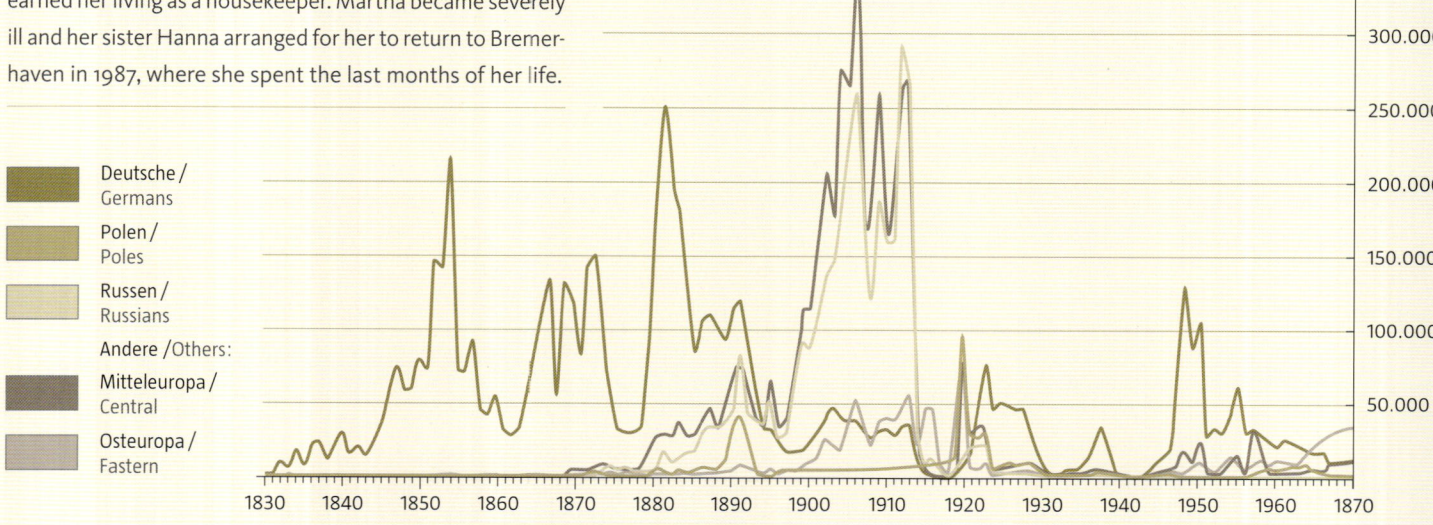

Deutsche / Germans
Polen / Poles
Russen / Russians
Andere /Others:
Mitteleuropa / Central
Osteuropa / Fastern

Deutsche und osteuropäische Einwanderung in die USA 1830 – 1970 / German and East European Immigrants to the United States of America 1830 – 1970

Quelle / Source: Report of the Immigration Commission, Vol. 3, New York, 1970

Mai Phuong Kollath

30.08.1963
Einwanderung 1981 nach Rostock
Immigration 1981 to Rostock

Mit 17 Jahren verwirklicht Mai Phuong Kollath aus Hanoi in Vietnam ihren großen Traum, ins Ausland zu gehen. 1980 reist sie als Vertragsarbeiterin in die DDR. Auch wenn in Vietnam die Arbeit in dem sozialistischen „Bruderland" als große Chance angesehen wird, stehen für Mai Phuong Kollath zunächst die Unabhängigkeit von der Familie und das Abenteuer im Vordergrund. Dass sie in der Großküche einer Hafenkantine anstatt, wie gedacht, in einem Hotel angestellt wird, erfährt sie allerdings erst nach ihrer Ankunft. Als sie schwanger wird, muss sie dies bis zum siebten Monat geheim halten, um nicht abgeschoben zu werden. Nach der Wende 1989 bleibt Mai Phuong Kollath in Deutschland und beginnt mit 37 Jahren zu studieren. Heute arbeitet sie als interkulturelle Beraterin.

Mai Phuong Kollath was 17 years old when she achieved her dream of going abroad. She left her home in Hanoi, Vietnam to work as a contract worker in the German Democratic Republic. Despite the fact that work in the socialist sister country was considered an excellent opportunity in Vietnam, the prospect of adventure and gaining independence from her family were Mai Phuong Kollath's main concerns. It was only after her arrival that she found out that she had been hired to work in the port canteen kitchen, instead of a hotel as she had assumed. She became pregnant and had to keep it secret until she was in her seventh month to avoid deportation. Mai Phuong Kollath stayed in Germany after the reunification in 1989, and began studying at the age of 37. Today she works as an intercultural advisor and coach.

Um sich ihren kargen Lohn in der DDR aufzubessern, nähen viele vietnamesische Vertragsarbeiter in der Freizeit Jeanshosen – so auch Mai Phuong Kollath. Es ist ein florierendes Geschäft. Eine neue falsche „Levis"-Jeans kostet mindestens 70 DDR-Mark. Wie bei den originalen „Levis"-Jeans gibt es auch hier ein kleines rotes Schildchen an der Gesäßtasche – nur ohne den Markennamen „Levis". / In order to improve their low salary in the GDR, many Vietnamese contract workers sewed jeans in their spare time: Mai Phuong Kollath too. It was a thriving business. A new fake "Levis" jeans cost at least 70 GDR Mark. Like the original "Levis," these jeans also featured a small red tag on the rear pocket – but without brandname "Levis."

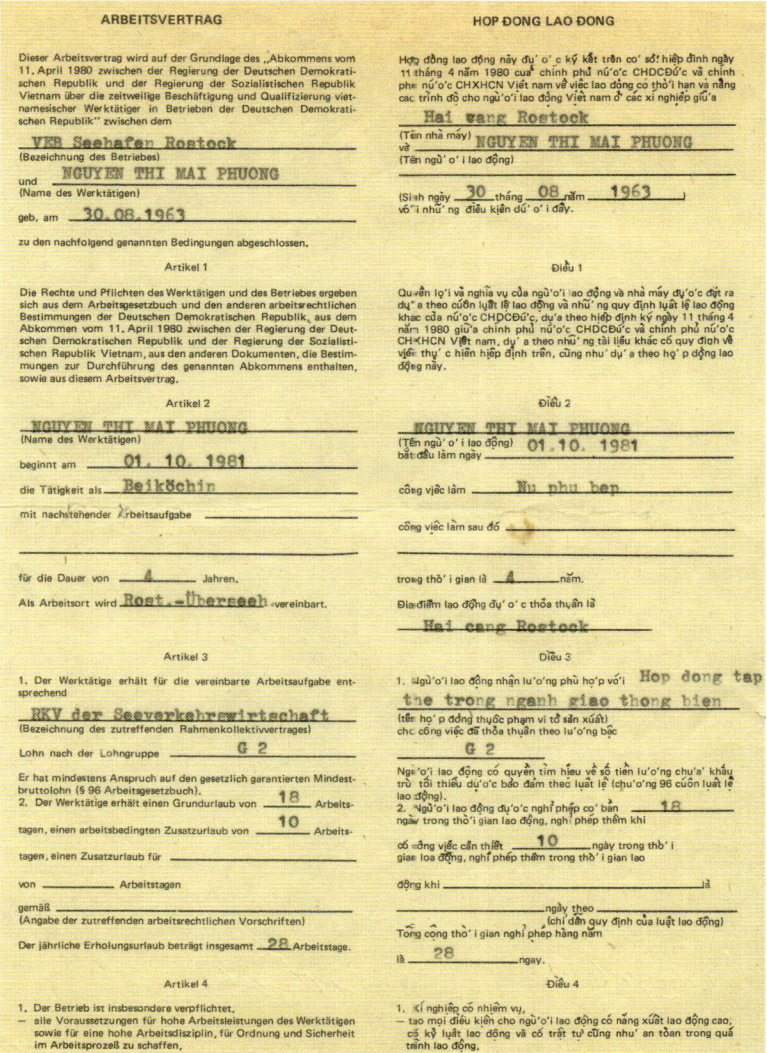

Sammlung Deutsches Auswandererhaus, Dauerleihgabe Mai Phuong Kollath

An dem Tag als sie in Rostock ihren ersten Arbeitsvertrag als Herdhilfe in der Hafenkantine unterschreibt, seien ihre Träume untergegangen, sagt Mai Phuong Kollath rückblickend. Bis dahin ging sie von einer Tätigkeit im Tourismusbereich aus. In Vietnam hätte sie Medizin studiert. 1985 schließt sie ihre Ausbildung zur Köchin ab und wird Schichtleiterin. / When Mai Phuong Kollath looks back on the day she signed her first work contract as an assistant cook in the port canteen in Rostock, she says that her dreams disappeared without a trace. Until then she expected to work in tourism. In Vietnam she would have studied medicine. In 1985, she completed her training as a cook and became shift manager.

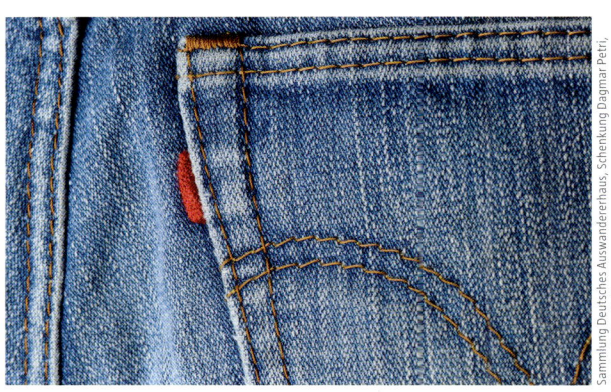

Sammlung Deutsches Auswandererhaus, Schenkung Dagmar Petri,
Photo: Stefan Volk

AUSWANDERER
EMIGRANT

Lebin Weckesser

18.01.1927
Auswanderung seiner Familie 1926 von Bremerhaven
Emigration of his family 1926 from Bremerhaven

Die russische Heimat seiner Eltern kennt Lebin Weckesser nur aus Erzählungen. Als die Familie 1926 nach Argentinien auswandert, ist seine Mutter im siebten Monat mit ihm schwanger. Seine Eltern sind Nachfahren deutscher Siedler, die sich im späten 18. Jahrhundert in der Wolgaregion in Russland niedergelassen hatten. Dort bewirtschaftet die Familie über Generationen einen Bauernhof. Mit Ausbruch der Russischen Revolution im Jahr 1917 und in den Wirren des darauf folgenden Bürgerkrieges verschlechtert sich die Situation grundlegend. Sie entschließen sich zur Rückkehr nach Deutschland, das sie nur aus Erzählungen kennen. Doch schon nach kurzer Zeit reist die Familie weiter nach Argentinien, wo sie auf bessere Bedingungen in der Landwirtschaft hofft. Deutsch lernt Lebin Weckesser von seinen Eltern und Geschwistern, sein Bruder und auch er führen in Buenos Aires eine Bandoneonwerkstatt.

Whatever knowledge Lebin Weckesser has about his parents Russian home is from stories. His mother was seven months pregnant with him when the family immigrated to Argentina in 1926. His parents were of German origin, but their ancestors had settled in the Russian Volga region in the late 18th century. The family farmed there for generations. However, the situation deteriorated dramatically with the outbreak of the Russian revolution in 1917, and the turmoil of the civil war that followed. They decided to return to Germany, a country known only to them from stories. The family soon migrated to Argentina where they hoped to find better farming conditions. Lebin Weckesser learned German from his parents and siblings; he and his brother run a bandoneon workshop in Buenos Aires.

Lebin Weckesser an der Kaje in Bremerhaven, 2007. Er ist bis dahin noch nie in Deutschland gewesen und steht nun an der Stelle, von der aus seine wolgadeutsche Familie nach Argentinien aufbrach. / Lebin Weckesser on the "Kaje" in Bremerhaven, 2007. He had never been to Germany and was now standing on the wharf from where his Volga German family embarked on their journey to Argentina.

Deutsches Auswandererhaus, © Ciro Cappellari

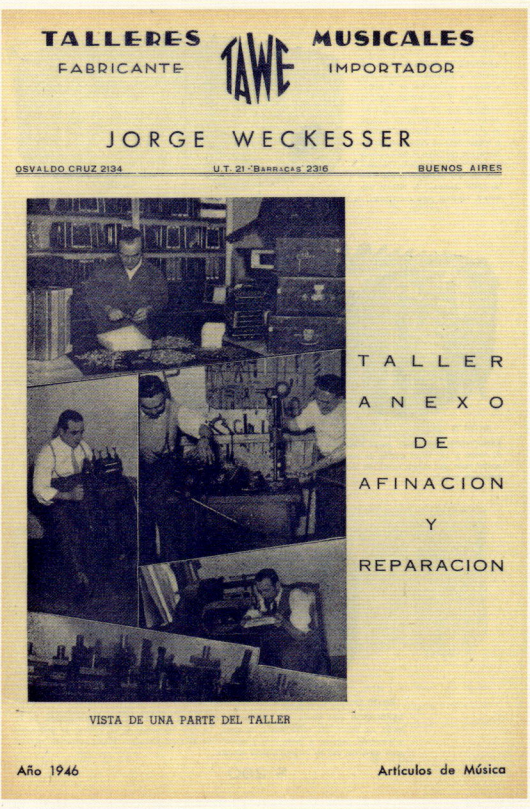

Sammlung Deutsches Auswandererhaus, Schenkung Familie

Instrumentenkatalog der Werkstatt Weckesser, Buenos Aires, 1946. Spare parts for bandoneons from the Weckesser workshop, 2007.

Sammlung Deutsches Auswandererhaus, Ankauf

Das von dem Deutschen Heinrich Band erfundene Bandoneon bringen Auswanderer zu Beginn des 20. Jahrhunderts auch nach Argentinien. Dort wird es bald das charakteristische Instrument des Tangos. Wie dieses 1925 im Erzgebirge gefertigte Bandoneon nach Argentinien gelangt, ist unbekannt. Familie Weckesser kauft und restauriert es 2008 in der eigenen Bandoneonwerkstatt in Buenos Aires. / Created by the German instrument dealer, Heinrich Band, the bandoneon was imported to Argentina at the beginning of the 20th century by emigrants. It soon became an essential instrument in tango ensembles. This bandoneon originated from the Erzgebirge. How it reached Argentina is unknown. The Weckesser's purchased it, and restored it in their bandoneon workshop in Buenos Aires in 2008.

Wilhelm Somplatzki

31.05.1863 – 1940
Saisonarbeiter 1881 – 1905 im Ruhrgebiet
Seasonal laborer 1881 – 1905 in the Ruhr Area

Das „schwarze Gold" des Ruhrgebietes lockt Wilhelm Somplatzki 1881 aus Ostpreußen nach Gelsenkirchen, denn der Ertrag aus der heimatlichen Landwirtschaft reicht gerade nur zum Überleben. Der 18-Jährige ist Masure. Die Masuren sind wie die Polen eine Minderheit im deutschen Ostpreußen. Beide Gruppen zieht es seit 1871 in die boomende Bergbauindustrie. Die Arbeit ist schwer und gefährlich, doch Wilhelm verdient „gutes Geld". Fortan geht er jedes Jahr in den Wintermonaten als Hauer in die Bergwerke im Ruhrgebiet. Für die Frühjahrs- und Sommermonate kehrt er zurück in seine Heimat, um die Felder zu bestellen. Bis zu Beginn des 20. Jahrhunderts pendelt Wilhelm Somplatzki dann bleibt er endgültig in Masuren bei seiner Familie. Sein Sohn Karl arbeitet nach dem Zweiten Weltkrieg erneut als Bergarbeiter im Ruhrgebiet. Er bleibt mit seiner Familie für immer.

Tempted by the "black gold" in the Ruhr region, Wilhelm Somplatzki left his home in East Prussia for Gelsenkirchen in 1881, where his native farm yielded barely enough to survive. The eighteen-year old was Masurian. Similar to the Poles, the Masurians were a minority in German East Prussia. The mining boom that began in 1871, attracted both groups to the Ruhr region. The work was hard and dangerous, but Wilhelm earned "good money." Every year from then on, he was a face worker in the mines of the Ruhr region during the winter. He returned home to his native farm for the spring and summer months to cultivate the fields. Wilhelm Somplatzki traveled back and forth until the early 20th century when he returned home to stay with his family. At the end of World War II his son Karl worked in a coalmine in the Ruhr region like his father. He and his family settled there and have been there ever since.

Wilhelm Somplatzki (2. Reihe, 2. v. li.) zu Beginn des 20. Jahrhunderts auf einer der großen Hochzeitsfeiern in Masuren. / Wilhelm Somplatzki (2nd row, 2nd from left) at the beginning of the 20th century, at one of the large wedding ceremonies in Masuria.

Wilhelm Somplatzkis Sohn Karl tritt in die Fußstapfen seines Vaters. Auch er wird Bergmann. Im Gegensatz zu seinem Vater geht er der schweren Arbeit unter Tage ganzjährig nach. Mit dieser Trinkflasche stillt er in den 1950er Jahren seinen Durst bei der Arbeit. Karl Somplatzki trägt sie immer an seinem Gürtel. Deswegen schlägt die Flasche in den engen Stollen oft an die steinigen Wände und ist stark zerbeult. / Wilhelm Somplatzki's son Karl followed in his father's footsteps. He also became a miner. In contrast to his father he worked underground all year round. In the 1950s, he quenched his thirst from this drinking flask. Karl Somplatzki wore it daily on his belt. Its battered condition is the result of banging against the stone walls of the narrow tunnels.

Hertha Nathorff

05.06.1895 – 10.06.1993

Flucht 1939 von Bremerhaven

Flight 1939 from Bremerhaven

Den Ärzten Erich und Hertha Nathorff, geb. Einstein, entziehen die Nationalsozialisten 1933 die Kassenzulassung. Im Zuge des Novemberpogroms 1938 wird Erich Nathorff verhaftet und für fünf Wochen ins Konzentrationslager Sachsenhausen verschleppt. Nach seiner Freilassung hält die Familie nichts mehr in Deutschland. Doch trotz der Bürgschaft der Hollywood-Legende Carl Laemmle, der wie Hertha Nathorff aus Laupheim stammt, stellt das amerikanische Konsulat die notwendigen Visa nicht aus. Zumindest ihr Sohn Heinz bekommt einen der begehrten Plätze in einem „Kindertransport" nach England. 1939 kann das Ehepaar Nathorff ebenfalls nach England flüchten. 1940 erhalten sie gemeinsam ihre Visa für die Einreise in die USA und emigrieren schließlich nach New York. Der sehr schwierige Neubeginn im Exil wird Hertha Nathorff ihr Leben lang belasten.

Erich and Hertha Nathorff, neé Einstein were medical doctors. In 1933, the Nazis withdrew their statutory health insurance accreditation. Erich Nathorff was arrested during the 1938 November pogrom, and transported to the Sachsenhausen concentration camp. There he was detained for five weeks. There was no reason for the family to remain in Germany after his release. Despite the bond offered by Hollywood legend Carl Laemmle, who came from Laupheim, the same town as Hertha Nathorff, the U.S. Consulate refused to issue the necessary visa. However, her son Heinz was given one of the coveted "Kindertransport" spots to England. Erich and Hertha Nathorff succeeded in fleeing to England in 1939. When they obtained their visa for the United States in 1940, and the family immigrated to New York. Their extremely difficult new start in exile burdened Hertha Nathorff for the rest of her life.

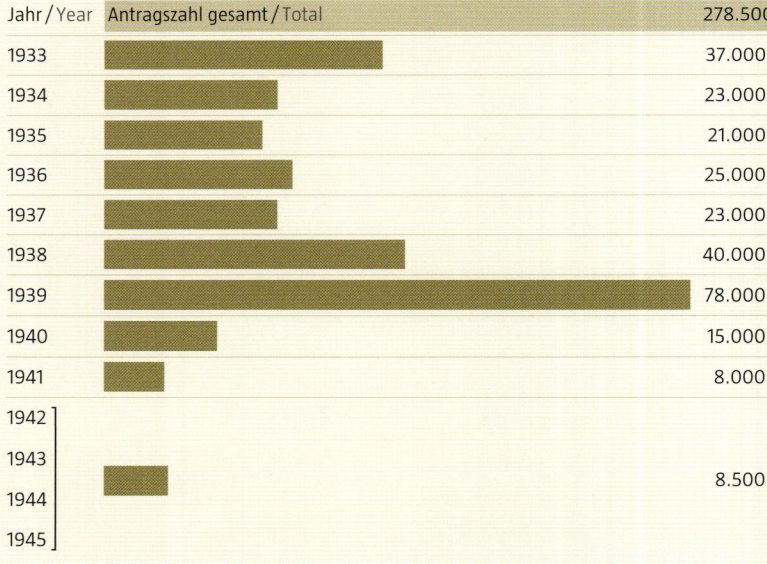

Hertha Nathorff nimmt in New York oft Reisende als Übernachtungsgäste in ihrer kleinen Wohnung in New York auf, so auch Winfried Wübbolt. Er bleibt nach seiner Rückkehr noch lange mit Hertha Nathorff in Briefkontakt. Dieser Brief aus dem Jahr 1971 verdeutlicht ihre Verbitterung über die erzwungene Auswanderung: Sie schreibt, sie wäre am Ende doch lieber vergast worden. / Hertha Nathorff often hosted travellers as overnight guests in her small apartment in New York. Winfried Wübbolt was one of them. Over the years, he regularly corresponded with Hertha Nathorff. This letter, dated 1971, shows her bitterness about the forced emigration. She writes that she would, after all, rather have been gassed.

Sammlung Deutsches Auswandererhaus, Schenkung Winfried Wübbolt

Jüdische Flucht aus Deutschland 1933 – 1945 / Jewish refugees from Germany 1933 – 1945

Jahr / Year	Antragszahl gesamt / Total	278.500
1933		37.000
1934		23.000
1935		21.000
1936		25.000
1937		23.000
1938		40.000
1939		78.000
1940		15.000
1941		8.000
1942		
1943		8.500
1944		
1945		

Quelle / Source: Schoeps, Julius H. (Hrsg / publisher.): Neues Lexikon des Judentums, Gütersloh, 2000.

Benz, Wolfgang (Hrsg./Ed.): Das Tagebuch der Hertha Nathorff. Berlin-New York. Aufzeichnungen 1933 bis 1945, Frankfurt am Main, 2010.

Jeanne Greber

09.04.1884 – 15.06.1981

Einwanderung 1919 nach Saarlouis
Immigration 1919 to Saarlouis

Nach der Rückgabe Elsass-Lothringens an Frankreich 1919 werden viele der dort ansässigen Deutschen vertrieben. Sie wandern daraufhin zumeist in die angrenzenden Regionen des Deutschen Reiches ein. Die strenge Ausweisungspolitik der französischen Behörden trennt binationale Familien: Im Jahr 1919 folgt die Französin Jeanne Greber zusammen mit den beiden Söhnen ihrem ausgewiesenen deutschen Mann Karl ins Saargebiet, denn ihre Ehe soll nicht zerbrechen. Die 1940er Jahre werden für Jeanne die schrecklichste Zeit ihres Lebens. Ihre beiden Söhne kämpfen auf deutscher Seite und fallen im Zweiten Weltkrieg, kurz darauf stirbt ihr Mann und die einzige Tochter erkrankt schwer an Tuberkulose. Jeanne bleibt unglücklich in Deutschland; ihre einzige Freude sind später ihre Enkelkinder.

After Alsace-Lorraine was returned to France in 1919, many of the Germans based there were forced to leave. Most of them immigrated to the neighboring regions of the German Reich. The strict policy of deportation on the part of the French authorities separated bi-national families. In 1919, together with her two sons, the French Jeanne Greber followed her German husband Karl to the Saar region of Germany. They did not want to be separated. The 1940s were the worst years of Jeanne's life. Both of her sons fought on the side of Germany and fell in battle. Shortly after, her husband died and her only daughter contracted tuberculosis. Jeanne was unhappy but she remained in Germany. In later life, her grandchildren were her only joy in life.

Jeanne Greber mit ihren beiden Söhnen Theodor (li.) und Franz (re.) während des Ersten Weltkrieges. Trotz der Bedrohung durch den Krieg sind es für sie glückliche Tage – in ihrer Heimat in Elsass-Lothringen. / Jeanne Greber and her sons, Theodor (left) and Franz (right), are shown during World War I. She was happy at home in Alsace-Lorraine despite the threat of the war.

Sammlung Deutsches Auswandererhaus, Dauerleihgabe Edith Behrens

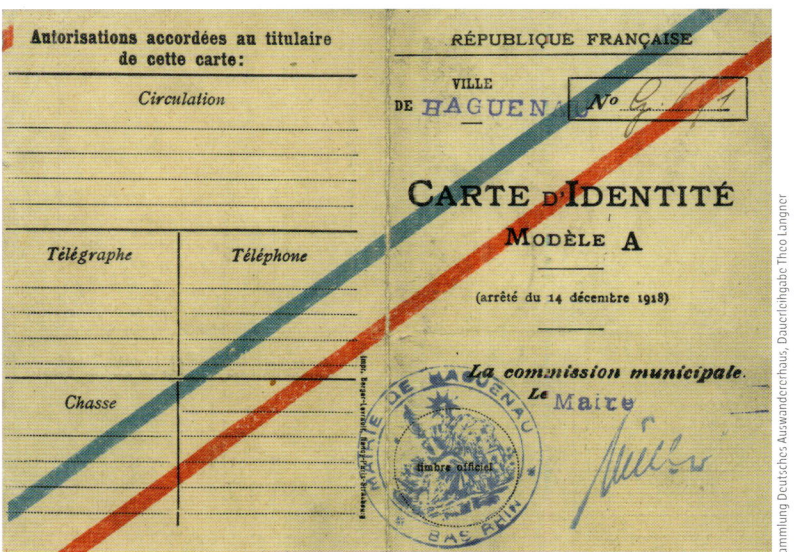

Sammlung Deutsches Auswandererhaus, Dauerleihgabe Theo Langner

Die „Carte d'Identité" bekommt nach dem Ende des Ersten Weltkrieges jeder Elsass-Lothringer. Jeanne Greber erhält ein „A", das sie als Französin legitimiert. Ihr ausgewiesener Mann Karl fällt unter die Kategorie „C", die ihn als Deutschen kennzeichnet. / At the end of World War I, every resident in Alsace-Lorraine was given this "Carte d'Identité." Jeanne Greber was given an "A," that proved she was a Frenchwoman. Her deported husband Karl, came under category "C," that identified him as a German.

BILDER DER AUSSTELLUNG
PICTURES OF THE EXHIBITION

BILDER DER AUSSTELLUNG
IMAGES OF THE EXHIBITION

SIMONE EICK, JULIAN HERBIG

Die Ausstellungsräume des Deutschen Auswandererhauses wirken auf die Besucher im ersten Moment wie Gemälde, in die man hineintritt und plötzlich ganz neue Sinneseindrücke sieht, hört und fühlt. Auf den zweiten Blick entdeckt man die zahlreichen Wissens- und Medienstationen, an denen Migrationsgeschichte vermittelt wird. Diese einzigartige Collage aus Inszenierung und Wissensvermittlung, aus Schauen, Erleben und Entdecken weckt bei den Besuchern eine neue Lust am Lernen.

Bewusst setzen die Museumsmacher neben der intellektuellen Wissensvermittlung auf Sinnlichkeit und Emotionalität, denn einzigartig am Thema Aus- und Einwanderung ist, dass neben vielen Fakten, wie Einreisebestimmung, Arbeitsmarktzahlen oder Integrationsleistungen, viele Ideen, Meinungen und Gefühle eine sehr große Rolle spielen. Während in den Einwanderungsländern die Gesellschaft ihre Werte und Normen diskutiert und Professoren, Politiker und Beamte Gesetze schreiben und erlassen, treffen die Migranten ihre Entscheidungen im Stillen und träumen leise ihre Träume. Diese oft sich widersprechenden Ideen, Meinungen und Gefühle darzustellen, gelingt im Deutschen Auswandererhaus, weil Ausstellungsräume, Objekte, Texte und Bilder verschiedene Blicke auf das Thema Migration bieten und unterschiedliche Meinungen zulassen.

At first glance, the exhibition spaces of the German Emigration Center appear to be paintings the visitors step inside of and suddenly experience new sensory impressions. At second glance, they discover the numerous knowledge and media stations that communicate migration history. This unique collage of staging and transfer of knowledge, of contemplating, experiencing and discovering awakens a new desire to learn in the visitors.

In addition to the intellectual transfer of knowledge, the museum deliberately focuses on sensibility and sentiment, because, apart from the many facts, including entry requirements, job figures or integration services, a unique aspect of the migration issue is that it involves many ideas, opinions and feelings. While society in the immigration countries discusses values and standards, and professors, politicians and civil servants write and pass laws, the migrants make their decisions in silence and quietly dream their dreams. The German Emigration Center successfully illustrates these often conflicting ideas, opinions and feelings because the exhibition spaces, the objects on display, texts and images highlight different views on the issue of migration and tolerate different opinions.

AUSWANDERUNG
IMMIGRATION

→ **Bremerhaven**

Über sieben Millionen Europäer sind von Bremerhaven nach Übersee gereist. Heute findet sich nur noch wenig Historisches in der Stadt. Deswegen rekonstruierte das Deutsche Auswandererhaus viele Original-schauplätze. / Over 7 million Europeans emigrated overseas through the port of Bremerhaven. Today, there are only a few historical sites in the city. This is why the German Emigration Center reconstructed many of the original locations.

AUSWANDERUNG
EMIGRATION

→ **Wartehalle / Waiting Hall**

Die Zeitreise durch die Auswanderungsgeschichte beginnt in einem Nachbau der Wartehalle, die der „Norddeutsche Lloyd" 1869 am Neuen Hafen
errichten ließ. Im Wartesaal für die Passagiere des Zwischendecks ver-
anschaulicht ein Modell die Hafenanlagen Bremerhavens im Jahr 1904.
The time journey through the history of emigration begins with a reproduction of the waiting hall the "North German Lloyd" had built at the
"New Harbor" in 1869. A model in the steerage passengers' waiting room
visualizes the docks in Bremerhaven in 1904.

Auswanderung

An der Kaje / On the Wharf

Bremerhaven. Es ist kalt und nass. Auswanderer aus allen Regionen
Europas drängen sich an der Kaje. Ihre Stimmen vermischen sich mit den
Geräuschen des Hafens. Vor ihnen erhebt sich die Bordwand der „Lahn" —
das Dampfschiff ist bereit zum Aufbruch in die Neue Welt. / Bremerhaven.
It is cold and wet. Emigrants from all regions of Europe force their way
to the wharf. Their voices blend in with the harbor sounds. The ship's
wall of the "Lahn" rises up in front of them — the steamer is ready to
begin its journey to the New World.

Galerie der 7 Millionen / Gallery of the 7 Million

Woher kamen sie? Warum gingen sie? Von den mehr als 7,2 Millionen Menschen, die Europa zwischen 1830 und 1974 über Bremerhaven verließen, sind hier 2.000 Namen von Auswanderern versammelt. Briefe, Fotos, Dokumente und Erinnerungsstücke geben Auskunft darüber, wer sie waren. Historische Bilder, Statistiken und Hörtexte erklären die politischen, wirtschaftlichen und gesellschaftlichen Ursachen der europäischen Massenauswanderung. / Where did they come from? Why did they leave? The names of two thousand emigrants, out of a total of 7.2 million people who left Europe between 1830 and 1974 from the port of Bremerhaven are collected here. Letters, photographs, documents and artifacts provide information about who they were. Historical pictures, statistics and audio texts illuminate the political, economical and social reasons that led to the wave of emigration from Europe.

Überfahrt / Crossing

Das rekonstruierte Zwischendeck eines Segelschiffes (um 1850), eines Dampfschiffes (um 1890) sowie eines Ocean Liners (um 1930) vermitteln die Überfahrtsbedingungen der Auswanderer hautnah. Eng und stickig war es immer, doch gegen Ende des 19. Jahrhunderts sank zumindest das Risiko, auf der Überfahrt zu erkranken oder zu sterben. The reconstructed steerage deck of a sailing vessel (about 1850), a steamer (about 1890) and an ocean liner (about 1930) offer a first hand experience of the conditions the emigrants endured during the crossing. It was always crowded and close, but the risk of contracting an illness or dying during the crossing fell towards the end of the nineteenth century.

Klaus Frahm

Ellis Island

Allen Auswanderern, die im Zwischendeck reisten, standen bei der Ankunft Kontrollen bevor: medizinische Untersuchungen und Befragungen durch die Behörden, denn arbeitsfähig und selbstständig sollten die Einwanderer sein, um niemandem zur Last zu fallen. Die größte und bedeutendste Einwanderungsstation der USA war Ellis Island bei New York. Auch in Kanada, den südamerikanischen Einwanderungsländern sowie in Australien befanden sich solche Stationen.

The emigrants who traveled steerage were subjected to inspections upon arrival. The authorities examined immigrants for medical fitness and asked questions. It was essential that they be fit for work, financially independent and not become a burden on the community. The largest and most significant immigration station in the United States was Ellis Island in the harbor of New York City. Similar stations were located in Canada and in the South American immigration countries, as well as in Australia.

Office of the New World

Was wussten die Auswanderer bereits vorab von ihren Zielländern? Auf welche Weise gelangten Informationen von der Neuen Welt zurück nach Europa? Auswandererführer, Werbebroschüren, Zeitungen sowie Briefe von bereits ausgewanderten Verwandten und Freunden waren wichtige Informationsqueller. Ob die dort gemachten Angaben über Verdienst- und Arbeitsmöglichkeiten, Klima oder andere Lebensbedingungen stimmten, konnten die Einwanderer häufig erst vor Ort feststellen.

What previous knowledge did the emigrants have of their destinations? How was information transmitted from the New World back to Europe? Important resources of information were emigration guides, advertizing brochures, newspapers and letters from friends and relatives who had already emigrated. However, the emigrants often could only determine whether the information provided about income and employment opportunities, climate or other conditions of life were accurate when they had reached their destination.

Goodbye New World

DEUTSCHE IN DEN USA· SÜDSTAATEN UM 1860
GERMANS IN THE USA·SOUTHERN STATES AROUND 1860
Eine eigene Farm/A farm of one's own

KAY Riechers

→ Grand Central Terminal

Endlich angekommen – doch wie geht es jetzt weiter? In dem 1913 er-
öffneten New Yorker Bahnhof „Grand Central Terminal" trafen sich täglich Hunderttausende Einwanderer und Alteingesessene, Arme und Reiche,
Europäer und Asiaten. In de n Nachbau der prächtigen Bahnhofshalle
erzählen 18 Biographien beispielhaft von Lebenswegen in der Neuen Welt;
Dioramen, zahlreiche Fotog afien und Lithographien dokumentieren
zusätzlich 300 Jahre deutsch er Einwanderungsgeschichte in den USA.
Here at last! – but what comes next? Every day, hundreds of thousands
of immigrants, long-time residents, rich and poor, Europeans and Asians
passed through Grand Central Terminal which opened in New York City
in 1913. In the reproduction of the splendid waiting hall, eighteen biographies recount the life sto ies of emigrants to the New World. Addition-
ally, dioramas, numerous photographs and lithographs document three
hundred years of German immigration history in the United States.

EINWANDERUNG
IMMIGRATION

→ **Kiosk / Kiosk**

Es ist der 24. November 1973, ein Tag nach dem „Anwerbestopp ausländischer Arbeitskräfte". Die aktuellen Zeitungen am Kiosk titeln mit dem Beschluss der Bundesregierung, der für eine Wende in der deutschen Einwanderungspolitik steht. Wie sah die Einwanderung nach Deutschland vor diesem Datum aus? Und was hat sich seitdem verändert?
The date is November 24, 1973, the day after the "recruitment ban for foreign workers." The current newspapers at the kiosk headline with the Federal Government's decision that marks a change in German immigration policy. What characterized immigration to Germany before this date? And what has changed since?

Ilka Seer

→ Einkaufszentrum / Shopping mall

Eine originalgetreue Ladenpassage aus den 1970er Jahren. In diesem ganz alltäglichen Einkaufszentrum ist viel Neues und vermeintlich Altbekanntes zu entdecken. Im Zentrum stehen dabei die bewegenden Lebensgeschichten von 15 Einwanderern und ihren Nachfahren. Neben den Verkaufsartikeln in den Schaufenstern finden sich – oft erst auf den zweiten Blick erkennbar – persönliche Erinnerungsobjekte der verschiedenen Einwanderergruppen. / A re-created 1970s shopping arcade. This ordinary shopping mall invites visitors to discover both new and nostalgic objects, while focusing on the moving stories of fifteen immigrants and their descendants. It often requires a second glance to notice the immigrants' personal items among the merchandise on display in the shopfront windows.

Aussehen

Constantin Heller

Frisörsalon / Hairdresser

In dem originalen Frisörsalon Matthieves von 1966, der aus der Nähe von Leverkusen stammt und bis Ende 2011 in Betrieb war, dreht sich alles um das Thema „Aussehen". Die Porträtfotos der 15 Einwanderer und ihrer Nachfahren, deren Geschichten in dem Museum erzählt werden, stehen in den Regalen und werfen Fragen auf: Wie begegnet man den neugierigen, fragenden Blicken, wenn man anders aussieht als die meisten? Wann wird man nicht mehr als Fremder wahrgenommen?
The focus is on "appearance" in the original Friseursalon Matthieves that dates back to 1966. It was situated near the city of Leverkusen and was open until 2011. The portraits of the fifteen immigrants and their descendants whose stories are told in the museum stand on the shelves. Their photos raise questions: how does one deal with curious, questioning glances when one's appearance is different from most of the others? When is one no longer perceived as a foreigner?

→ Antiquariat / Second-hand bookstore

Das Antiquariat atmet den Zeitgeist der späten 1960er Jahre. Studentenrevolte und Marxismus sind die scheinbar alles dominierenden Themen. Inmitten der damals aktuellen Bücher und Plakate liegt das, was immer zeitlos und wertvoll sein wird: Erinnerungsstücke an die Familie und Freunde, an die alte Heimat oder den eigenen Glauben.
The second-hand bookstore reflects the spirit of the late 1960s. Student revolts and Marxism apparently are the dominant themes. Amidst contemporary books and posters, one encounters items which will forever remain timeless and valuable: Memorabilia of family and friends, the native country, or of one's personal faith.

EINBÜRGERUNG
NATURALIZATION
03 AA-ZZ

Constantin Heller

→ **Behördengang / Trip to the authorities**

Zwei zentrale Hürden gibt es für Einwanderer, die nach Deutschland
kommen: die Einreise und das Aufenthaltsrecht. Die Einbürgerung bleibt
freiwillig. Der „Behördengang" und Auszüge des „Einwanderungstests"
aus dem Jahr 2012 eröffnen Einblicke in die bürokratischen Vorausset-
zungen für eine Ein- oder Zuwanderung in die Bundesrepublik Deutschland. Audiostationen vermitteln historische Hintergrundinformationen
zu 300 Jahren Einwanderungsgeschichte nach Deutschland und den
15 bedeutendsten Einwanderergruppen. / Immigrants to Germany are
faced with two major hurdles: entry requirements and right of residence.
The 'trip to the authorities' gives insight into the bureaucratic requirements for immigration to the Federal Republic of Germany. Audio stations provide historical background information on the three hundred
years of migration to Germany and the fifteen most significant groups
of immigrants.

Roxy Kino und Foyer / The Roxy cinema

Das Museumskino „Roxy" strahlt den Charme eines Lichtspieltheaters der 1950er Jahre aus. Hier werden eigene Filmproduktionen des Deutschen Auswandererhauses über deutsche Auswanderer und ihre Nachfahren und Einwanderer in Deutschland gezeigt. Die Filme erzählen von Heimweh und Fernweh, Heimat und Zuhause. Es sind Dokumente über das persönliche historische Bewusstsein emigrierter Menschen, die die Identität der kulturellen Vielfalt in Einwanderungsländern zeigen. / The museum cinema, the "Roxy", captures the charm of a 1950s movie theater. Here visitors can watch films produced by the German Emigration center about German immigrants and their descendants and immigrants in Germany. The films deal with homesickness and wanderlust, home and "Heimat." Both these films document the personal and historical awareness of people who have emigrated and their contribution to the cultural diversity of the immigration countries.

DIE ARCHITEKTUR DES DEUTSCHEN AUSWANDERERHAUSES
THE ARCHITECTURE OF THE GERMAN EMIGRATION CENTER

Skizze: / Sketch: Andreas Heller

ANDREAS HELLER

Ein Gemälde aus dem späten 19. Jahrhundert steht am Anfang der Gestaltung für die Architektur des Deutschen Auswandererhauses: Eine Menschenmenge steht an der Kaje, verabschiedet ein Schiff mit vielen Menschen an Bord, die Europa in Richtung Amerika für immer verlassen. Eine Frau sticht aus dieser Menge heraus. Sie schwenkt ein weißes Tuch, winkt zum Abschied – für die Entwicklung der Formensprache der Architektur ein bleibender und prägender Eindruck. Diese Geste, die sich aus der Menge erhebt, ist Sinnbild für die Hoffnung, sich eines Tages wiederzusehen.

Die aufragenden Schwingen des Gebäudes symbolisieren dieses winkende Tuch: hoch geschwungen und für ihre Größe zart. Eingebettet sind die Schwingen, manchmal auch Segel genannt, in eine runde, weiche Gebäudeform. Alles aus Sichtbeton.

In the beginning of the conceptual design for the architecture of the German Emigration Center there was a nineteenth-century painting depicting a crowd on the wharf bidding a shipful of passengers farewell as the ship casts off, heading for America. One woman stands out. She is waving a white hanky, waving farewell. This one little detail left a lasting and indelible impression, consequently influencing the development of the museum's architectural concept considerably. This small gesture, standing out from the crowd, was a symbol of hope; the hope that one day people would see each other again.

The soaring wings of the structure symbolize that white handkerchief being waved in the air. Embedded in the round, soft shape of the building these wings, also called sails, rise high above the building, yet they are delicate for their size. The basic structure and the wings are made of exposed concrete.

RER

DEUTSCHE
AUSWANDE
HAUS

ERWEITERUNG 2012
EXTENSION 2012

Skizze: / Sketch: Andreas Heller

Ein- und Auswanderung braucht beides: Zuversicht und den Mut zur Entbehrung. Diese Eigenschaften spiegelt auch die Architektur des Deutschen Auswandererhauses wider. In die weiche, ovale Grundform aus Sichtbeton des Haupthauses schiebt sich das holzbeplankte Obergeschoss als kantiger Block. Beide Elemente erscheinen als Gegenpole und sind doch untrennbar miteinander verbunden. Auch die aufragenden Betonschwingen betonen die gegensätzlichen Facetten von Migration. Sie stilisieren ein winkendes Tuch, das ein zentrales Symbol des Abschieds und zugleich der Hoffnung auf ein Wiedersehen ist.

Der würfelförmige Erweiterungsbau – eine hölzerne „Box", ein Aufbewahrungsgebäude – beherbergt diejenigen Biographien, anhand derer das Migrationsmuseum die Einwanderungsgeschichte nach Deutschland von 1685 bis heute erzählt. Eine Brücke verbindet beide Gebäudekomplexe: die europäische Auswanderungsgeschichte und die deutsche Einwanderungsgeschichte. Symbolhaft wird hiermit gezeigt, dass die Unterscheidung von Aus- und Einwanderung in erster Linie eine Frage der Perspektive ist.

Emigration and immigration require two things: hope and courage, the courage to do without. The architecture of the German Emigration Center reflects these two qualities. The wood planked upper level, an angular block, fits into the soft basic oval, exposed concrete design of the main building. The two elements appear to be opposing poles, yet they are inseparably connected to each other. The soaring concrete wings emphasize the opposite aspects of migration and represent a stylized waving kerchief, a symbol synonymous with bidding farewell but at the same time evoking the hope of seeing one another again.

The cube-shaped extension wing, a wooden "box," a building for safekeeping, contains the biographies of the newly presented history of immigration. A bridge connects both structures and hence the history of emigration to the history of immigration, symbolically illustrating that the difference between emigration and immigration is, above all else, a question of perspective.

DAS SEEAMT
UND DIE BIBLIOTHEK

THE MARITIME
BOARD OF INQUIRY
AND THE LIBRARY

TANJA FITTKAU

Im Jahr 2007 ermöglicht die großzügige Unterstützung der „Max Kade Foundation", New York, die Restaurierung der Räumlichkeiten im ehemaligen Seeamt Bremerhaven. Der alte Gerichtssaal wird nun zum „Max-Kade-Saal". Max Kades 1944 gegründete Stiftung fördert wissenschaftliche Einrichtungen auf beiden Seiten des Atlantiks. Vermittelt wird die Spende durch die „Stiftung Deutsches Auswandererhaus", die ihren Sitz 2007 in dem historischen Bau nimmt. Im Juni 2007 bezieht die wissenschaftliche Abteilung des Deutschen Auswandererhauses die Büroräume im Erdgeschoss.

2013 wird im „Max-Kade-Saal" die Präsenzbibliothek des Deutschen Auswandererhauses eröffnet.

In 2007 the ground floor of the former Marine Board of Inquiry was restored with the generous support of the "Max Kade Foundation" in New York. The ancien courtroom became the "Max-Kade-Saal." Founded in 1944, the Max Kade Foundation sponsors research institutions on both sides of the Atlantic. This donation was secured by the "German Emigration Center Foundation" and the historical building became their headquarters in 2007. The research department of the German Emigration Center moved into the offices on the ground floor in June 2007.

The German Emigration Center's reference library opens in the "Max-Kade-Saal" in 2013.

Ilka Seer

Bibliothek zur deutschen Ein- und Auswanderungsgeschichte am Deutschen Auswandererhaus / Library of German immigration and emigration history in the German Emigration Center

Die Bibliothek umfasst über 6.000 Sammelbände, Fachbücher, Enzyklopädien, Auswandererführer und Monographien aus Deutschland, den USA und Südamerika.
The library includes over 6.000 anthologies, science books, encyclopedias, emigration guides and monographs from Germany, the United States and South America.

SONDERAUSSTELLUNGEN (AUSWAHL)
SPECIAL EXHIBITIONS (SELECTION)

SONDERAUSSTELLUNGEN 2006–2016
SPECIAL EXHIBITIONS 2006–2016

SIMONE EICK, TANJA FITTKAU, KARIN HESS, KATRIN QUIRIN

Die Sonderausstellungen am Deutschen Auswandererhaus bieten die Gelegenheit, bestimmte Themen der Aus- und Einwanderungsgeschichte Deutschlands zu vertiefen, wie beispielsweise Umweltmigration, Fremdheitserfahrungen und neue deutsche Sehnsuchtsländer wie Australien. Dabei werden nicht nur Fotos, Dokumente und Objekte aus der Sammlung des Deutschen Auswandererhauses, sondern auch zahlreiche Leihgaben aus Museen und Archiven in Europa und aus Übersee gezeigt.

Oftmals produziert das Deutsche Auswandererhaus für seine Sonderausstellungen kurze Dokumentationsfilme, wie beispielsweise in New Orleans oder Buenos Aires, und publiziert Kataloge mit Beitragen von Historikern, Politikern und Schriftstellern.

The special exhibitions at the German Emigration Center provide the opportunity for deepening one's knowledge of certain aspects of the history of migration in Germany, for example environmental migration, the foreignness immigrants experience, or new destinations for Germans such as Australia. These exhibitions include photographs, documents and objects from the collection of the German Emigration Center as well as numerous loans from European and US American museums and archives.

The German Emigration Center frequently produces short documentaries – for instance in New Orleans or Buenos Aires – to accompany its special exhibitions and publishes catalogues with contributions by historians, politicians and authors.

Pacific Palisades

Kalifornien, USA
California, U.S.A.

Deutsches Auswandererhaus

SCHRIFTSTELLER IM EXIL
WRITERS IN EXILE

Thomas Mann, Lion Feuchtwanger, Vicki Baum, Bertolt Brecht und Theodor W. Adorno gehörten zu der Gruppe von Schriftstellern, die sich während der nationalsozialistischen Diktatur im Ort Pacific Palisades in Kalifornien im Exil niederließen. Lebens- und Arbeitsbedingungen in der englischsprachigen Fremde stellten für alle deutschsprachigen Schriftsteller eine Herausforderung dar. Pacific Palisades – eine Hügellandschaft im Norden von Los Angeles – wurde zum „Weimar unter Palmen". Doch das Paradies hatte seine Schattenseiten: Nicht allen Schriftstellern gelang es, in Amerika Fuß zu fassen. / Thomas Mann, Lion Feuchtwanger, Vicki Baum, Bertolt Brecht and Theodor W. Adorno numbered among the writers who fled Germany and its Nazi dictatorship to live in exile in Pacific Palisades. The living and working conditions in an English-language environment far away from home posed a challenge for these German-language writers. Pacific Palisades, in the hills north of Los Angeles, soon became a "tropical Weimar" of sorts. What at first glance may have appeared to be paradise definitely had its drawbacks. Not all of the émigré writers managed to cope with their new lives in the U.S.A.

.. .. 28/01/2006–02/04/2006

Pacific Palisades – Der Weg deutsch-sprachiger Schriftsteller ins kalifornische Exil 1932–1941 / Pacific Palisades – German-Language Writers on the Road to Exile in California 1932–1941
In Kooperation mit dem Buddenbrookhaus Lübeck. Außerdem gezeigt im Literaturhaus München, Buddenbrookhaus Lübeck und Erich Maria Remarque-Friedenszentrum Osnabrück. / In cooperation with the Buddenbrookhaus Lübeck. Also shown at Literaturhaus Munich, Buddenbrookhaus Lübeck and Erich Maria Remarque-Friedenszentrum Osnabrück.

Deutsches Auswandererhaus

....

Zu dieser Sonderausstellung ist ein Katalog in der edition DAH erschienen. / A catalogue of this special exhibition was published by edition DAH.

Deutsches Auswandererhaus

Buenos Aires

Hauptstadt Argentiniens
Capital of Argentina

EINE STADT VOLLER HISTORISCHER GEGENSÄTZE
A CITY FULL OF HISTORIC CONTRASTS

Die deutschen Einwanderer in Argentinien waren lange Zeit sehr präsent in der Öffentlichkeit: Zeitungen, Gebäude, Firmen und Siedlungen mit deutschen Namen gab es zahlreiche. Sie alle wiesen hin auf die knapp 100.000 Deutschen, die ins Land gekommen waren, um dort als Bauern, Arbeiter und Handwerker ein neues Leben zu beginnen. Mit Beginn der nationalsozialistischen Diktatur traten zwei andere Einwanderergruppen in den Vordergrund: jüdische Flüchtlinge, später dann NS-Verbrecher. So begegneten sich in der Stadt Opfer, Täter und argentinische Sympathisanten des Nationalsozialismus. Die Geschichte fand eine tragische Fortsetzung: Nachkommen der jüdischen Flüchtlinge wurden zu Opfern der argentinischen Militärdiktatur in den 1970er Jahren. Exklusiv für das Museumskino entstand der Kurzfilm „24h Buenos Aires" von Grimme-Preisträger Ciro Cappellari. Drei argentinische Biographien sind auch in der Dauerausstellung vertreten. / German immigrants to Argentina were very present in public life in Argentina for a long time. Newspapers, buildings, businesses and settlements with German names were numerous, all indicative of the nearly 100,000 Germans who came to the country to start a new life as farmers, blue-collar workers and workmen. With the beginning of the Nazi dictatorship two new emigrant groups came to the fore – Jewish refugees and, later, Nazi criminals. Buenos Aires became a place where victims, perpetrators and sympathizers of the Nazi dictatorship encountered one another. History repeated itself tragically when descendants of the Jewish refugees became victims of the military dictatorship in Argentina in the 1970s. The short film 24h Buenos Aires was created by Grimme award-winning director Ciro Cappellari exclusively for the museum's Ocean Cinema. The permanent exhibition features three Argentinean biographies.

.... 21/01/2008–21/09/2008

Nach Buenos Aires! Deutsche Auswanderer und Flüchtlinge im 20. Jahrhundert/Off to Buenos Aires! German Emigrants and Refugees in the 20th Century
Zu dieser Sonderausstellung ist ein Katalog in der edition DAH erschienen. / A catalogue of this special exhibition was published by edition DAH.

New Orleans
Louisiana, U.S.A.

K. Quirin

Deutsches Auswandererhaus

DIE AUSGEWANDERTE STADT
THE CITY LEFT BEHIND

Der Wirbelsturm „Katrina" erreichte am 29. August 2005 New
Orleans. 1.836 Menschen starben und 1,3 Millionen flohen
aus der Stadt und ihrer Umgebung. New Orleans fehlen 2009
40 Prozent seiner ehemaligen Bewohner. Die meisten leben
im ländlichen Louisiana und in Texas. Binnenmigration aufgrund von Klimakatastrophen ist ein neues Migrationsphäno-
men, das die nächsten Jahrzehnte bestimmen wird. / Hurri-
cane Katrina hit New Orleans on 29 August 2005 killing 1,836
people and forcing 1.3 million to flee the city and its surround-
ings. In 2009, New Orleans is still missing forty percent of its
former population. The majority has taken up residence else-
where in the state of Louisiana or relocated to Texas. Domestic
migration due to climate disaster is a migration phenomenon
destined to mark the coming decades.

.... 02/02/2009–10/05/2009

*Nach der Flut die Flucht. New Orleans – die
ausgewanderte Stadt / The Flight after the
Flood. New Orleans – The City Left Behind*
*Zur Sonderausstellung wurden Kurzfilm-
biographien gedreht. / Short biographical films
were produced for the special exhibition.*

J. Meier

Hoffnungsträger
Bearer of Hope

„HOFFNUNG – DIE ZWEITE SEELE DER UNGLÜCKLICHEN?"* "HOPE—THE SECOND SOUL OF THE UNHAPPY?"*

Europas ausgewanderte 1848er Revolutionäre, Arbeiterführer, Frauenrechtlerinnen, Zionisten und Shoa-Überlebende einte eines: die Hoffnung, dass in einer neuen Heimat etwas besser werden würde. Ihre kulturellen Wurzeln, die abrahamitischen Religionen Judentum, Christentum und Islam, predigen die Hoffnung. Der stärkste atheistische Hoffnungsmythos ist derjenige der Pandora. Die Annäherung an die treibende Kraft der Auswanderer, die Hoffnung, steht ganz im Zeichen der Zeit und muss immer wieder neu erfolgen. (* J. W. von Goethe in „Maxime und Reflexionen", 1833.) / One thing united European émigrés – revolutionaries from 1848, labor leaders, women's suffragettes, Zionists and Shoa survivors – the hope of having a better life in a new country. Their cultural roots, the Abrahamic religions Judaism, Christianity and Islam, are based on hope. The strongest atheist myth of hope is Pandora's Box. The emigrant's driving force – hope – is quite a sign of the times and must be approached over and over again. (* J.W. von Goethe in *Maxime und Reflexionen*, 1833.)

28/02/2007–30/04/2007

Hoffnung – Die zweite Seele der Unglücklichen? / Hope – The Second Soul of the Unhappy

Zur Ausstellung erschien ein Magazin

A magazin was published for the exhibition

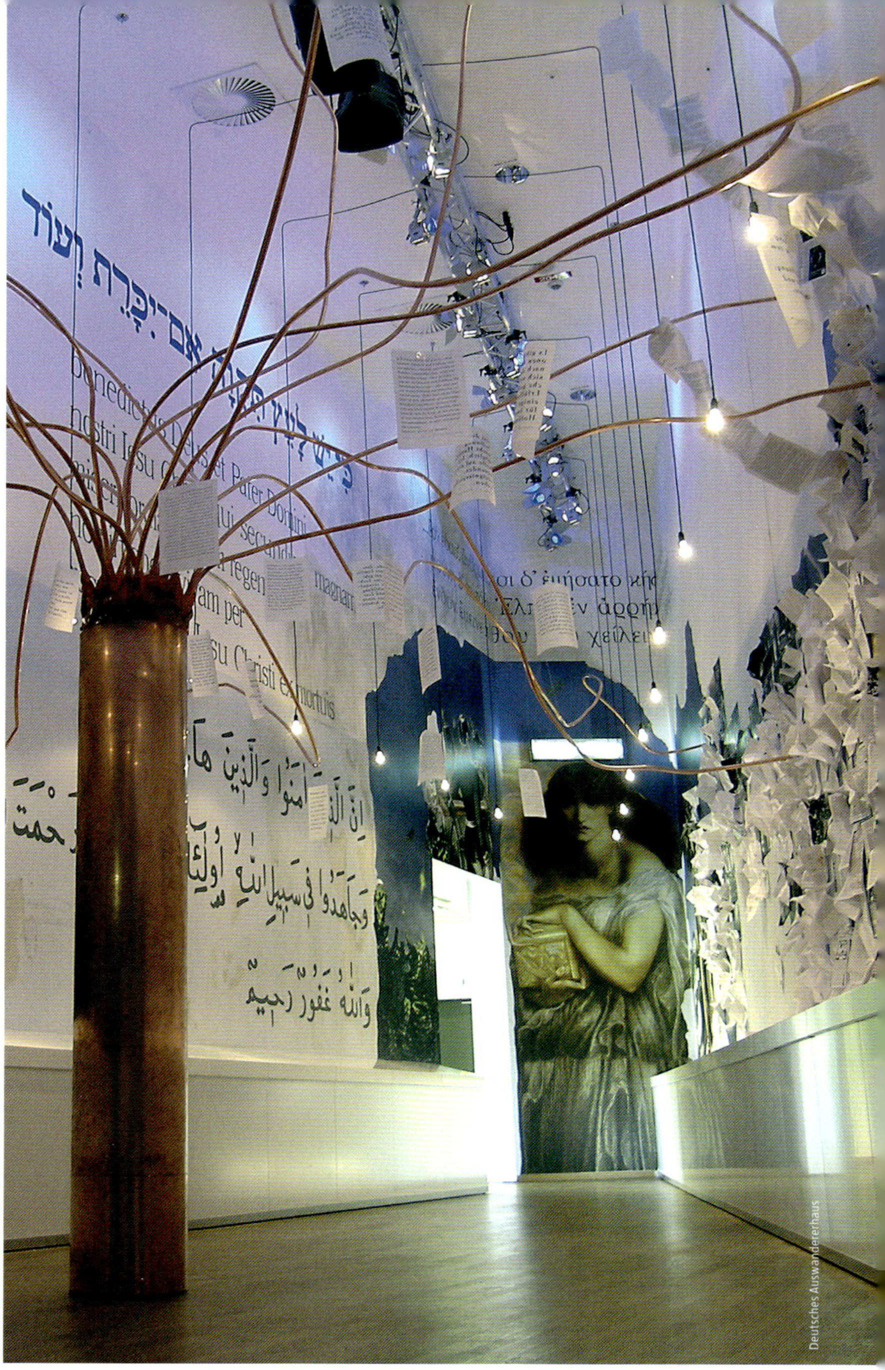

Deutsches Auswandererhaus

Hoffnungen machen den Mund groß, Erfahrungen machen ihn klein.
Hoffnung braucht man nicht zu kaufen.
Wer auf Hoffnung traut, hat auf Eis gebaut

10 Hoffnung KULTUR Hoffnung und Mut sind allzeit gut.

Wer von Hoffnung lebt, stirbt vor Hunger.
Den Narren macht die Hoffnung reich.
Im Lande der Hoffnung wird man nicht fett.
Ein leerer Magen verdaut keine Hoffnung.
Bei Hoffnung ist immer Zweifel.
Wer liebt, hat alle Taschen voll Hoffnung.
Die Hoffnung ist der Trägheit Tochter.
Je dürrer die Zeit, je grüner die Hoffnung.
Die Hoffnung ist ein süßes Leiden.
Wenn das Glück uns verlässt, so bleibt uns die Hoffnung.
Hoffnung macht graue Haare. (Weil man darüber alt wird)
Die Hoffnung ist ein langes Seil.
Wo Hoffnung aufhört, fängt Furcht an.

Biografien · Lou Andreas-Salomé
SELBSTBEWUSST, UNABHÄNGIG, WEIBLICH

Biografien · Ruth Elias
DER GESTANK VON AUSCHWITZ

Biografien · Halina Birenbaum
DAS LEBEN ALS HOFFNUNG

Zeitung zum Ausstellungsprojekt „Hoffnung – Die zweite Seele der Unglücklichen?"

Hoffnung

März/April 2007 · www.dah-bremerhaven.de

Politik · Wirtschaft · Kultur · Sport

3,80 Euro

DEUTSCHES AUSWANDERERHAUS BREMERHAVEN

Hoffnung – Gedanken über ein Phänomen

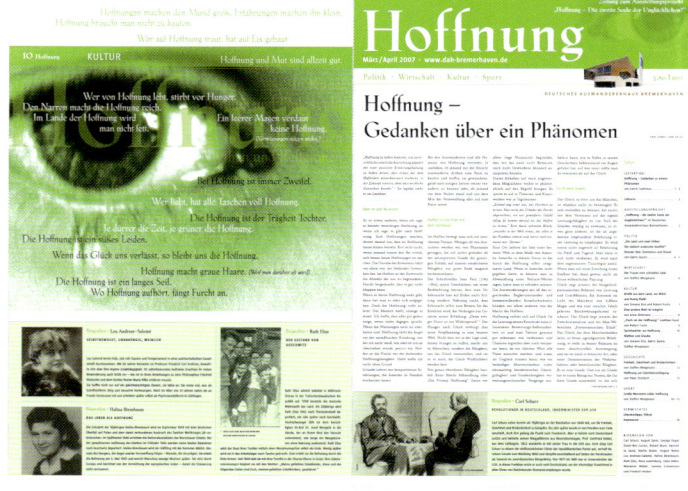

Friesen in Amerika
Frisians in America
Amrum, Föhr

In fast jeder Familie auf den beiden Nordfriesischen Inseln Amrum und Föhr finden sich ein oder sogar mehrere Auswanderer. Statt in das nahe gelegene Hamburg zu ziehen, gingen viele von ihnen in den 1950er und 1960er Jahren für einige Zeit nach New York, weil sie dort Familie oder Freunde hatten. Dort verdienten sie „gutes Geld" – zum Beispiel im Deli, einem der vielen kleinen Lebensmittelgeschäfte, die es in „Big Apple" auch heute noch an jeder Ecke gibt. Nach einigen Jahren kehrten die „Auswanderer auf Zeit" zurück auf die Inseln: aus Heimweh, um ihre Familien zu unterstützen oder den elterlichen Hof zu übernehmen. Von sechs spannenden Lebenswegen von Amrum und Föhr nach Amerika und zurück erzählte die Sonderausstellung: Hörstationen, Objekte und Fotos von damals und heute ließen dieses ungewöhnliche Kapitel deutscher Auswanderungsgeschichte wieder aufleben. / Nearly every family on the North Frisian islands of Amrum and Föhr has one or more relatives who have moved away. Instead of going to the nearby city of Hamburg, many of them immigrated to New York in the 1950s and 1960s, where they had family or friends and earned "good money." They worked in the "delis," one of the countless, small grocery stores that can still be found on every corner of the "Big Apple." As a result of homesickness, a need to support their families or to take over their parent's farm, the "temporary immigrants" returned to the islands after a few years. This special exhibition gives insight into the fascinating life stories of six individuals who journeyed from Amrum and Föhr to America and back. Audio stations, artifacts and photos from then and now rekindled this unusual chapter of German emigration history.

Deutsches Auswandererhaus

.... 14/08/2011–30/11/2011

Nach New York: „In Hamburg kannten wir doch keinen."/*Destination New York. "We knew nobody in Hamburg"*
Nach der Finnisage im Deutschen Auswandererhaus Bremerhaven wanderte die Ausstellung für einige Monate ins „Dr.-Carl-Häberlin-Friesen-Museum" nach Wyk auf Föhr./After the closing at the German Emigration Center, the exhibition traveled to the "Dr.-Carl-Häberlin-Friesen-Museum" in Wyk on the island of Föhr where it was on display for a few months.

Zu dieser Sonderausstellung ist ein Katalog in der edition DAH erschienen./A catalogue of this special exhibition was published by edition DAH.

Lena

Stefan Volk

PORTRAIT EINER
SPÄTAUSSIEDLERIN
PORTRAIT OF A
LATE REPATRIATE

Lena lebte 2008 in Paderborn und arbeitete als Erzieherin in einem Kindergarten. 2004 verließ sie ihre sibirische Heimatstadt Slawgorod und kam über das Grenzdurchgangslager Friedland nach Deutschland. Der Fotograf Stefan Volk begleitete Lena auf ihrem Weg in die neue Heimat über fünf Jahre. Ein einzigartiges Portrait, das beispielhaft für den Weg der rund 4,4 Millionen Aussiedler und Spätaussiedler steht. Stefan Volk wurde 1971 in Münster geboren. Nach einer Fotografenlehre studierte er Fotodesign an der FH Bielefeld. Stefan Volk lebt in Hamburg und arbeitet in den Bereichen Reportage, Reise und Portrait, u. a. für „GEO", „Stern" und „Brigitte". / Lena lived in Paderborn in 2008 where she worked as a kindergarten teacher. In 2004 she left her hometown Slavgorod in Siberia, entering Germany through the Border Repatriation Center in Friedland. Photographer Stefan Volk accompanied Lena for five years on her path to a new homeland. A unique portrait, exemplary of the path of some 4.4 million ethnic Germans and late repatriates of German origin. Stefan Volk was born in Münster in 1971. After apprenticing with a photographer he studied Photographic Design at the Bielefeld University of Applied Sciences. Stefan Volk lives in Hamburg and carries out reportage, travel and portrait assignments for magazines such as *GEO, Stern* and *Brigitte*.

....23/11/2008–15/01/2009
25/05/2009–31/12/2009

Lena. Portrait einer deutsch-russischen
Auswanderung 2003–2008 / Lena. Portrait of
a German-Russian Emigrant 2003–2008

Stefan Volk

Stefan Volk

Stefan Volk

Auf der Flucht
On the Flight

SIEBEN LEBENSWEGE NACH DEUTSCHLAND 1980–2010
SEVEN LIVES WAY TO GERMANY 1980–2010

„Gib niemals auf!" – das war das Lebensmotto des 22-jährigen A an Kadiew. Geflohen mit 13 Jahren aus der russischen Republik Dagestan, lebte er 2010 mit dem Aufenthaltsstatus der Duldung in Deutschland. In der Sonderausstellung „Auf der Flucht. Sieben Lebenswege nach Deutschland 1980 – 2010" standen Flüchtlinge aus Dagestan, dem Iran, Kamerun, Togo, der Türkei und Sri Lanka im Mittelpunkt, die 2010 in Bremerhaven lebten. Jeder Protagonist hatte sein liebstes Erinnerungsstück an die Heimat oder die Ankunft und das neue Leben in Deutschland für die Ausstellung zur Verfügung gestellt: A an Kadiew beispielsweise die Medaillen, die er in seinem Schwimmverein bei Wettkämpfen in Bremerhaven gewonnen hatte. / "Never give up!" – That is the credo 22-year-old Alan Kadiev lives by. Having fled from the Russian Republic of Dagestan at the age of 13, in 2010 he lives in Bremerhaven under a tolerated residence permit. "On the Flight. Seven Paths Leading to Germany 1980– 2010" focuses on refugees from Dagestan, Iran, Cameroon, Togo, Turkey and Sri Lanka, all of whom live in Bremerhaven in 2010. Each protagonist named his favorite souvenir or memento that reminds her or him of his o d or new l fe. Alan Kadiev for exemples presents the medlas he won in swimming events in Bremerhaven.

.... 31/01/2010–02/05/2010

Auf der Flucht. Sieben Lebenswege nach Deutschland 1980–2010 / On the Flight. Seven lives way to Germany 1980–2010
In Kooperation mit dem Pädagogischen Zentrum e. V. in Bremerhaven. Die eindringlichen Ausstellungsporträts stammen von dem Hamburger Fotografen Stefan Volk. / In Cooperation with *Pädagogischen Zentrum e. V. in Bremerhaven.* The striking portraits are the work of Hamburg photographer Stefan Volk.

Stefan Volk

„Fluchtgeschichten. Aus und nach Deutschland. Biographien und Hintergründe 1933 – 2011"
Das Buch erschien 2012 und knüpft an das Ausstellungsprojekt an.
The book was published in 2012 and continues the research work of the exhibit.

Der Gelbe Schein
The Yellow Ticket

MÄDCHENHANDEL 1860–1930
TRAFFIC IN GIRLS 1860–1930

„Der Gelbe Schein" war der Ausweis der Prostituierten in Russland vor 1917. Für Jüdinnen bildete er oft die einzige Möglichkeit einer legalen Existenz in einer russischen Großstadt. Er ist zugleich ein Symbol der Zwangslage vieler junger Frauen um die Wende des vorigen Jahrhunderts. Zehntausende von ihnen wanderten zwischen 1860 und 1930 aus Europa aus. Sie suchten Arbeit in Haushalten, Gaststätten oder Tanzpalästen, doch ihr Weg führte nicht selten in die Prostitution. Mit Gewalt verschleppt, mit märchenhaften Versprechen verführt oder aus freien Stücken? Die Diskussion darüber war schon damals vehement geführt worden. Die Ausstellung präsentierte Spuren und Dokumente ihrer Lebenswege: Fotos, Briefe, Polizeiprotokolle, Zeitungsnotizen und Audiodokumente bildeten eine berührende Schau, in der ihre Hoffnungen, Ängste und Nöte spürbar werden. / "The yellow ticket" was a pass carried by the prostitutes in Russia before 1917. For Jewish women it often provided the only legal chance of survival in a Russian city. It is also a symbol for the predicament of many young women at the turn of the last century. Tens of thousands of them emigrated from Europe between 1860 and 1930. They looked for work in private homes, restaurants or dance halls but they often ended up as prostitutes. Were they forcibly abducted, tempted by fantastic promises or did they go voluntarily? This was already a subject of argument back then. The exhibition presents evidence and documents of their lives: photographs, letters, police reports, newspaper articles and audio documents form a moving exhibition that reveals their hopes, fears and hardships.

...................................27/08/2012–28/02/2013

Der Gelbe Schein. Mädchenhandel 1860–1930 / The Yellow Ticket. Traffic in Girls 1860–1930
Zu dieser Sonderausstellung ist ein Buch in der edition DAH erschienen. / A book of this special exhibition was published by edition DAH.

Constantin Heller

Irene Stratenwerth

DER GELBE SCHEIN

Mädchenhandel 1860 bis 1930

Simone Blaschka-Eick / Hermann Simon (Hrsg.)

edition DAH

Kay Riechers

Deutsche
in Australien
Germans
in Australia

15 lange Wochen dauerte es in den meisten Fällen, um Mitte des 19. Jahrhunderts von Bremerhaven nach Australien zu segeln. Die beschwerliche Reise unternahmen vor allem junge Männer, die das Gold des Fünften Kontinents ab 1851 anlockte. Aber auch Entdecker und Wissenschaftler wie Ludwig Leichhardt zog es in das unerforschte Australien. Sie trugen dazu bei, das Land geografisch und naturkundlich zu erschließen. Hundert Jahre später erreichte die deutsche Einwanderung ihren Höhepunkt. Nun kamen Handwerker und Facharbeiter, die im kriegszerstörten Deutschland keine Zukunft sahen. Heute übt Australien seinen Reiz vor allem auf junge Deutsche aus, die den Kontinent mit „work & travel" erkunden. Derzeit sind mehr als 90 Prozent der dort lebenden Bevölkerung europäischer Abstammung. Erstmals zeigte das Deutsche Auswandererhaus in einer Sonderausstellung, welchen Reiz Australien über die Jahrhunderte auf die Deutschen ausübte, was sie dorthin führte und wie ihre Reiserouten aussahen. / In the mid-nineteenth century, the passage from Bremerhaven to Australia for sailing vessels averaged fifteen long weeks. By 1851, passengers, who undertook the difficult voyage, were mainly young men tempted by the gold finds in Australia. However, explorers and scientists such as Ludwig Leichhardt were drawn to the unexplored continent as well. Their studies of Australia's geography and natural history contributed to the development of the country. German emigration reached its peak a hundred years later. Craftsmen and skilled workers had no prospects in war-damaged Germany and now sought their fortune in Australia. Today, Australia attracts young Germans who visit the continent with "work & travel" programs. Currently, ninety percent of the population there is of European descent. In this special exhibition, the German Emigration Center illustrates the attraction Australia has held for Germans over the past centuries, what led them there and what routes they traveled.

.... 29/09/2013–02/03/2014

Deutsche in Australien. 1788–heute
Germans in Australia. 1788–today

Kay Riechers

Sammlung Deutsches Auswandererhaus,
Schenkung Karl-Heinz Dietzel

Zu dieser Sonderausstellung ist ein Katalog in der edition DAH erschienen. / A catalogue of this special exhibition was published by edition DAH.

Displaced Persons

Die Ausstellung präsentierte 30 Schwarz-Weiß-Porträts des deutschstämmigen Fotografen Clemens Kalischer. Sie zeigen die Ankunft von Displaced Persons – ehemalige KZ-Häftlinge, Zwangsarbeiter und Kriegsgefangene – am Hafen von New York kurz nach dem Zweiten Weltkrieg. Es sind Überlebende des Holocaust, die von Deutschen oder deren Helfern aus ihrer Heimat deportiert oder verschleppt worden sind und nun nicht mehr dorthin zurückkehren möchten. Stattdessen wandern sie aus, um neu anzufangen. Allein 550.000 Displaced Persons schiffen sich dabei über Bremerhaven ein. / The exhibition presents 30 black-and-white portraits taken by Clemens Kalischer, a photographer of German origin. His pictures portray the arrival of Displaced Persons – former concentration camp prisoners, forced laborers and prisoners of war – in the harbor of New York shortly after World War II. They are survivors of the Holocaust, who were deported or displaced from their homeland by Germans or their helpers and now no longer wish to return. Instead they emigrate seeking a new beginning. Alone 550,000 Displaced Persons departed from the port of Bremerhaven.

… ……………………………… 14/07/2014 – 30/11/2014

Displaced Persons. Überlebende des Holocaust 1938 – 1951 / Displaced Persons. Survivors of the Holocaust 1938 – 1951

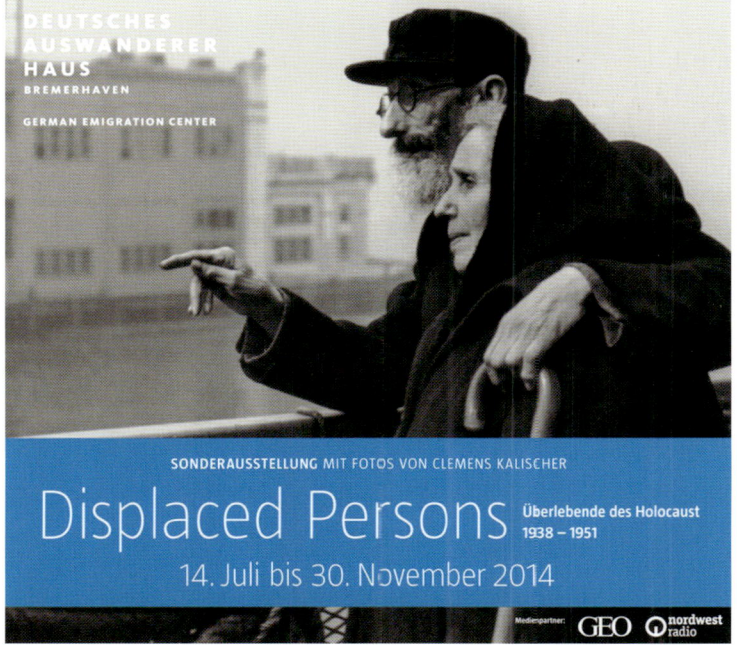

DEUTSCHES AUSWANDERER HAUS
BREMERHAVEN

GERMAN EMIGRATION CENTER

SONDERAUSSTELLUNG MIT FOTOS VON CLEMENS KALISCHER

Displaced Persons Überlebende des Holocaust 1938 – 1951

14. Juli bis 30. November 2014

Medienpartner: GEO nordwest radio

Plötzlich da ...
Suddenly here ...

DEUTSCHE BITTSTELLER 1709, TÜRKISCHE NACHBARN 1961
GERMAN PETITIONERS 1709, TURKISH NEIGHBORS 1961

„Was sollen wir mit ihnen tun?", fragte der britische Schrift-steller Daniel Defoe, als 1709 über 10.000 Deutsche plötzlich nach London kamen, im Glauben, dass Queen Anne ihner Land in ihren neuen amerikanischen Kolonien schenker würde. „Was sollen wir mit ihnen tun?", fragten sich ab 1973 auch deutsche Politiker, als hunderttausende türkische „Gast-arbeiter" plötzlich ihre Familien nachholten und begannen, ihr Leben in der Bundesrepublik einzurichten.

Anhand dieser sehr unterschiedlichen Beispiele zeigte die Son-derausstellung, wie das Zusammenleben in einer Einwande-rungsgesellschaft aussieht, wenn Migration als bloßes Instru-ment wirtschaftspolitischer Maßnahmen behandelt wird.

Die Sonderausstellung war der erste Teil der dreiteiligen Reihe „deutsch und fremd?", in der sich das Deutsche Auswande-rerhaus auch damit beschäftigte, wie man in der Bundesre-publik Einwanderer zu Fremden „macht" und warum sich Ein-wanderer hier oftmals zugleich deutsch und fremd fühlen. / The British author, Daniel Defoe asked, "What shall we do with them?" when 10,000 Germans suddenly arrived in London in 1709, in the belief that Queen Anne would give them land in her new American colonies. In 1973, German politicians also asked, "What shall we do with them?" when hundreds of thousands of Turkish "guest workers" were suddenly joined by their families and began to settle in the Federal Republic of Germany.

Based on these very different examples, the special exhibi-tion illustrated what defines coexistence in an immigration society when migration is treated solely as an instrument for economic strategy.

The special exhibition was the first part of the three-part series "German and foreign?" in which the German Emigration Center takes a look at how the Federal Republic of Germany "turns" immigrants into foreigners, and why immigrants here often feel German and foreign at the same time.

.... 07/12/2015 – 31/05/2016

Plötzlich da ... Deutsche Bittsteller 1709, Türkische Nachbarn 1961 / Suddenly here ... German petitioners 1709, Turkish neigh-bors 1961

Kay Riechers

Zu dieser Sonderausstellung erschienen ein Katalog in der edition DAH und der Dokumentarfilm „Deutsch-Türkische Liebe". / A catalogue of this special exhibition was published by edition DAH and a short documentary "Deutsch-Türkische Liebe" came out.

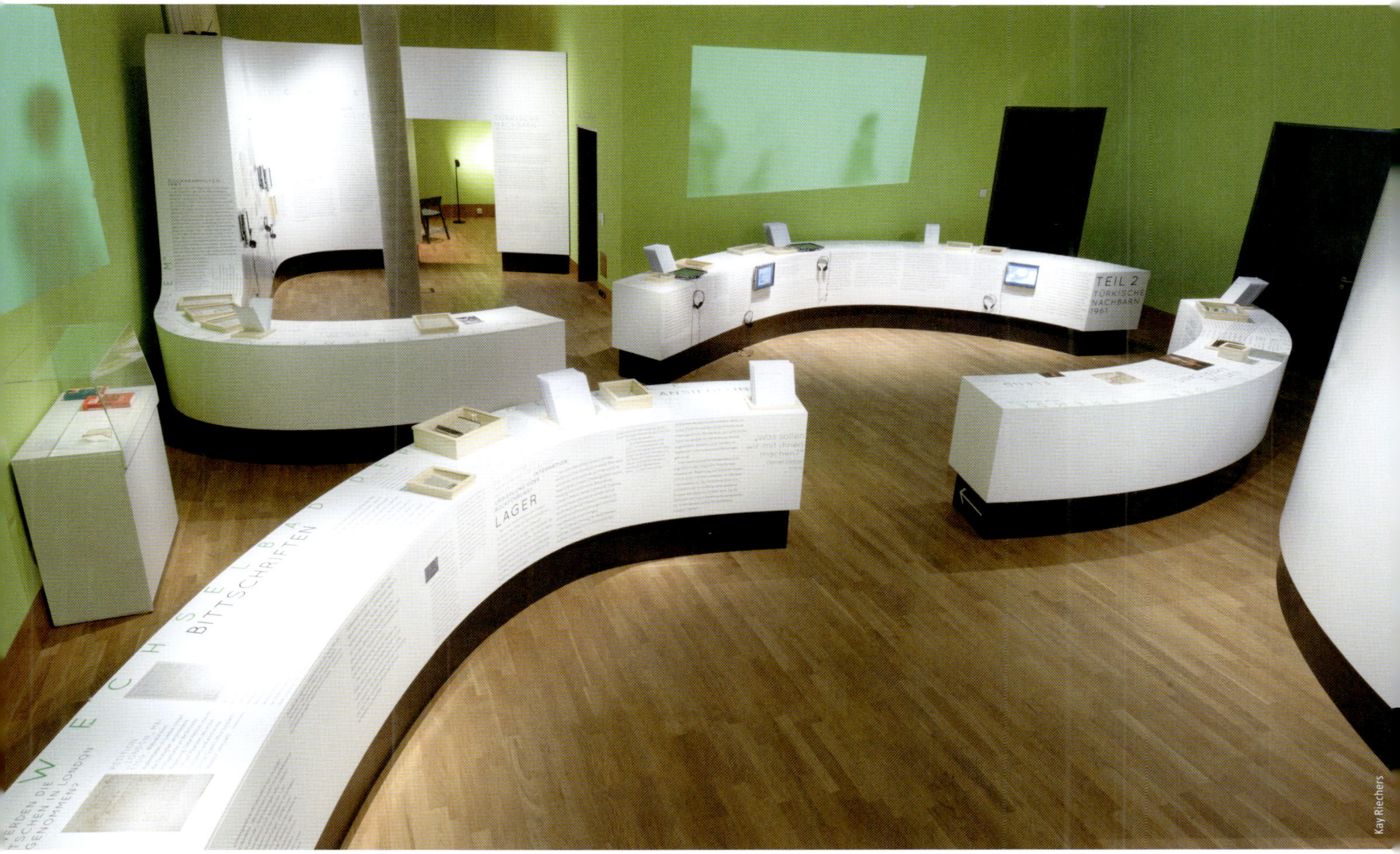

Kay Riechers

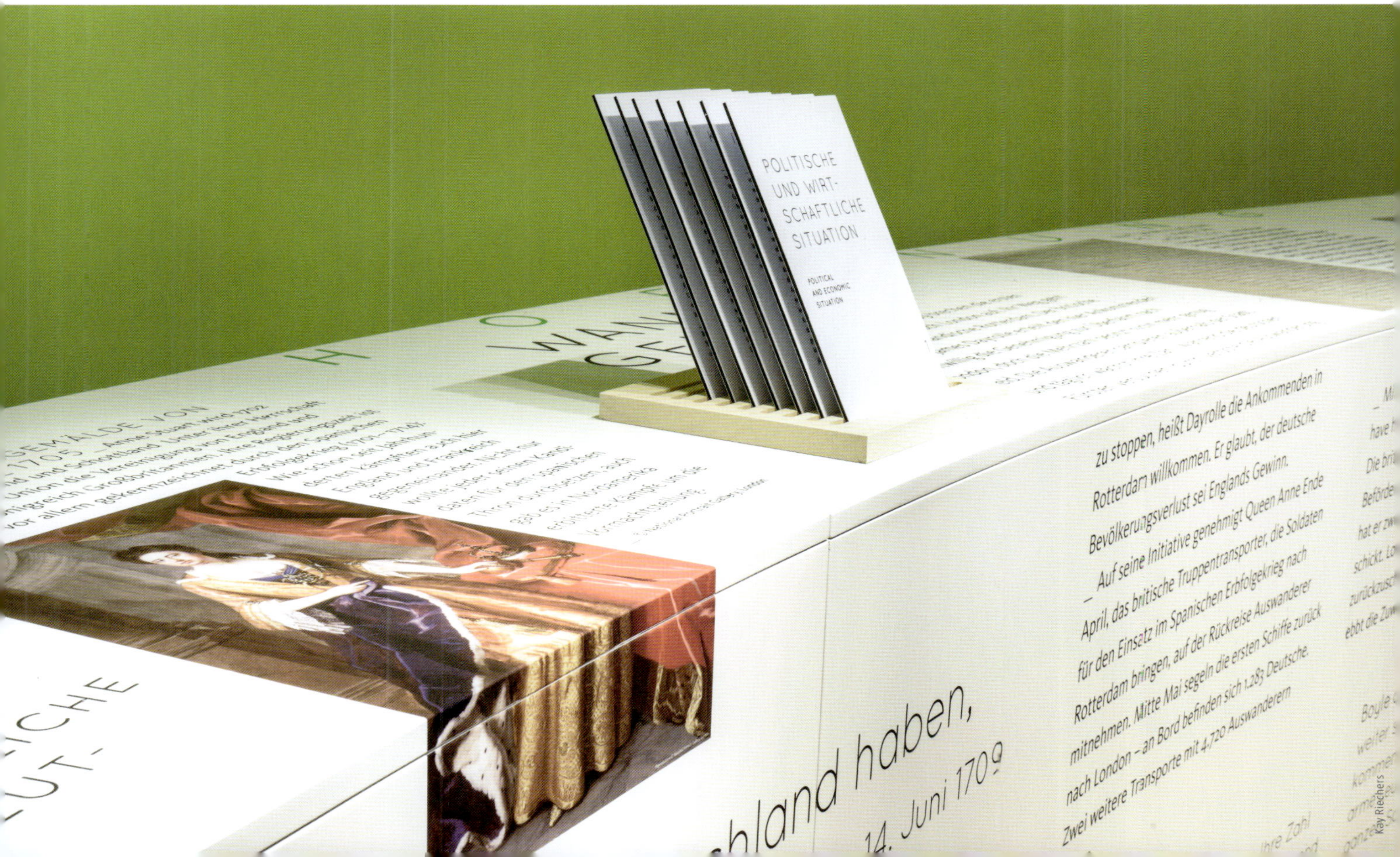

Kay Riechers

DIE SAMMLUNG
THE ARTIFACTS COLLECTION

KANN MAN HOFFNUNG VERMESSEN?
Forschung und Sammlung des Deutschen Auswandererhauses

CAN HOPE BE MEASURED?
Research and collection of the German Emigration Center

SIMONE EICK

Ein Teddybär, ein Schiffsticket und ein Eisbecher – drei von tausenden von Objekten, die das Deutsche Auswandererhaus seit 2005 von Deutschen, Amerikanern, Italienern und vielen anderen für seine Museumssammlung überreicht bekommen hat.

Der Teddy tröstete ein Mädchen auf der Flucht 1945, die Fahrkarte war das Ticket nach New York, und im Eisbecher wurden italienische Leckereien serviert. Alle drei stehen für etwas, das Auswanderer und Flüchtlinge antreibt: die Hoffnung auf ein besseres Leben. Man sucht eine Chance, möchte mehr Geld verdienen oder in Sicherheit leben.

Ob in den USA oder in Deutschland: Wer eingewandert ist, kann aufgrund dieser Erfahrung mal Spannendes, mal Trauriges, mal Großartiges berichten, vor allem in Briefen, Anekdoten und Erzählungen, die an Kinder und Enkel weitergegeben werden. Zusätzlich bewahren die Familien oft auch einzigartige Erinnerungsobjekte auf, wie den Teddy, das Ticket oder den Eisbecher.

Jede dieser Geschichten erklärt einen neuen Aspekt von Migration. All diese vielen kleinen Puzzleteilchen zu einem großen Bild zusammenzusetzen, ist die Aufgabe der Forschung am Deutschen Auswandererhaus. Damit leistet das Museum seinen Beitrag zur Aufarbeitung der deutschen Migrationsgeschichte.

Zahlen und Statistiken können helfen, die Größenordnungen von Zuwanderung in verschiedenen Jahren einzuschätzen, Zusammenhänge zwischen Einkommen, Bildung und Migration festzustellen oder als Politbarometer die Einstellung der Mehrheitsgesellschaft zu Migrationsfragen

A teddy bear, a steamship ticket, and an ice cream bowl – these are just three of thousands of objects that Americans, Germans, Italians and many others have presented to the German Emigration Center for its museum collection.

The embarkation card was the ticket to New York, the teddy bear comforted a fleeing child in 1945, and Italian treats were served in the ice cream bowl. All three stand for the major drivers of migrants and refugees – the hope for a better life. They seek opportunities, want to improve their economic situation or live in safe societies.

Based on what they have experienced, whether in the United States or in Germany, migrants can share fascinating stories, sometimes sad and sometimes magnificent, especially in letters, anecdotes and narratives, and pass them on to their children and grandchildren. In addition, the families often keep unique mementos such as the teddy bear, the ticket or the ice cream bowl.

Each of these stories explains a new aspect of migration. The central role of research at the German Emigration Center is to build a large picture made up of these small puzzle pieces. In doing so, the museum contributes to the reappraisal of German migration history.

Figures and statistics can help assess the levels of immigration in different years, determine the relationship between income, education and migration, or act as a barometer by reflecting the mindset of civil society with regard to migration issues. However, statistics and figures cannot provide the following: Why is it that some people emigrate and others, who are in exactly the same economic situation, do not?

widerzuspiegeln. Eines jedoch können Zahlen und Statistiken nicht leisten – nämlich Fragen beantworten wie: Warum wandern manchen Menschen aus und andere, die sich exakt in der gleichen wirtschaftlichen Lage befinden, nicht? Die Facetten der Persönlichkeit prägen Migrations- und Integrationsentscheidungen von Einwanderern und ihren Kindern ebenso mit wie wirtschaftliche oder politische Gründe. Es ist vor allem diese Individualität und Emotionalität, die die Erforschung von Migration so besonders macht; denkt man doch im Allgemeinen, dass Gefühle und Forschung nicht miteinander vereint werden können. Hoffnung kann man nicht vermessen. Wie man als Migrationsforscher aber eben nicht nur analytisch, sondern auch emphatisch sein kann, finden die Wissenschaftler am Deutschen Auswandererhaus tagtäglich aufs Neue heraus.

Die Sammlung des Deutschen Auswandererhauses ist in der europäischen Museumslandschaft einzigartig. Sie weiter zu erforschen und dabei auch neue Wege zu gehen, ist ein großes Ziel für die nächsten Jahre.

Auszüge aus diesem Text erschienen bereits im Magazin „Roots" der Nordsee-Zeitung im August 2015.

Both an individual's personality traits, as well as economic or political reasons have a major impact on the migration and integration behavior of immigrants and their children. The distinctiveness and emotional aspects are what make migration research so unique – one generally does not expect emotions and research to be united. Hope cannot be measured. Every day, the researchers at the German Emigration Center experience how their work as migration researchers is both analytical and also emphatic.

The collection of the German Emigration Center is unique among European museums. A major goal for the coming years is to continue research while breaking new ground.

Excerpts from this text have appeared in the magazine "Roots," published by the Nordsee-Zeitung in August 2015.

Erinnerungsstücke
Memorabilia

Teddy Bär / Teddy Bear

Teddybär von Sabine Schastok. Das Stofftier war auf der Flucht von Oberschlesien nach Bad Zwischenahn 1945 dabei. Als Sabine Schastok 1958 erst nach Großbritannien und 1960 dann in die USA auswanderte, nahm sie den Teddy mit und kleidete ihn später neu ein.

Sabine Schastok's teddy bear. This cuddly toy was with her when she fled to Bad Zwischenahn from Upper Silesia in 1945. When Sabine Schastok immigrated to Great Britain in 1958 and then to the United States in 1960, she took her teddy bear with her and later gave it a new set of clothes.

Sammlung Deutsches Auswandererhaus, Schenkung Sabine Schastok

Brosche / Brooch

Das Familienerbstück von Martha Hüner hat eine weite Reise hinter sich: Von Bremerhaven wandert die Brosche 1923 mit Martha Hüner nach New York – und kehrt 1985 mit ihr wieder zurück.
Marthas Schwester Hanna bewahrt sie auf, bis sie 2012 in die Sammlung des Deutsches Auswandererhauses übergeben wird.

Martha Hüner's family heirloom has traveled a long way. The brooch accompanied her when she emigrated from Bremerhaven to New York in 1923, and returned to Germany in 1985.
Martha's sister kept the brooch in her possession until it became part of the collection of the German Emigration Center in 2012.

Sammlung Deutsches Auswandererhaus, Schenkung Hanna Wolff

Erinnerungsstücke
Memorabilia

Koffer / Suitcase

Anneliese Banholzer wandert als junges Mädchen 1952 in die USA aus. Auf der Überfahrt lernt sie Mormonen kennen und entschließt sich, zunächst einige Monate in Salt Lake City (Utah) zu verbringen. Doch lange hält es sie dort nicht.
Ihr Koffer – gekauft bei „Bloomingdales" in New York – zeugt von ihren vielen Reisen quer durchs Land.

As a young girl, Anneliese Banholzer emigrated from Germany to the United States in 1952. She made the acquaintance of Mormons on the journey and decided to spend a few months in Salt Lake City. However, she did not stay in Utah for very long.
Her suitcase, purchased at Bloomingdale's in New York is evidence of her many travels throughout the country.

Sammlung Deutsches Auswandererhaus, Schenkung Anneliese Banholzer

Keksdose / Cookie tin

Carl Cabos ist gelernter Bäckermeister und Nachfahre des protestantischen Glaubensflüchtlings Etienne Cabos, der Ende des 18. Jahrhunderts aus Frankreich flieht.
Der Hugenotte eröffnet um 1864 die „Wiener Cakes- und Biskuits-Fabrik". Kaiserin Sissi ist begeistert von seinen Backwaren und so wird er zum kaiserlich-königlichen Hoflieferanten ernannt.

Carl Cabos, a master baker and descendant of the Protestant religious refugee Etienne Cabos, fled from France at the end of the 18th century.
The Huguenot opened the "Wiener Cakes- und Biskuits-Fabrik" in 1864. Empress Sissi was so enthralled by his bakery products that he was granted the title of "Official Supplier of the Imperial Royal Court."

Sammlung Deutsches Auswandererhaus

Wasserkessel / Water kettle

Im Februar 1962 brechen in Hamburg völlig unerwartet die Deiche und überschwemmen einen Großteil der Stadt. Auch die Familie Brandt wird im Schlaf von dem eiskalten Nass überrascht. Ihnen gelingt es, sich auf das Dach eines Hauses zu retten.

Sie gehören zu den Migranten, die weltweit aufgrund von Naturkatastrophen ihren Wohnsitz ändern müssen. Ihren aus den Fluten geretteten Wasserkessel bewahren sie auf.

In February 1962, Hamburg's dykes broke without any fore-warning and floodwater swept over a large part of the city. The Brandt family was awakened in the middle of the night by the icy water. They were able to escape to a rooftop.

They belong to the migrants worldwide who are compelled to move as a result of natural disasters. The Brandts salvaged their water kettle from the floods.

Sammlung Deutsches Auswandererhaus, Schenkung Gerda Brandt

Kindergartenausweis
Identification card

Ayaz Koto wird 2005 im syrischen Aleppo geboren. Im April 2014 flieht er mit seiner Familie über die Türkei nach Bulgarien. Ayaz nimmt seinen Kindergartenausweis als Erinnerung mit. In Bulgarien verbringen die Kotos sechs Monate in Flüchtlingslagern. Im Dezember 2014 kommen sie nach Deutschland.

Ayaz Koto was born in Aleppo in Syria in 2005. In April 2014 the Koto's flight from Syria led them via Turkey to Bulgaria. Ayaz took along his kindergarten ID as a memento. The Kotos spent six months in refugee camps in Bulgaria. In December 2014 they arrive in Germany.

Sammlung Deutsches Auswandererhaus, Schenkung Khalil Koto

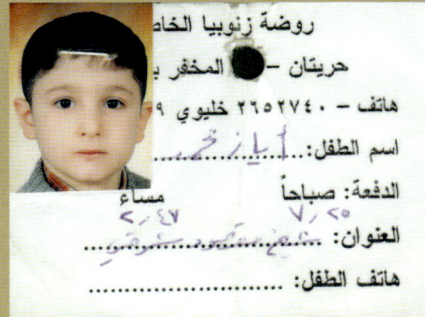

Urkunde / Certificate

Die Entlassung aus der Preußischen Staatsangehö-rigkeit ist Voraussetzung für die legale Auswande-rung und die Ausstellung eines Reisepasses. Dieser Auswandererkonsens von 1879 zeugt von der Schuldenfreiheit des Inhabers, der Erfüllung seiner Militärpflicht, den Verlust der Staatsangehörigkeit und schließt seine Rückkehr in Armut aus.

The release from the Prussian citizenship was a prerequisite for legal emigration and the issuance of a passport. This emigration consensus dated 1879 proves that the owner is free of debt, has fulfilled his milita-ry duties, has lost his citizenship and rules out his return in poverty.

Sammlung Deutsches Auswandererhaus, Schenkung Annegret Lorenzen

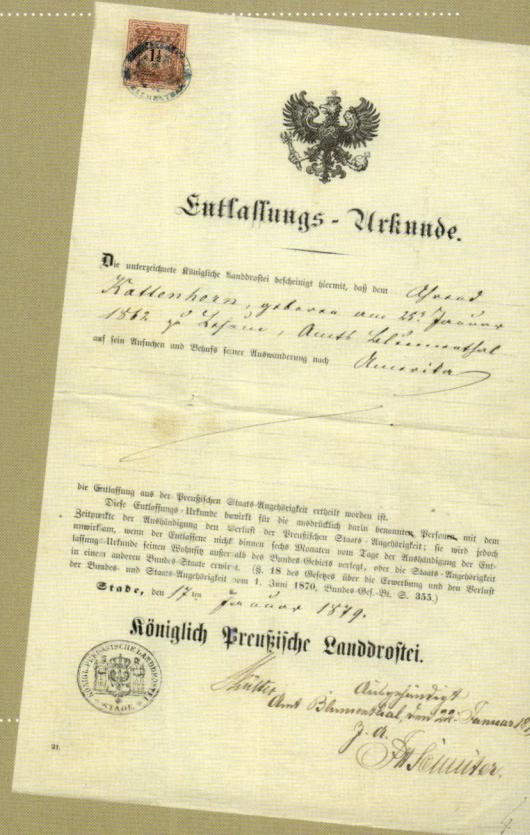

BRINGEN SIE UNS IHRE ERINNERUNGSSTÜCKE! / BRING US YOUR MEMORABILIA!

Erzählen Sie uns die Geschichte Ihrer ausgewanderten Vorfahren oder Ihrer eigenen Migration. Helfen Sie uns, unsere einzigartige Sammlung an Lebensgeschichten und den dazugehörigen Dokumenten, Fotografien und Objekten zu vergrößern. Wir freuen uns auf Ihre Geschichte. / Tell us the story of your ancestors who emigrated or the story of your own migration. Help us enlarge our unique collection of familiy stories with the documents, phothgraphies and objects that go with them. We look forward to hearing your personal account.

GLOSSAR

....

A

Abschiebung → Zurückgewiesene

AEMI – The Association of European Migration Institutions > Das Kooperationsforum europäischer Institutionen und Organisationen, die sich mit historischer und aktueller Migration befassen, organisiert internationale Symposien und gemeinschaftliche Forschungsprojekte.
> www.aemi.eu

Akkulturation / Assimilation > Akkulturation ist ein Begriff aus der Migrationsforschung, der Integrationsprozesse in Einwanderungsgesellschaften beschreibt. Ethnologen, Soziologen und Historiker bezeichnen damit die Angleichung verschiedener Kulturen innerhalb einer Gesellschaft. Diesen Prozess des kulturellen Austauschs durchleben sowohl die Immigranten als auch die einheimischen Bürger des Aufnahmelandes. Er kann mehrere Generationen und damit Jahrzehnte dauern. Ein erster Austausch zeigt sich beispielsweise in der Übernahme und/oder dem Tolerieren von Essgewohnheiten oder religiösen und politischen Feiertagen. Jeder Einwanderer verfolgt dabei eine eigene Strategie: Während einige die Integration, also die Eingliederung in die Aufnahmegesellschaft, wünschen, separieren und isolieren sich andere. Der Idealfall ist eine Integration unter Beibehaltung eigener kultureller Wurzeln. Über Erfolg oder Misserfolg der Integration entscheiden Gesellschaft und Politik des Aufnahmelandes.
Der Begriff der Assimilation gilt in der heutigen Migrationsforschung als veraltet. Er bezeichnet die Aufgabe der ursprünglichen kulturellen Identität von Einwanderern. Die Vorstellung, dass die Einwanderer beim Grenzübertritt ihr kulturelles Gepäck abgeben, hat sich bei der Untersuchung verschiedener Einwanderungsgesellschaften wie den USA, aber auch Deutschland als falsch erwiesen. Siehe auch **→ Melting Pot / Salad Bowl**

Arbeitsmigranten > Sie planen eine Auswanderung auf Zeit, um in einem anderen Land zu arbeiten. Schon immer waren wirtschaftliche Motive Hauptgrund für eine Auswanderung. Während des sogenannten Wirtschaftswunders der 1950er Jahre herrschte in der Bundesrepublik Deutschland ein Mangel an Arbeitskräften. Vom Ende der 1950er Jahre bis zum Anwerbestopp 1973 kamen rund 14 Millionen Arbeitsmigranten vor allem aus der Türkei, Italien und Spanien ins Land. Elf Millionen kehrten in ihr Heimatland zurück, die anderen blieben, holten ihre Familien nach und siedelten dauerhaft in der BRD an. Auch in der DDR wurden in geringem Umfang ausländische Arbeitskräfte beschäftigt, vor allem aus Vietnam.

Asyl > Schon seit Jahrhunderten bieten Freistädte, Hospize oder Klöster schutzbedürftigen und verfolgten Menschen Unterschlupf. Heute versteht man unter Asyl vor allem die Anerkennung politischer Flüchtlinge. In Artikel 16 des Grundgesetzes der Bundesrepublik Deutschland ist das Grundrecht auf Asyl für politisch Verfolgte festgeschrieben. Dieses weltweit offenste Asylrecht wurde 1993 jedoch stark eingeschränkt. Seitdem hat kaum noch eine Chance auf Asyl, wer aus „verfolgungsfreien" Ländern stammt oder über „sichere Drittstaaten" in die Bundesrepublik eingereist ist. Während ihres Verfahrens, das zwischen zwei Wochen und mehreren Jahren dauern kann, müssen Asylsuchende in ihnen zugewiesenen Unterkünften wohnen und dürfen ihren Aufenthaltsort nicht ohne Genehmigung verlassen. Sie erhalten geringere Sozialleistungen als üblich und in manchen Bundesländern statt Geld Lebensmittelgutscheine oder -pakete. Seit 2001 dürfen Asylbewerber und geduldete Ausländer nach einem Jahr Wartezeit arbeiten, wenn sich für die Stelle kein deutscher Arbeitnehmer oder ein Ausländer mit Aufenthaltsbewilligung findet. Asylberechtigte bekommen zunächst eine Aufenthaltserlaubnis für drei Jahre, danach, wenn kein Widerruf erfolgt, eine Niederlassungserlaubnis.

Aussiedler / Spätaussiedler > Aussiedler sind Angehörige deutschstämmiger Minderheiten, deren Vorfahren sich seit dem Mittelalter bis in das 19. Jahrhundert auf den Gebieten nahezu aller Staaten Ost- und Südosteuropas angesiedelt hatten – dem Ruf nach Arbeitskräften und Siedlern vor allem der russischen Zaren folgend. Seit 1950 hat die Bundesrepublik Deutschland über vier Millionen Aussiedler vor allem aus der Sowjetunion bzw. der GUS aufgenommen. Das „Bundesvertriebenen- und Flüchtlingsgesetz" von 1953 sicherte ihnen die deutsche Staatsangehörigkeit und integrationsfördernde Maßnahmen zu. Seit 1993 werden Aussiedler aus anderen Staaten als der GUS nur anerkannt, wenn sie eine Benachteiligung aufgrund ihrer deutschen Volkszugehörigkeit nachweisen können. Antragsberechtigt sind seither außerdem nur noch vor 1993 geborene Spätaussiedler. Als zusätzliche Barriere wurde 1996 ein Sprachtest eingeführt, der seit 2005 auch für mitreisende Familienangehörige nichtdeutscher Herkunft verpflichtend ist.

Auswanderer > Menschen, die die Absicht haben, sich für immer in einem fremden Land niederzulassen.

Auswandereragenten > Für Reedereien und Schiffsmakler übernahmen Auswandereragenten überall in Europa die Anwerbung von Ausreisewilligen.

Auswandererhaus > Als bis dahin weltweit einmalige Einrichtung 1849 von dem Bremer Kaufmann Johann Georg Claussen in Bremerhaven eröffnet, bot das Auswandererhaus, auch „Karlsburg" genannt, bis zu 2.000 Reisenden Kost und Logis zu erheblich günstigeren Preisen und in besseren hygienischen Verhältnissen als in den hafennahen Wirtschaften und Spelunken.

Auswanderungshäfen > Die bedeutendsten Einschiffungshäfen für deutsche Auswanderer waren bis in die Mitte des 19. Jahrhunderts Rotterdam (Holland), Antwerpen (Belgien), Le Havre (Frankreich) sowie Liverpool und Southampton (England). Auswanderer aus Süd- und Südosteuropa reisten zumeist von Genua (Italien) ab. Dank der **→ Bremer Verordnung,** der Einrichtung eines **→ Auswandererhauses** und der weltweit erfolgreichen Reederei **→ Norddeutscher Lloyd** begann Mitte des 19. Jahrhunderts Bremerhavens Aufstieg zum größten Auswandererhafen des europäischen Festlands. Der „Norddeutsche Lloyd" hatte seinen Heimathafen in Bremerhaven, seine Schiffe fuhren jedoch unter Bremer Flagge,

Die Auswandererhallen auf der Veddel in Hamburg, 1908. Links die Abfertigungshalle, rechts die Unterkunftshallen. / The emigration halls on Veddel Island in Hamburg, 1908. The passenger terminal on the left, the living quarters on the right.

da Bremerhaven zum Staat Bremen gehörte und immer noch gehört. Insgesamt wanderten zwischen 1830 und 1974 7,2 Millionen Menschen von Bremerhaven in die Neue Welt aus.

Während in der Segelschiffzeit und in der frühen Dampfschiffzeit auch von Hamburg Auswandererschiffe in die Neue Welt aufbrachen, änderte sich dies Ende des 19. Jahrhunderts: In Hamburg lag der Sitz der Passagierdampfschifffahrtsgesellschaft → **Hapag**, deren Schiffe ab 1889 größtenteils vom verkehrstechnisch günstiger gelegenen Cuxhaven abfuhren. Insgesamt reisten auf Schiffen unter der Hamburger Flagge 5,5 Millionen Passagiere in die Neue Welt.

Das südfranzösische Marseille erlangte vor allem während der Zeit des Nationalsozialismus als Flüchtlingshafen Bedeutung.

Auswanderungswellen > Wanderungsstatistiken werden oft als Liniendiagramme dargestellt. Die Aufwärtsbewegungen im Wanderungsgeschehen werden dabei als Wellen bezeichnet. Sucht man nach Gründen für solche Höhepunkte der Auswanderungen, zeigt es sich oft, dass die Menschen mit einer Verzögerung von fünf bis zehn Jahren auf Wirtschaftskrisen reagieren. Im 19. Jahrhundert kamen Missernten und die darauf folgenden Hungersnöte als weitere Auswanderungsgründe hinzu. Am verheerendsten trafen die Ernteausfälle Irland: Ausgelöst durch aufeinander folgende Kartoffel-Missernten zwischen

1846 und 1851 verhungerten etwa eine Million Menschen, eine weitere Million Iren verließen das Land. Siehe auch → **Kettenwanderung**

· ·

B

Ballin, Albert > Der jüngste Sohn eines jüdischen Kaufmanns (1857–1918) begann seine Karriere bei der → **Hapag** im Jahre 1886. Schnell übertrug die Hamburger Reederei ihrem Angestellten leitende Aufgaben. Bereits 1888 war er Direktor, 1899 Generaldirektor der Hapag. Ballin trug einen wesentlichen Anteil zum Aufstieg Hamburgs als Auswandererhafen bei. Siehe auch → **Veddel**

Bandoneon (-ion) > Das Bandoneon gehört zur Gruppe der Handbalginstrumente. In den 1870er Jahren gelangte es von Deutschland nach Argentinien. Dort entwickelte sich das Instrument schnell zum festen Bestandteil des Tangos.

Belgranodeutsch > Ein Sprachgemisch aus Deutsch und Spanisch, das in Argentimien noch heute von den deutschen Einwanderern und ihren Nachkommen gesprochen wird. Namensgeber ist der stark von Deutschen geprägte Stadtteil Belgrano in Buenos Aires.

Bibliothek zur deutschen Ein- und Auswanderungsgeschichte am Deutschen Auswandererhaus > Durch Schenkungen und Ankäufe verfügt

das Deutsche Auswandererhaus über eine eigene über 4.000 Bände umfassende Bibliothek zur europäischen und im speziellen deutschen Migrationsgeschichte. Gemeinsam mit der über 2.000 Bände umfassenden Bibliothek des Freundeskreises des Museums (→ **Freundeskreis**) bildet sie die Bibliothek zur deutschen Ein- und Auswanderungsgeschichte am Deutschen Auswandererhaus. Die Präsenzbibliothek ist einmal im Monat für Besucher geöffnet.
> www.dah-bremerhaven.de/bibliothek

Blaues Band > Die Verleihung des „Blauen Bandes" für die schnellste Atlantiküberquerung war im Zeitalter der Dampfschifffahrt für Reedereien eine bedeutende Ehrung. 1838 erhielt die „Sirius" als erstes Schiff diese Auszeichnung. Bis zur Jahrhundertwende dominierten die Schiffe englischer Gesellschaften das Feld, dann brach das Jahrzehnt der großen Schiffe des → **Norddeutschen Lloyd** und der → **Hapag** an. Als letzter großer Dampfer holte sich 1952 die „United States" das „Blaue Band".

Bremer Verordnung > Als erste staatliche Maßnahme zum Schutze der Auswanderer in Deutschland begründete die Bremer „Verordnung wegen der Auswanderer mit hiesigen oder fremden Schiffen" von 1832 Bremerhavens guten Ruf als Auswandererhafen entscheidend mit: Erstmals waren Reeder per Gesetz verpflichtet,

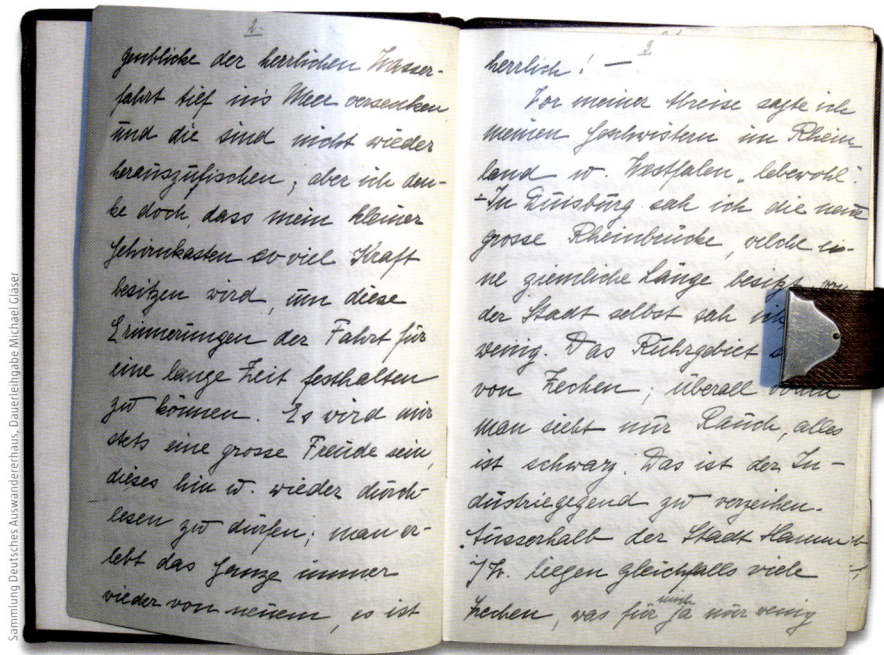

Reisebericht von Emmy von Hove über ihre Auswanderung nach Amerika, 1910. / Emmy von Hove's journal of her journey to America, 1910.

die Seetüchtigkeit ihrer Schiffe nachzuweisen, Passagierlisten zu führen, ausreichend Proviant auch für die Passagiere des Zwischendecks mitzuführen und weitere Mindeststandards auf den Schiffen einzuhalten.

C

Castle Garden > Castle Garden war Amerikas erste Einwanderungsstation. Sie lag für die Schiffe gut erreichbar an der Südspitze Manhattans. Der zentrale Ankunftsort bot den Einwanderern Schutz vor Wucherern und sie hatten dort die Möglichkeit, Eisenbahnfahrkarten für die Weiterfahrt ins Landesinnere zu erwerben. Hier wurden die Einwanderer auch in Ankunftslisten pro Schiff erfasst. Diese Ankunftslisten, im Englischen „Manifests" oder „Passenger Lists", dienen noch heute Familienforschern in aller Welt, um nach ihren Vorfahren zu suchen (siehe auch → **Datenbanken / Familienrecherche**). Von 1855 bis 1890 reisten über Castle Garden etwa acht Millionen Menschen nach Amerika ein. Abgelöst wurde Castle Garden von → **Ellis Island**.

Colonia Liebig > liegt im nördlichen Teil der Provinz Corrientes in Argentinien. Am 27. Januar

1924 wurde die Deutsch-Südamerikanische Kolonie und Handelsvereinigung (Cooperativa) „Neu Karlsruhe", wie das Dorf zuerst hieß, gegründet. Ursprünglich war das genossenschaftliche Siedlungsprojekt für Paraguay geplant worden. Die Pläne scheiterten und die ersten 200 bis 300 deutschen Siedler erhielten in Corrientes Land der Liebig-Gesellschaft („*Liebig Extract of Meat Company*"), nach der der Ort benannt wurde. Im Dezember 1926 erfolgte dann die Gründung der „*Cooperativa Agrícola de la Colonia Liebig*", deren erster Präsident Walter Ostermann war. Bis heute produziert die Genossenschaft Mate-Tee.

Cunard Line > 1839 wurde die „Cunard Line" als „British and North American Royal Mail Steam Packet Company" (Umbenennung 1878) von dem Kanadier Samuel Cunard gegründet. Zunächst sollte sie eine zuverlässige Postzustellung zwischen Großbritannien und Nordamerika ermöglichen. Schon 1840 wurden die ersten vier Dampfschiffe in Betrieb genommen und ein wöchentlicher Service von Liverpool nach Halifax und Boston eingerichtet. Von Anfang an konnten auch regelmäßig Passagiere mitgenommen werden. Bis in die 1870er Jahre dominierte die „Cunard Line" das Post- und Passagiertransportwesen, litt aber unter den teils strengen Auflagen der Geldgeber.
1932 fusionierte die von der Weltwirtschaftskrise getroffene „Cunard Line" auf Druck der bri-

tischen Regierung mit der → **White Star Line** zur „Cunard White Star Line" und konzentrierte sich zunehmend auf das Geschäft mit Kreuzfahrten. 1998 schloss sie sich dem Kreuzfahrtenimperium der „Carnival Corporation" an.

Cuxhaven > Seit 1889 fertigte die Hamburger Reederei → **Hapag** ihre Schnelldampfer Richtung New York von der damals hamburgischen Stadt an der Elbemündung ab. Dafür ließ der Hamburger Staat die Hafenanlagen Cuxhavens ausbauen. 1902 wurde die Hapag-Halle als Überseebahnhof fertiggestellt. Als Dependance von Hamburg liegen bisher keine gesicherten Gesamtzahlen zur Auswanderung über Cuxhaven vor. Die meisten Schiffe steuerten Häfen in Nordamerika an.
Nach dem Zweiten Weltkrieg nahm 1948 die „Cunard White Star Line" (→ **Cunard Line**) als erste Reederei ihren Liniendienst wieder auf. Von September 1948 bis März 1950 brachten ihre Schiffe „Samaria" und „Scythia" auf 27 Reisen 26.700 → **Displaced Persons** nach Kanada. 1968 kam in Cuxhaven durch die immer größere Konkurrenz durch den → **Luftverkehr** das Aus für die überseeischen Liniendienste.

D

Datenbanken / Familienrecherche > Verschiedene Datenbanken ermöglichen eine Recherche nach ausgewanderten Vorfahren im Internet:

Bremer Passagierlisten 1920–1939 (Die MAUS)
> www.passagierlisten.de
Im Archiv der Handelskammer Bremen lagern heute noch 2.953 Passagierlisten von Bremer Schiffen. Dies sind 70 Prozent der Passagierlisten von Schiffen, die zwischen 1920 und 1939 von Bremerhaven in die USA, nach Kanada, Südamerika und Australien gefahren sind. Seit Juli 1999 wurden diese Listen von der „Gesellschaft für Familienforschung Bremen e.V.", die MAUS, im Staatsarchiv Bremen erfasst. Alle weiteren Bremer Passagierlisten sind – bis auf wenige Ausnahmen – vernichtet worden. Die Listen nach 1945 stehen noch unter Datenschutz. Die Datenbank steht im Internet zur freien Verfügung.

Ancestry

> www.ancestry.com/.de

Die US-amerikanische Firma Ancestry arbeitet mit dem Nationalarchiv in Washington zusammen: Im Archiv lagern die Passagierlisten der Schiffe, die aus aller Welt in US-amerikanische Häfen einliefen. Daneben sind auch die Hamburger Passagierlisten zu finden. Ebenfalls befinden sich dort die US-amerikanischen Listen der Volkszählungen, die seit 1790 alle zehn Jahre durchgeführt werden. Darüber hinaus bietet die Datenbank die Einsicht in ausgesuchte deutsche Auswandererregister, deutsche Telefon- und Adressbücher sowie die Bremer Musterungslisten und Seeleuteregister.

Ancestry verarbeitet die Passagierlisten (bis 1957) und Volkszählungslisten elektronisch: Mit Scannern werden die Daten digitalisiert und im Internet zur Verfügung gestellt. Daneben gibt es Einsicht in Militärregister, Geburts-, Heirats- und Todeslisten sowie US-amerikanische Telefonbücher.

Die Nutzung im Internet ist gebührenpflichtig.

Castle Garden

> www.castlegarden.org

→ **Castle Garden** ist die erste offizielle Einwandererstation der USA und Vorläufereinrichtung von → **Ellis Island**. Sie bestand zwischen 1850 und 1890. In der Datenbank sind für die Zeit zwischen 1830 und 1892 über zehn Millionen Einwanderungseinträge gesammelt.

Die Nutzung im Internet ist frei.

Ellis Island Passenger Records

> www.ellisisland.org

2001 wurde im Rahmen der Stiftung „The Statue of Liberty – Ellis Island Foundation, Inc." das „American Family Immigration History Center" gegründet. In diesem Recherchezentrum auf → **Ellis Island**. können Besucher in 25 Millionen Datensätzen nach ausgewanderten Vorfahren recherchieren, die zwischen 1892 und 1924 über New York in die USA eingewandert sind. Die Datenbank steht im Internet frei zur Verfügung, nachdem man sich ein persönliches Passwort eingerichtet hat.

Displaced Persons (DPs) > Englisch für „Heimatlose". Der Fachbegriff wird vor allem in Deutschland für jene über acht Millionen Menschen auf dem Gebiet der heutigen BRD verwendet, die die westlichen Alliierten im Mai 1945 in ihren Besatzungszonen antrafen. Zwischen 1933 und 1945 aus allen Teilen Europas nach Deutschland verschleppt oder deportiert, konnten oder wollten sie nach Kriegsende nicht mehr in ihre Heimat zurückkehren. Die Zwangsarbeiter und überlebenden KZ-Häftlinge, aber auch Kriegsgefangene und osteuropäische Fremdarbeiter wurden zunächst in DP-Camps in Deutschland untergebracht. Oft nutzte man dafür ehemalige Konzentrationslager, so dass die Menschen unter der täglichen Erinnerung an die grauenvolle Zeit des Holocausts, unter der Enge und Ungewissheit über ihre Zukunft litten. Hunderttausende emigrierten nach Großbritannien, in die USA und nach Kanada. Allein von Bremerhaven fuhren über 550.000 Displaced Persons ab.

E

Einreise- und Aufenthaltsbestimmungen für Argentinien > Die bereits in der ersten Hälfte des 19. Jahrhunderts beginnende staatliche Förderung der europäischen Einwanderung wurde durch die Verfassung von 1853 im Artikel 20 der Republik Argentinien festgelegt. Eine „Masseneinwanderung" erfolgte jedoch erst mit der politischen Stabilisierung des Landes nach 1870. Die Zunahme der sozialistischen und anarchistischen Organisationen und Arbeiterstreiks ab den 1890er Jahren führte 1902 als Reaktion auf den ersten Generalstreik zum Aufenthaltsgesetz („*Ley de Residencia*"). Dieses ermöglichte, Ausländern die Einreise zu verweigern oder sie auszuweisen, wenn sie als gefährlich für die öffentliche Ordnung betrachtet wurden. Trotz dieser negativen Entwicklungen, für die eingewanderte Arbeiter verantwortlich gemacht wurden, galt die staatliche Förderung der Einwanderung weiterhin als bedeutend.

Erst mit dem Militärputsch gegen Präsident Hipólito Yrigoyen im Jahr 1930 endete die liberale Ära und veränderte die bis dahin weitgehend restriktionsfreie Einwanderungspolitik. Am 1. Januar 1933 trat ein neues Gesetz in Kraft, welches die Einwanderung auf Familiennachzug („*llamadas familiares*") und Kolonisten in landwirtschaftlichen Ansiedlungen beschränkte. Infolge der Konferenz in Evian wurde in Argentinien am 12. Juli 1938 das „Circular 11" unterzeichnet, eine geheime Direktive, welche die Einwanderung von „Unerwünschten" (vor allem jüdischen Flüchtlingen) nach Argentinien unterbinden sollte.

Einwanderungshäfen > In der Neuen Welt gab es eine Reihe bedeutender Einwanderungshäfen. So war vor allem die Ostküste der USA bevorzugte Anlaufstelle europäischer Einwanderer. Neben New York als größtem Einwanderungshafen der USA gingen über zwei Millionen Menschen in Baltimore von Bord, über eine Million in Philadelphia. Darüber hinaus gehörte Boston ebenso zu den beliebtesten Anlaufstellen wie New Orleans und Galveston im Süden der USA, die vor allem von jenen aufgesucht wurden, die nach Texas weiterreisen wollten. Da der Hafen von Galveston dank seiner Wassertiefe von größeren Schiffen angelaufen werden konnte, löste er ab 1855 New Orleans in seiner Bedeutung ab. Bis 1900 gingen über 100.000 Einwanderer in Galveston an Land, ein Großteil davon Deutsche, die über Bremerhaven gekommen waren. Auch Südamerika lockte Einwanderer an: Zwischen 1850 und 1940 wanderten 6,6 Millionen Europäer in Argentinien ein, die meisten über den Hafen von Buenos Aires. Ein gesuchtes Einwanderungsland war auch Brasilien, dessen Häfen in Rio de Janeiro und Santos zwischen 1819 und 1974 Menschen aus mehr als 50 Nationen aufnahmen, darunter vor allem Italiener, Portugiesen, Spanier und Deutsche. Eine weitere große Einwanderungsstadt war Montevideo in Uruguay, deren Hafen 1868 als fortschrittlichster Umschlagplatz Südamerikas eröffnet wurde.

Für die Einwanderung nach Kanada spielten die Häfen von Quebec und Halifax eine entscheidende Rolle, von denen letzterer zum größten Hafen des Landes wurde. Rund sechs Millionen Menschen gingen über die beiden Häfen an Land. Zu den klassischen Einwanderungsländern gehörte seit Beginn der Massenauswanderung auch Australien. Hier waren es vor allem die Häfen von Melbourne und Sydney, über die Millionen Einwanderer den Fünften Kontinent erreichten.

Ellis Island > Größte Einwanderungsstation der USA. Mit dem starken Ansteigen der Ein-

wanderung vor allem aus Osteuropa ab den 1880er Jahren wurde die Einwanderungsstation → **Castle Garden** an der Südspitze Manhattans zu klein. Mit der Einführung einheitlicher Einwanderungsbedingungen in den USA wurde 1892 die Einwanderungsstation Ellis Island, eine kleine Insel vor New York, eröffnet.

Die großen Passagierdampfer mit den europäischen Auswanderern an Bord legten zunächst am Pier in Hoboken an, wo die Passagiere der I. und II. Klasse aussteigen konnten. Sie waren bereits an Bord überprüft worden. Die Einwanderer, die in der III. Klasse gereist waren, mussten sich auf Ellis Island dem umfangreichen Einwanderungsverfahren unterziehen: einer Prüfung ihrer Gesundheit sowie einer Befragung durch die Inspektoren der Einwanderungsbehörde. Bis 1954 wurden über 16 Millionen Menschen auf Ellis Island registriert, was die Station zur größten Anlaufstelle der USA machte. Etwa zwei bis drei Prozent der Menschen wurde am Ende der Einwanderungsprozedur die Einreise verweigert. Geschichten über → **Zurückgewiesene** brachten Ellis Island den Beinamen „Insel der Tränen" ein.

Exil > In der Migrationsforschung wird das Exil, im Unterschied zur Auswanderung, als eine exterritoriale, aber auf die Rückkehr in das Heimatland zielende Form der Wanderung beschrieben. Die USA sind demnach ein Emigrationsland, kein Exilland, denn die vorübergehende Aufnahme von Flüchtlingen aus politischen oder religiösen Gründen ist gesetzlich nicht vorgesehen.

···

F

Flüchtiger > Im Gegensatz zum → **Flüchtling** die Bezeichnung für eine juristisch verfolgte Person, die sich auf der Flucht befindet. In diese Kategorie fallen beispielsweise die (ehemaligen) deutschen Nationalsozialisten wie Adolf Eichmann, Josef Mengele und Erich Priebke.

Flüchtling > Im Unterschied zu Auswanderern verlassen Flüchtlinge ihr Land unfreiwillig für begrenzte Zeit oder auf Dauer, da sie verfolgt werden oder ihnen Verfolgung droht. Laut → **Genfer Flüchtlingskonvention** von 1951 gilt als Flüchtling, wer sich aufgrund einer begründeten Furcht vor Verfolgung außerhalb des Staates

aufhält, dessen Staatsangehörigkeit er besitzt, oder sich als Staatenloser außerhalb seines gewöhnlichen Aufenthaltsstaates befindet. Anerkannte Verfolgungsgründe sind Ethnie, Religion, Nationalität, Zugehörigkeit zu einer bestimmten sozialen Gruppe und politische Überzeugung.

Freundeskreis Deutsches Auswandererhaus e.V. > Der Freundeskreis ist 2005 aus dem 1985 gegründeten „Förderverein Deutsches Auswanderermuseum e.V." entstanden. Während sich der „Förderverein" 20 Jahre aktiv für die Errichtung eines Auswanderermuseums in Bremerhaven einsetzte, bereichert der Freundeskreis seit der Eröffnung des Deutschen Auswandererhauses im August 2005 das Veranstaltungsprogramm des Hauses durch Vorträge und Informationsveranstaltungen rund um das Thema Migration. Inhaltlich beschäftigen sich die Veranstaltungen vor allem mit den Auswandererhäfen Bremerhaven und Bremen. Die mit über 2.000 Bänden sehr umfangreiche Bibliothek des Freundeskreises ist als Dauerleihgabe inzwischen Teil der → **Bibliothek zur deutschen Ein- und Auswanderungsgeschichte am Deutschen Auswandererhaus**.

Freundeskreis
**DEUTSCHES
AUSWANDERER
HAUS** *e.V.*

···

G

Genealogie > Sie beschäftigt sich mit der Abstammung von Menschen, sowohl in aufsteigender (Vorfahren) als auch absteigender Linie (Nachfahren). Sobald die Forschung über rein biologische Zusammenhänge hinausgeht, spricht man von **Familienforschung**. Umgangssprachlich wird die Genealogie auch Ahnenforschung genannt.

Genfer Flüchtlingskonvention > Ziel der „Genfer Flüchtlingskonvention", die im Juli 1951 auf einer UN-Sonderkonferenz verabschiedet wurde, ist es, einen einheitlichen Rechtsstatus für → **Flüchtlinge** zu schaffen, die keinen diplomatischen Schutz ihres Heimatlandes genießen. Die 146 Vertragsstaaten verpflichten sich unter anderem, Flüchtlingen → **Asyl** zu gewähren. Die „Genfer Flüchtlingskonvention" und das Protokoll von 1967 sind die Rechtsgrundlage für das „Amt des Hohen Flüchtlingskommissars der Vereinten Nationen" (UNHCR).

Globalisierung > Die zunehmende weltweite Vernetzung der Menschen und Gesellschaften wirkt sich sowohl auf wirtschaftliche Beziehungen (z. B. Firmenzusammenschlüsse) als auch auf den privaten Bereich (z. B. Internet) aus. Globalisierungskritiker weisen darauf hin, dass durch die Globalisierung Arbeitsplätze in Länder mit geringem Lohnniveau transferiert werden; vor allem Großunternehmen in den reichen Ländern profitieren, während Länder mit geringerer Wirtschaftskraft verlieren. Befürworter sehen in den zusammenwachsenden Märkten und Gesellschaften die Möglichkeiten für wirtschaftliche und soziale Vereinigungen auf den unterschiedlichsten Ebenen.

···

H

Hapag / Hapag-Lloyd > Ausgelöst durch die rasch wachsende Bedeutung Bremerhavens als Auswandererhafen wurde 1847 in Hamburg die „Hamburg-Amerikanische Packetfahrt-Actien-Gesellschaft" (Hapag) gegründet. Ziel war es, mit einer direkten Segelschiff-Verbindung von Hamburg nach Nordamerika am Geschäft mit der Beförderung von Auswanderern teilzunehmen. Hatte der → **Norddeutsche Lloyd** (NDL) von Beginn an auf Dampfschiffe gesetzt, führte die Hapag erst 1889 Schnelldampfer ein. Gleichzeitig bot die Reederei Kreuzfahrten für Urlauber an. 1901 eröffnete die Hapag in Hamburg die Auswandererstadt, die bis zu 5.000 Menschen beherbergen konnte (siehe auch → **Veddel**). Sowohl nach dem Ersten als auch nach dem Zweiten Weltkrieg verloren die Hapag und der NDL ihre gesamte Flotte, die als Reparationszahlung an die Alliierten ging. Beim Wiederaufbau der

Flotten und Liniendienste ab 1954 kooperierten beide Reedereien, um eine Konkurrenz zu vermeiden. 1970 fusionierte die Hapag mit dem NDL zur „Hapag-Lloyd AG". Bedeutende Schiffe der Hapag: die „Augusta Victoria" (1889), die „Fürst Bismarck" (1891) und das damals schnellste Schiff auf der Nordamerika-Linie. Die „Deutschland" errang auf der Jungfernreise 1900 das → **Blaue Band**, der „Imperator" (1913) und der „Vaterland" (1914) waren beide die größten Schiffe ihrer Zeit.

Heimat > ist für viele Menschen ein geographischer Ort, mit dem sie sich sehr verbunden fühlen, den sie als Zuhause empfinden, an dem sie sich nicht erklären müssen. Heimat steht damit im Gegensatz zu Fremde und Exil. Heimat ist häufig, aber nicht unbedingt der Ort, an dem man geboren ist (Wahlheimat). Im Englischen lässt sich Heimat mit „homeland" oder „native land" übersetzen.
Das Wort Heimat hat seinen Ursprung in der Romantik. In Deutschland ist der Begriff umstritten, weil er für viele durch die historische Entwicklung einen völkischen und nationalen Beiklang hat.

Hyphen-Americans > (dt.: „Bindestrich-Amerikaner") Viele ethnische Gruppierungen in den USA verspüren trotz ihrer amerikanischen Staatsbürgerschaft eine starke Verbundenheit mit ihrem Herkunftsland und halten kulturelle Traditionen und Gewohnheiten aufrecht. Italian-Americans, African-Americans, Polish-Americans und andere Hyphen-Americans sind den USA gegenüber sehr loyal, definieren ihre Staatsbürgerschaft als primär politisch und empfinden sich als Mitglied der amerikanischen Einwanderungsgesellschaft.

I

IMIS – Institut für Migrationsforschung und Interkulturelle Studien > Das interdisziplinäre und interfakultative Forschungsinstitut der Universität Osnabrück beschäftigt sich mit historischen und gegenwärtigen Migrationsbewegungen sowie mit politischen, sozialen und kulturellen Aspekten der Migration und Integration.
> www.imis.uni-osnabrueck.de

Initiativkreis Deutsches Auswandererhaus e. V. > Das Engagement von Unternehmern und Privatpersonen ist prägend für die Geschichte des Deutschen Auswandererhauses. 1985 gründeten Bremerhavener Bürger den „Förderverein Deutsches Auswanderermuseum" (→ **Freundeskreis Deutsches Auswandererhaus e.V.**), 1998 folgte der von lokalen Unternehmern ins Leben gerufene „Initiativkreis Erlebniswelt Auswanderung"– heute „Initiativkreis Deutsches Auswandererhaus e. V.". Dieser engagierte sich besonders in der Politik für die Errichtung des Museum und unterstützt heute Vorhaben der → **Stiftung Deutsches Auswandererhaus** sowie museumspädagogische Programme für Bremerhavener Schulen.

Integration → Akkulturation / Assimilation

K

Kai / Kaje > sind Begriffe für ein durch Mauern befestigtes Ufer. Der Begriff Kaje stammt aus dem Niederländischen. Er wird in der Region um Bremerhaven, aber auch in anderen deutschen Küstenregionen verwendet. Die Kaje hat den Wasserzugang auf einer Seite – im Gegensatz zum Pier, das beidseitig einen Wasserzugang hat.

Kettenwanderung > Berichte von geglückten Neuanfängen vieler Auswanderer gelangten durch Briefe und Zeitungsartikel in die alte Heimat. Ermuntert von ausgewanderten Familienmitgliedern und Bekannten folgten Hunderttausende nach. Vielerorts, etwa in Preußen, Mecklenburg oder Württemberg kam es durch Kettenwanderungen in einer Reihe von Ortschaften zu erheblichen Bevölkerungsrückgängen.
Das große Ansteigen der Auswandererzahlen aus Europa in der zweiten Hälfte des 19. Jahrhunderts wird unter anderem auf die „Multiplikator-Effekte" der Kettenwanderung zurückgeführt, die sich bis zu Beginn des 20. Jahrhunderts zu dem am weitesten verbreiteten Auswanderungsmuster entwickelte.
Mit Beginn des 21. Jahrhunderts ist der Brief als Transmitter für positive Nachrichten in die Heimat längst durch SMS, Twitter und Skype abgelöst worden. Statt Wochen, die ein Brief brauch-

te, um beim Adressaten anzukommen, fließen Nachrichten im World Wide Web heute in Bruchteilen von Sekunden. Dementsprechend haben sich auch Wanderungsbewegungen beschleunigt, wie auch das Jahr 2015 in der Bundesrepublik Deutschland zeigte, als innerhalb weniger Wochen hunderttausende Flüchtlinge und Migranten ankamen. Untersuchungen haben ergeben, dass die Menschen vor, während und nach der Flucht intensiven Kontakt in die Heimat und in das Zielland via Smartphone hielten und so auch Kettenwanderungen auslösten.

L

Luftverkehr > In den 1960er Jahren verlor das Geschäft mit der Auswanderung per Schiff an Bedeutung. Bremerhaven und Hamburg hatten als Auswandererhäfen ausgedient. Ein zentraler Grund dafür ist neben den nordamerikanischen Einwanderungsbeschränkungen die Möglichkeit, seit Ende der 1950er Jahre den Atlantik per Flugzeug in wesentlich kürzerer Zeit zu überqueren. Die „Deutsche Lufthansa AG" als staatliche Fluggesellschaft wurde 1926 durch einen Zusammenschluss der „Deutschen Aero Lloyd" mit dem „Junkers Luftverkehr" gegründet. Nach dem Zweiten Weltkrieg erfolgte 1955 die Neugründung der Lufthansa Zwischen 1994 und 1997 wurde die Fluglinie komplett privatisiert.

M

Meier, Hermann Heinrich > Der Bremer Geschäftsmann und Politiker (1809–1898) gründete 1857 den → **Norddeutschen Lloyd**, der sich zu einer der größten Reedereien weltweit entwickelte.

Melting Pot / Salad Bowl > Die USA wurden in der Soziologie lange Zeit als „Melting Pot" beschrieben, als „Schmelztiegel", in dem sich die verschiedenen ethnischen Herkünfte seiner Einwanderer zu einer neuen eigenständigen Kultur vermischen. Diese Sichtweise wird jedoch zunehmend berichtigt. An ihre Stelle tritt das multikulturelle Konzept der „Salatschüssel" („Salad Bowl") als nicht homogene, aber in sich strukturierte und harmonierende Einheit.

Dokumententasche des Auswandereragenten Friedrich Missler, um 1920. / Emigration agent Friedrich Missler's document case, about 1920.

Migration > Wanderungsbewegungen von Einzelnen oder Gruppen, die mit einem kurzfristigen, längerfristigen oder dauerhaften Wohnortwechsel verbunden sind. Man unterscheidet zwischen Emigration (Auswanderung) und Immigration (Einwanderung). Bei Wohnortwechseln innerhalb eines Staates spricht man von Binnenwanderung, das Durchqueren von Staaten bezeichnet man als Transitwanderung.

Die Gründe und der Grad der Freiwilligkeit der jeweiligen Emigration sind sehr unterschiedlich, darum unterscheidet man bei Migranten zwischen → **Auswanderern**, → **Arbeitsmigranten**, → **Flüchtlingen** und → **Vertriebenen**.

Missler-Hallen > Um das Unterbringungsproblem der in Bremen auf ihre Abfahrt nach Bremerhaven wartenden Auswanderer zu lösen, ließen der → **Norddeutsche Lloyd** und sein Hauptagent Friedrich Missler 1906/1907 im Bremer Stadtteil Findorff Auswandererhallen errichten. Sie sollten insbesondere den Ost- und Südosteuropäern ausreichendes und billiges Quartier bieten. Das Modell Auswandererhallen hatte sich bereits in Hamburg auf der Veddel bewährt. 1907 wurden die neuen – im Volksmund „Missler-Hallen" genannten – Quartiere mit Platz für mehr als 2.700 Menschen fertiggestellt. Nach dem Tod Misslers 1922 übernahm der „Norddeutsche Lloyd" die Gebäude, nun „Lloydheim" genannt, für die Betreuung seiner Fahrgäste.

N

New Immigrants > (dt.: Neue Einwanderer) Um die Jahrhundertwende kamen immer mehr süd- und osteuropäische Auswanderer nach Amerika: vorwiegend Italiener, Griechen sowie Katholiken und Juden aus Osteuropa. Erstmals im Jahre 1896 überstieg ihre Anzahl die der „alten Einwanderer" aus nord- und nordwesteuropäischen Ländern. Viele Amerikaner beobachteten diese Entwicklung kritisch, die „New Immigrants" wurden als Bedrohung für die amerikanische Gesellschaft angesehen und marginalisiert. Es folgte eine lebhafte Diskussion um Einwanderungsbeschränkungen, die letzlich im → **Quota Act** von 1921 mündete. Er regelte die gesamte Einwanderung nach einem Quotensystem, bei dem die ost- und südosteuropäischen Einwanderer benachteiligt waren.

Norddeutscher Lloyd (NDL) > Die 1857 in Bremen gegründete Dampfschifffahrtsgesellschaft war die erste Reederei, die einen regelmäßigen Schiffsverkehr zwischen Deutschland und New York aufbaute. Im Deutschen Kaiserreich (1871–1918) stieg der NDL zu einer der größten Reedereien der Welt auf. Seine Schiffe befuhren Routen in die USA, nach Südamerika und Australien. Die meisten Passagiere waren Auswanderer, aber auch amerikanische und deutsche Touristen reisten auf Schiffen des NDL.

Heimathafen der Bremer Reederei war Bremerhaven. 1869 eröffnete sie am „Neuen Hafen" die erste Wartehalle, die zweite Wartehalle folgte 1897 an der Kaiserschleuse. Da die Bremerha-

vener Hafen- und Schleusenanlagen für die immer größer werdenden Schiffe zu klein wurden, fuhren die Schiffe des NDL zwischen 1890 und 1896 von Nordenham ab, das am westlichen Weserufer gegenüber von Bremerhaven liegt. Aus der ersten Werkstatt des NDL, in der die Schiffe gewartet und repariert werden konnten, entwickelte sich die „Lloyd Werft Bremerhaven", die bis heute existiert und in den Bereichen Schiffsverlängerung und Umbau zu den bekanntesten Werften zählt. Zu den berühmtesten Schiffen des NDL gehörten der erste Vierschornsteindampfer „Kaiser Wilhelm der Große", die „Columbus", die „Europa" und die „Bremen", die 1929 das

Passagierliste der „Seydlitz" von ihrer Fahrt von Bremerhaven nach New York, Abfahrt 17.03.1923. / Passenger list of the *Seydlitz* en route from Bremerhaven to New York, depatrture 17 March 1923.

→ **Blaue Band** für die schnellste Atlantiküberquerung errang. 1970 fusionierten der NDL und die Hapag, einst größte Konkurrenten des Passagierverkehrs auf See, zur → **Hapag-Lloyd**.

P

Pilgrim Fathers > (dt.: „Pilgerväter") Als religiöse Separatisten in England verfolgt, wanderten die puritanischen Pilgerväter im 17. Jahrhundert nach Amerika aus. Sie waren die ersten englischen Siedler in Neuengland.
Legendär ist die Geschichte der „Mayflower". Im Jahre 1602 brachte das Segelschiff 102 Menschen, vorwiegend Pilgrims, nach Amerika. Die Überfahrt von Plymouth (England) nach Plymouth (Massachusetts) dauerte vom 16. September bis zum 11. November.

Pogrom > Im weiteren Sinne bezeichnet Pogrom (russ.: Verwüstung, Zerstörung, Krawall Ausschreitungen gegenüber religiösen, nationalen und ethnischen Minderheiten. Eng verbunden ist der Begriff mit antijüdischen Gewalttaten und Plünderungen. Im zaristischen Russland lösten wiederholte Pogrome zwischen 1880 und 1913 große Auswanderungswellen russischer Juden in die USA und nach Palästina aus. Im nationalsozialistischen Deutschland wurden die antijüdischen Novemberpogrome 1938 von staatlicher Seite initiiert. Das letzte große Pogrom gegen Juden in Europa fand 1946 im polnischen Kielce statt.

Q

Quota Act > Mit dem „Emergency Quota Act" vom 19. Mai 1921 schränkten die USA die jährliche Zuwanderung massiv ein und bevorzugten Einwanderer aus Nord- und Westeuropa. Jährlich war nur noch eine Zuwanderung von drei Prozent jeder 1910 in den USA lebenden Herkunftsnationalität erlaubt: den Census-Daten nach insgesamt 357.802 Einwanderer, von denen mehr als die Hälfte aus nord- und westeuropäischen Ländern stammte. Für Einwanderer aus Süd- und Osteuropa bedeutetete der „Quota Act" eine Reduktion um 75 Prozent im Vergleich zu den Vorjahren. In dem an der Herkunftsnation orientierten Quotensystem schlug sich die

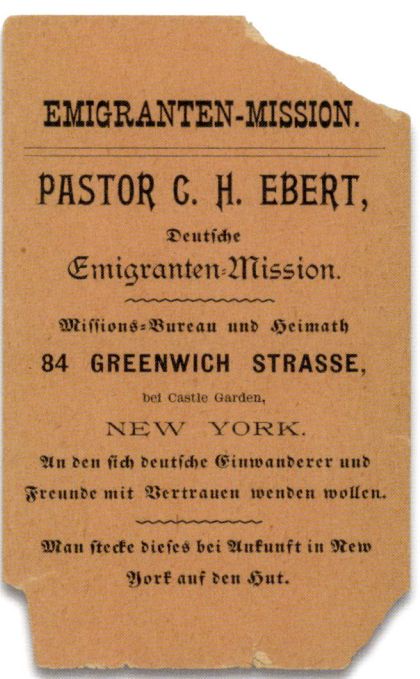

EMIGRANTEN-MISSION.

PASTOR C. H. EBERT,

Deutsche

Emigranten-Mission.

Missions=Bureau und Heimath

84 GREENWICH STRASSE,

bei Castle Garden,

NEW YORK.

An den sich deutsche Einwanderer und Freunde mit Vertrauen wenden wollen.

Man stecke dieses bei Ankunft in New York auf den Hut.

Sammlung Deutsches Auswandererhaus, Schenkung Dorothea und Christoph Präckel

seit Jahrzehnten zunehmende Fremdenangst nieder. Die USA verschärften 1924 mit dem „National Origins Act" – insgesamt 164.000 Zuwanderer jährlich bei maximal zwei Prozent aus jeder Herkunftsnationalität von 1890 – ihre restriktive Einwanderungspolitik noch weiter.

R

Raphaels-Werk > Bis heute ist der 1871 gegründete christliche Verein zum Schutz katholischer Auswanderer – benannt nach dem Erzengel Raphael, der als Beschützer der Reisenden verehrt wird – eine Beratungsstelle für Menschen, die Deutschland vorübergehend oder dauerhaft verlassen wollen. Auch die zur Diakonie gehörende „Evangelische Auswandererberatung e.V." (heute Auslandsberatung) bietet Auswanderungswilligen Beratung an.

> www.raphaels-werk.de
> www.ev-auslandsberatung.de

Rattenlinie > (engl.: ratline) Vom US-amerikanischen Geheimdienst geprägter Begriff, der den Fluchtweg führender Vertreter des NS-Regimes nach dem Ende des Zweiten Weltkrieges beschreibt. Die Route führte über Italien, Süditalien oder auch Rom, nach Südamerika – dort insbesondere nach Argentinien. Auf diese Weise

Solche Karten von Hilfsorganisationen steckten sich Männer bei ihrer Ankunft an ihre Hutbänder. Anhand der Farbe und des Aufdrucks erkannten die zuständigen Helfer ihre „Schützlinge", um 1900. / Supplied by relief organizations the men put these cards in their hatband on arrival; the helpers responsible identified their "charges" according to the color and the print, around 1900.

entkamen viele Nazis zunächst ihrer Strafe für die begangenen Verbrechen während der nationalsozialistischen Diktatur in Deutschland (1933–1945).

S

Sammlung Deutsches Auswandererhaus > Die Sammlung des Deutschen Auswandererhauses umfasst 3.000 Familienkonvolute, die neben den Migrantenbiografien auch dazugehörige Dokumente, Fotografien und persönliche Erinnerungsstücke beinhalten. Monatlich kommen Schenkungen hinzu von Menschen, die dem Museum ihre Familiengeschichte anvertrauen. → Siehe auch „Kann man Hoffnung vermessen? Forschung und Sammlung am Deutschen Auswandererhaus", Seite 118 ff.

Schiffsklassen > Die technische Entwicklung der Schiffe veränderte die Überfahrtsbedingungen der Auswanderer erheblich – vor allem für Passagiere der III. Klasse: Auf den Segelschiffen waren sie meist zu Hunderten in stickigen und engen Zwischendecks untergebracht, in denen katastrophale hygienische Zustände herrschten. Viele Menschen fanden auf der bis zu 15 Wochen dauernden Atlantiküberfahrt den Tod. Mit Einführung der Schnelldampfer ab 1880 verringerte sich die Reisedauer nach Amerika auf acht bis 15 Tage. Passagieren der III. Klasse standen zudem Neuerungen wie Sanitäranlagen zur Verfügung. Dank größerer Maschinen und verbesserter Antriebstechnik bewältigten die vom → **Norddeutschen Lloyd** ab 1897 eingesetzten Liner die Atlantiküberquerung in sechs Tagen. Diese Schiffe waren erheblich sicherer. Sie boten den III. Klasse-Passagieren ab 1906 einen eigenen Speisesaal. Ab Ende der 1920er Jahre ersetzten Mehrbettkabinen die Massenunterkünfte, zusätzlich wurde eine Touristenklasse eingeführt.

Stiftung Deutsches Auswandererhaus > Um aufwändige und umfangreiche wissenschaftliche Projekte zu unterstützen und die Ziele des Deutschen Auswandererhauses international zu verankern, wurde im Januar 2006 die Stiftung Deutsches Auswandererhaus gegründet. Stiftungsgeber sind: „Initiativkreis Erlebniswelt Auswanderung Bremerhaven e. V.", Vertreter der Bremerhavener Wirtschaft, der Stadt Bremerhaven und der Betreibergesellschaft des Deutschen Auswandererhauses.

Stiftung DEUTSCHES
AUSWANDERER
HAUS

Die Stiftung soll das Haus in die Lage versetzen, die Geschichte der Migration in ihrer historischen und aktuellen Bedeutung umfassend zu erforschen und durch Ausstellungen und Publikationen einer breiten Öffentlichkeit im In- und Ausland zu vermitteln. So sieht der Stiftungszweck vor, Exponate und Sammlungen zum Thema zu erwerben und den wissenschaftlichen Aufbau wie die Pflege der Datenbank und einer Archivbibliothek zu unterstützen. Darüber hinaus fördert die Stiftung Tagungen. Der Austausch von Studierenden aus den europäischen Nachbarländern und Übersee sowie die Vergabe von Forschungsstipendien sind weitere Aufgaben der Stiftung, um die Inhalte des Deutschen Auswandererhauses auch wissenschaftlich zu verankern. Seit 2015 verleiht die Stiftung alle zwei Jahre den mit 10.000 € dotierten Kalliope-Preis für angewandte Migrationsforschung.

> www.stiftung-dah.org

Kalliope: Ausschnitt aus einem Bilderbogen.
Cesare Ripa, Paris, 1677

T

Transitwanderung > Ende des 19. Jahrhunderts und in der Zeit der Weimarer Republik (1919–1933) durchquerten viele Auswanderer aus Süd- und Osteuropa das Gebiet des Deutschen Reichs, um von Hamburg oder Bremerhaven aus die Fahrt über den Atlantik anzutreten.

V

Veddel > Um den immer größer werdenden Strom der Auswanderer am Stadtzentrum vorbeizuleiten, ließ die Hamburger Reederei → **Hapag** ab 1898 auf der zwischen Norder- und Süderelbe gelegenen Insel Veddel Auswandererhallen errichten. 1901 eröffnet, wurde die Unterkunft stetig erweitert und umfasste letztlich ein Areal von 55.000 Quadratmetern mit rund 30 Einzelgebäuden. Die dezentrale Lage sowie die für die damalige Zeit vorbildlichen hygienischen Bedingungen resultierten daraus, dass man russische Auswanderer für den Ausbruch der Cholera-Epidemie von 1892 verantwortlich machte. Auf der Veddel wurde jeder ankommende Auswanderer zunächst einer Gesundheitsprüfung unterzogen und blieb bis zu 14 Tage in Quarantäne. Zugleich verhinderte man, dass mittellose Auswanderer ins Stadtzentrum gelangten.

Neben Schlaf- und Wohnpavillons umfasste die Anlage einen großen Speisesaal, Bäder und eine Desinfektionsanstalt. Auch eine Kirche für beide christlichen Konfessionen und eine Synagoge standen den Auswanderern zur Verfügung. Nach der Erweiterung 1906/1907 wurden jüdische und christliche Auswanderer in separaten Küchen und Speisesälen versorgt. Während des Ersten Weltkrieges dienten die Auswandererhallen als Lazarett. Zwischenzeitlich wieder für Auswanderer geöffnet, wurden die Auswandererhallen 1934 von der SS in Besitz genommen. Vorher wanderten vor allem jüdische Flüchtlinge über Hamburg nach Amerika aus. Die Hallen wurden später als Lager genutzt und größtenteils abgerissen. Im Juli 2007 wurde hier unter dem Namen „BallinStadt" ein Museum eröffnet.

Vertreibung / Vertriebene > Vertreibung ist eine erzwungene Auswanderung einzelner Personen oder ganzer ethnischer Gruppen aus von ihnen besiedelten Gebieten. Nach dem Zweiten Weltkrieg wurden Deutsche aus den ehemaligen Ostprovinzen und den deutschen Siedlungsgebieten in Ost- und Südosteuropa vertrieben. Schon vor Kriegsende beschlossen die Alliierten die Rückführung der deutschen Minderheiten, um zukünftige kulturelle und ethnische Konflikte zu verhindern. Siehe auch → **Aussiedler / Spätaussiedler**

Visum > Eine behördliche Erlaubnis zum Überschreiten der Grenze eines Landes. Der Erhalt eines Visums war und ist Voraussetzung für die Einwanderung und Teil des Einwanderungsverfahrens.

W

White Star Line > Im Zuge des australischen Goldrausches wurde 1845 die „Aberdeen White Star Line" gegründet, um Gold und andere Waren aus Australien nach Europa zu bringen. Den Durchbruch im transatlantischen Geschäft erlebte die Reederei erst, nachdem sie von hölzernen Segelschiffen auf eiserne Dampfer umstieg. Mehrere Schiffe gewannen das → **Blaue Band** (unter anderem die „Adreatic" 1872, „Germanic" 1875, „Teutonic" und „Majestic" 1891), bis ein neuer Eigner auf Größe und Luxus statt auf Geschwindigkeit setzte. Nach dem Verlust der beiden bekanntesten Schiffe, der „Titanic" und des Schwesternschiffes „Britannic", stand die „White Star Line" immer wieder vor dem Ruin und wurde schließlich mit der → **Cunard Line** zur „Cunard White Star Line" vereint.

Wolgadeutsche > Diese Sammelbezeichnung fasst deutsche Bevölkerungsgruppen aus dem Wolga- und Schwarzmeergebiet zusammen. Die russische Zarin Katharina die Große rief 1762/1763 deutsche Kolonisten zur Landbesiedlung nach Russland. Allein bis 1864 wurden über 300 Kolonien gegründet. Durch die Reformen Alexanders II. verloren die Kolonisten seit 1871 einen Großteil ihrer Sonderrechte. Dies veranlasste eine größere Anzahl zur Auswanderung auch nach Nord- und Südamerika. Die Aufrechterhaltung ihrer kulturellen (und sprachlichen) Eigenständigkeit gehörte zu den Motiven ihrer Auswanderung.

Z

Zurückgewiesene > Nicht jeder Passagier, der die Neue Welt erreichte, durfte auch tatsächlich einreisen. In einem Einwanderungsverfahren legten die aufnehmenden Staaten fest, welche Bedingungen erfüllt werden mussten. Meist führten bestimmte Krankheiten, körperliche oder geistige Behinderungen sowie fehlende Bürgschaften oder eine kriminelle Vorgeschichte des Antragstellers zu einer Ablehnung. In allen Fällen wurden die Kosten für die Rückreise der jeweiligen Reederei auferlegt. Kinder ab zehn Jahren mussten alleine zurückreisen, wenn der Rest der Familie aufgenommen wurde. Die Ablehnungsquote war allerdings recht gering. So betrug sie etwa in New York auf der Einwandererstation → **Ellis Island** nur zwei bis drei Prozent. In der Bundesrepublik Deutschland werden Zurückgewiesene heute Abgeschobene genannt, die in einem sogenannten Abschiebeverfahren meist per Flugzeug in ihre alte Heimat zurückgeführt werden, wenn ihr Asylantrag endgültig negativ beschieden wurde.

GLOSSARY

A

Acculturation / Assimilation > Acculturation is a term used in migration research referring to the various processes of integration in immigrant societies. Ethnologists, sociologists and historians alike use this word to denote the assimilation and adaptation of various cultures in one common society. Immigrants and local citizens experience mutual cultural exchange and interchange in the country of assimilation. Completion of this process may involve several generations and thus decades. The first step in this exchange involves the acceptance or tolerance of eating habits, and religious and political holidays. Immigrants have different strategies according to individual preference. Whereas some wish to become integrated and accepted in the society of assimilation as quickly as possible, others tend to separate or isolate themselves from the members of the host society. Ideally, integration takes place while maintaining one's cultural roots. The success or failure of the integration process depends on the society and politics of the country of assimilation.

The term assimilation is considered outdated in modern migration research as it denotes the abandonment of the immigrant's original cultural identity. Studies in various countries of immigration such as the U.S.A., but also Germany, have shown that the concept of immigrants dispensing with their original cultural background after migrating to a new country is wrong. See also → **Melting pot / Salad bowl**

AEMI – The Association of European Migration Institutions > A cooperation forum of European institutions and organizations which focuses on historic and current migration, organizes international symposia and joint research projects. > www.aemi.eu

Air travel > When the heyday of ocean-going vessels as a form of emigrant transportation receded in the 1960s, Bremerhaven and Hamburg lost their importance as major ports of emigration. In addition to the tightening of U.S. immigration restrictions, transatlantic crossings had become easier and faster with the introduction of air travel. In 1926, *Deutsche Aero Lloyd* and *Junkers Luftverkehr* merged to create the German national airline *Deutsche Lufthansa AG*. After the Second World War *Lufthansa* was newly founded in 1955. The airline underwent complete privatization between 1994 and 1997.

Asylum > For centuries free states, hospices, convents and monasteries have granted sanctuary to those in need of protection due to persecution. Today, asylum has come to mean the recognition of political refugees. Pursuant to Article 16 of the German Constitution every person has a right to political asylum. This right of asylum, the freest anywhere in the world, was greatly amended in 1993. As a result, virtually no one from a country "free of persecution" or anyone entering the Federal Republic of Germany by way of "a third, safe country" has a right to asylum. During the court hearing determining a person's right to political asylum, which may last any-

where from two weeks to several years, asylum seekers must live in designated accommodations and may not leave their place of residence without prior approval. Social benefits are reduced and in some German federal states asylum seekers receive food stamps or food packages instead of money. Since 2001, asylum seekers and tolerated foreigners are allowed to work provided the job cannot be filled by a German national or a foreign resident with a residence permit. Those entitled to political asylum first receive a temporary residence permit for three years. If this is not revoked they then receive a permanent residence permit.

Aussiedler / Spätaussiedler > So-called *Aussiedler* are people of German extraction who have moved back to Germany from East and Southeast Europe, where their families have sometimes been living for generations, notably from the Middle Ages up until the nineteenth century, following a call by the Russian czars for laborers, craftsmen and settlers. Since 1950 over four million *Aussiedler* have "returned" to Germany, mainly from the Soviet Union and CIS countries. Pursuant to the *Federal Eviction and Refugee Act* of 1953 they were entitled to German citizenship, and their integration in the population promoted. As of 1993, *Aussiedler* from countries outside the CIS are only recognized if they are able to provide proof of discrimination due to their ethnic German origin. In addition, only *Spätaussiedler* are entitled to apply for German citizenship if born prior to 1993. In 1996, a further obstacle was introduced, a language test, which is a so mandatory for members of the family traveling with the person involved who are not of German descent.

B

Ballin, Albert > The youngest son of a Jewish merchant (1857–1918) who began his career with → **Hapag** in the year 1886. The Hamburg shipping line was quick to assign managerial tasks to this young employee. By 1888 Ballin had risen to an executive position, in 1899 he became the managing director of Hapag. Ballin contributed enormously to Hamburg's rise as a port of emigration. See also → **Veddel**

Bandoneon (-ion) > The bandoneon, a type of accordion, is part of the concertina family of instruments. German sailors and emigrants to Argentina brought the instrument with them in the 1870s where it soon played an essential role in the tango orchestra.

Belgranodeutsch > A mixture of German and Spanish originally spoken by German emigrants who settled predominantly in the district by the same name and still spoken today by the German community living in the Belgrano neighborhood of Buenos Aires.

Blue Ribbon > Winning the *Blue Ribbon* for the fastest transatlantic crossing was in the age of the steamship a major honor for shipping com-

Bremen Decree > The first government-enforced regulation designed to protect emigrants in Germany. The Bremen Decree of 1832 was crucial in promoting Bremerhaven's good reputation as a port of emigration. Shipping lines were now legally obligated to document the seaworthiness of their ships, carry sufficient provisions and maintain minimal standards for passengers on board.

C

Castle Garden > America's first receiving station. As a central point of arrival Castle Garden offered incoming immigrants protection from profiteers and the opportunity to purchase train tickets for their journey inland. Here, too,

Sammlung Deutsches Auswandererhaus, Schenkung Graff M. Sieghold

Fotopostkarte der „Bremen" an der Columbuskaje in Bremerhaven. Der Dampfer bekam auf seiner Jungfernfahrt von Bremerhaven nach New York im Jahr 1929 das „Blaue Band" für die schnellste Antlantiküberquerung. / Photo postcard of the *Bremen* anchored at the Columbus wharf in Bremerhaven. The steamer received the *Blue Ribbon* for the fastest transatlantic crossing on its maiden voyage from Bremerhaven to New York in 1929.

panies. The *Sirius* was the first steamer to receive this award in 1838. Up until the turn of the century English ships had dominated this field, then the era of the great ships of the → **North German Lloyd** (*Norddeutscher Lloyd*) and → **Hapag** shipping lines dawned. The last great steamship to win the *Blue Ribbon* was the *United States* in 1952.

immigrants were registered in individual ship manifests. These passenger records, known as "manifests," are valuable documents for family and genealogical researchers the world over. (→ **Databases / Family research**). An estimated eight million immigrants entered America by way of Castle Garden between 1855 and 1890. Castle Garden was later replaced by → **Ellis Island**.

Chain Migration > Emigrants who reported back home of successful new lives or sent letters and clippings from the New World encouraged hundreds of thousands of friends and relatives to follow in their footsteps. In many towns and areas, particularly in Prussia, Mecklenburg and Württemberg chain migration caused the population to drop drastically. Invariably the phenomenal increase in emigrants from Europe during the latter half of the nineteenth century and continuing up through the early twentieth century is attributed to the multiplier effect of chain reaction emigration and represents the most widespread pattern of emigration there has ever been.
The onset of the 21st century brought about a major change in the form of communication: SMS, Twitter and Skype replaced letters home bearing good news. Instead of taking weeks for a letter to be delivered, today the World Wide Web transmits news in a fraction of seconds. The migration movements are picking up speed accordingly, as exemplified by the arrival, within a matter of weeks, of hundreds of thousands of refugees and migrants in 2015 in the Federal Republic of Germany. Studies have shown that people used their smartphones to remain in close contact with their country of origin and their destination country before, during and after their flight, triggering chain migrations.

Collection German Emigration Center > In the last four years our collection has grown to more than 2,800 exhibits, consisting to a great extent of photos and letters. However, there are also pieces of luggage, passenger lists, passports, souvenirs and personal documents which make up a significant part of our archive.
In most cases, visitors who have toured the museum come to us afterwards having remembered a forgotten memento or treasure in their attic at home or who recall a long-forgotten part of their family story. That is how we come to possess the exciting stories of all these "adventurers." We are not only interested in the abstract vita of an emigrant, but rather in the many objects which formed a part of a migrant's life and make these individual fates come alive for our visitors. That is why our exhibition combines display object and life story. The one without the other would make our museum far less expressive and vivid.

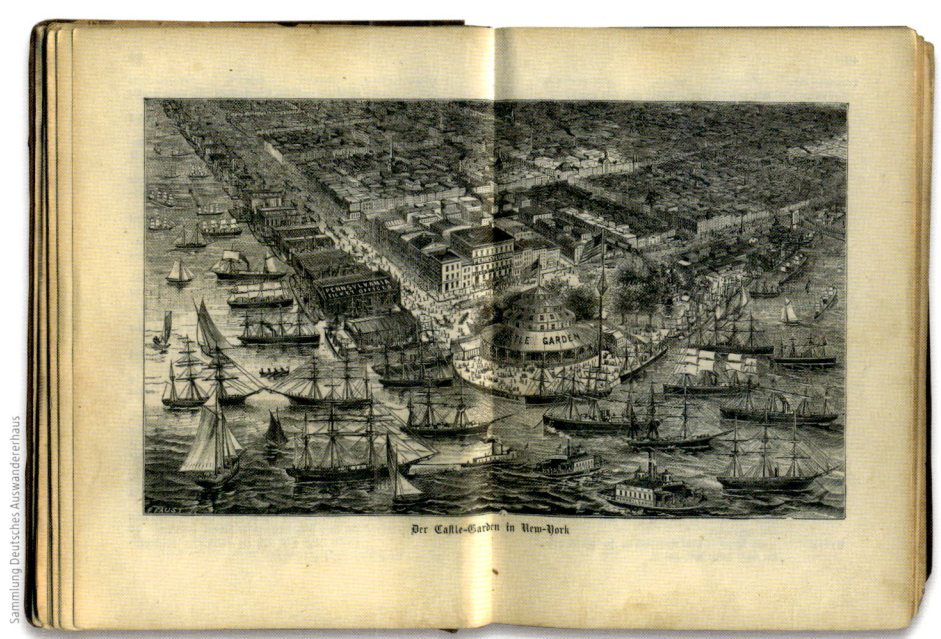

Castle Garden in New York. Aus: Adolf Ott: „Der Führer nach Amerika", Basel 1882. / Castle Garden in New York. Excerpt from Adolf Ott: *Der Führer nach Amerika* (The Guidebook to America), Basle 1882.

Colonia Liebig > Located in the northern part of the Corrientes province in Argentina. On 27 January 1924, the German-South American colony and cooperative *Neu Karlsruhe*, as the town was first named, was founded. When this settlement project, originally planned for Paraguay, failed, the first two to three hundred German settlers obtained land in Corrientes from the Liebig Company (*Liebig Extract of Meat Company*) which gave the colony its name. The founding of the *Cooperativa Agrícola de la Colonia Liebig* followed in December 1926, Walter Ostermann was the company's first president. To this day, the cooperative produces mate tea.

Cunard Line > The *British and North American Royal Mail Steam Packet Company* (renamed in 1878), formed by the Canadian Samuel Cunard in 1839 as a reliable mail service between Great Britain and North America. The first four steamships were put into service as early as 1840 and a regular weekly mail service set up from Liverpool to Halifax and Boston. Passengers were welcome to travel on these steamships from the start. The *Cunard Line* dominated mail and passenger transport service up through 1870, yet suffered from the very demanding conditions made by the line's financial backers.

Hurt by the Great Depression and under pressure from the British government, the *Cunard Line* merged with the **→ White Star Line** in 1932, thus becoming the *Cunard White Star Line* and focusing increasingly on passenger cruises. The Cunard Line joined the leading passenger cruise line *Carnival Corporation* in 1998.

Cuxhaven > Since 1889 the Hamburg-based Hapag shipping line **→ Hapag** had cleared its fast steamships to New York in Cuxhaven in the mouth of Elbe River, which at that time belonged to Hamburg. In return, Hamburg paid for the completion of Cuxhaven's harbor facilities. In 1902, the Hapag Hall overseas train station was completed. To date there are no final figures as to the total number of emigrants who passed through Cuxhaven. Most ships sailing from there were headed for ports in North America. The *Cunard White Star Line* (**→ Cunard Line**) was the first shipping line to resume regular service after World War II in 1948. From September 1948 until March 1950, the two liners *Samaria* and *Scythia* made 27 crossings transporting a total of 26,700 **→ Displaced Persons** to Canada. The port of Cuxhaven was unable to compete with the steady growth of **→ Air travel** hence discontinuing overseas liner service in 1968.

D

Databases / Family research > Researching ancestors who emigrated to other countries is possible on a number of Internet databases:

Bremen Passenger Records 1920–1939 (Die MAUS)
> www.passagierlisten.de
The archives of the Bremen Chamber of Commerce number 2,953 passenger records of ships departing from the Port of Bremen, 70 percent of which date back to between 1920 and 1939 and refer to ships departing from Bremerhaven for the U.S.A., Canada, South America and Australia. Since July 1999, these passenger lists have been collected and recorded by the Society of Genealogical Research of Bremen in the State Archives of Bremen. The passenger records for ships departing from the Port of Bremen were, with very few exceptions, all destroyed. The passenger records from 1945 on are still subject to data protection.
This data source is accessible online.

Ancestry
> www.ancestry.com / ancestry.de
The U.S. database Ancestry works together with the National Archives in Washington, D.C. where the passenger records for ships landing in U.S. ports from all over the world are filed, among them the passenger lists for ships sailing from Hamburg. In addition, the National Archives also keep a record of the U.S. federal censuses which have been carried out every 10 years since 1790. In addition it contains selected German emigration records, German telephone and address directories and the Bremen records of muster rolls and registers of seamen. Ancestry processes the passenger (through 1957) and census records electronically. The data is scanned and made available online. Ancestry.com also features other data on its web site, e.g. military records, birth, marriage & death records and U.S. phone directories. Meanwhile, papers and documents from German archives and former German-language archives located in Eastern Europe have become available. A fee is charged for using ancestry's online material.

Das historische Auswandererhaus wurde bereits wenige Jahre nach seiner Eröffnung 1865 aufgrund zu weniger Übernachtungsgäste wieder geschlossen. Heute ist ein Teil der ehemaligen „Karlsburg" in den Neubau der Hochschule Bremerhaven integriert. / The historic Emigrants' Hostel was closed in 1865, just years after it opened, because of too few overnight guests. Today, structural remnants of the former Karlsburg have been integrated in the new University of Applied Sciences of Bremerhaven building.

Castle Garden
> www.castlegarden.org
Castle Garden, the first official receiving station in the United States from 1850 until 1890 was the predecessor to Ellis Island. Its database features over 10 million entries for immigrant applications for the period from 1830 till 1892.
Online use of the web site is free of charge.

Ellis Island Passenger Records
> www.ellisisland.org
The *American Family Immigration History Center* was founded in 2001 as part of the *Statue of Liberty—Ellis Island Foundation, Inc.* In 25 million data records available at this research center on Ellis Island visitors can trace ancestors who immigrated to the U.S. between 1892 and 1924 and entered the country through New York.
After setting up a personal password, users have free online access to the database.

Deportation > Not every emigrant passenger who arrived in the New World was actually allowed to enter the country. The countries of immigration laid down specific immigration requirements which those seeking immigration were required to fulfil. The most common reasons for refusal and hence deportation were certain diseases, physical or mental disabilities, lack of sponsors in the country of immigration or a criminal record. Shipping companies were obligated to pay for the passenger's return ticket to his or her country of origin. Children over the age of 10 had to travel alone in the event the rest of the family had been allowed entrance. The percentage of entrance refusals was, fortunately, low and accounted for only two percent in New York. See also **→ Rejected refugees**

Displaced Persons (DPs) > This term is also used in Germany and refers to the approximately seven million persons the western Allied forces encountered in their zones of occupation in May 1945. Either displaced or deported to Germany from all over Europe between 1933 and 1945, the DPs neither wished for nor were able to return to their homes once the war was over. Survivors of concentration camps and labor camps, prisoners of war and laborers from East European countries were initially placed in DP camps in various areas of Germany. Former concentration camps were frequently used for this purpose which caused DPs great suffering as they were reminded daily of the horrors of the Holocaust in addition to the close living quarters and uncertainty as to their future. Hundreds of thousands emigrated to Great Britain, the U.S.A. and Canada. From Bremerhaven alone over 800,000 Displaced Persons set out for new lives in new countries.

E

Ellis Island > The largest receiving station in the U.S. With the influx of immigrants particularly from Eastern Europe as of 1880, **→ Castle Garden** on the southern tip of Manhattan soon became too small. The receiving station at Ellis Island, a small island off Manhattan, was opened in 1892. The large passenger steamships bringing in European immigrants first docked at Hoboken in Manhattan where first- and second-class passengers were allowed to disembark as they had already undergone immigration formalities on board. The steerage passengers, however, disembarked at Ellis Island where they underwent a medical examination and were processed by immigration inspectors before receiving permission to enter the U.S. More than 16 million arrivals registered on Ellis Island by 1954, it had become the largest receiving station in the United States. An estimated two to three percent were refused entrance to the country. Stories of those who were deported (**→ Deportation**) back to their native countries soon gave Ellis Island the name *Island of Tears.*

Emigrants > People who intend to settle in a foreign country on a permanent basis.

Emigration agents > So-called emigration agents were hired by shipping lines and ship brokers to recruit willing emigrants throughout Europe.

Emigration Center > This set-up, unique in the world, was established by the Bremen merchant Johann George Claussen in Bremerhaven in 1850 and offered up to 2,000 travelers affordable room and board and better sanitary facilities than the taverns and honky-tonks in the harbor area.

Emigration waves (mass emigration) > Migration statistics are frequently portrayed as line charts and the upward trends referred to as

waves. In researching the reasons causing peak migratory movement there is often evidence of a delayed reaction to economic crises, with emigration commonly setting in about five to ten years later. Crop failure and ensuing famine were additional reasons for the onset of emigration in the nineteenth century. Ireland was hardest-hit by this occurrence. Several potato crops failed in short succession between 1846 and 1851; close to one million people died of starvation, a further million emigrated to the United States. See also → **Chain Migration**

Entry and residence regulations for Argentina > The government-aided program for European emigration to Argentina, beginning during the first half of the 18th century and stipulated in Article 20 of the Constitution of 1853. "Mass emigration," however, did not take place until 1870 when the country had become politically stable. The increase in socialistic anarchistic labor strikes beginning in 1890 led to the Law of Residency (*ley de residencia*) which entitled the authorities to expel immigrants or refuse their entry to the country if they were considered a threat to public order. Despite these negative developments, blamed entirely on immigrant laborers, the government-aided immigration program continued to be significant.

It wasn't until 1930 and the military coup against President Hipólito Yrigoyen that the liberal era and, largely with it, the unrestricted immigration policy ended. A new law went into effect on 1 January 1933 restricting immigration to family unification (*llamadas familiares*) and colonists in agricultural settlements. As a result of the Évian Conference the *Circular 11* was signed in Argentina on 12 July 1938, a secret directive designed to stop the immigration of "undesired persons" (Jewish refugees, in particular) to Argentina.

Exile > In contrast to the term "emigration" migration researchers define the term "exile" as a form of extraterritorial migration with the objective of returning to the native country. Hence the U.S.A. is a country of emigration and not of exile as no legal provision has been made for the temporary acceptance of people seeking political or religious asylum.

Expulsion / Expelled > Expulsion is the forced emigration of individuals or entire ethnic groups from areas populated by them. After the war, ethnic Germans were expelled from historically Eastern German areas in present-day Poland, the Czech Republic, Slovakia, Hungary, Yugoslavia, the German province of Eastern Prussia, the later Kaliningrad Oblast of Russia, Lithuania, and other East European countries.

The decision for a population transfer of German minorities to the Allied occupation zones in post-war Germany to avoid cultural and ethnic conflicts and violence in the future was made before the war was over. See also → **Aussiedler / Spätaussiedler**

Auslaufender Dampfer mit Auswanderern, vermutlich in einem englischen Hafen, um 1880. Gemälde von Charlie W. Wyllie. / Steamship with emigrants on board sailing out of an harbor, possibly in England, about 1880. Painting by Charlie W. Wyllie.

F

Fugitives > In contrast to refugees, a fugitive is a person fleeing justice. (Former) German Nazis who fall into this category are Adolf Eichmann, Josef Mengele and Erich Priebke.

G

Genealogy > The study of ancestry and lineage. One speaks of family research when research exceeds the purely biological background of mankind.

Geneva Convention > The purpose of the *Geneva Convention*, adopted at a U.N. special conference in July 1951, is to create a uniform legal status for all → **refugees** who are not awarded diplomatic protection in their native country. All 146 member states are committed to granting → **asylum** to refugees. The *Geneva Convention* and its 1967 Protocol are the legal foundation for the *United Nations High Commissioner for Refugees* (UNHCR).

German Emigration Center Foundation > The *German Emigration Center Foundation* was formed in January 2006 with the aim of promoting large, cost-intensive projects and in the interest of promoting the museum's aims on an international scale. The *German Emigration Center Foundation* is also a public-private partnership project, formed by the joint efforts of the *Initiativkreis Deutsches Auswandererhaus e.V.* (German Emigration Center Initiative), representatives of the Bremerhaven business community, the city of Bremerhaven and the German Emigration Center's operating company.

The purpose of this foundation is to enable the German Emigration Center in Bremerhaven to carry out profound research on the history of

migration, thereby focusing specifically on its historic and current significance and to arrange special events, exhibitions, projects and publications, and to make these accessible to a broad public in Germany as well as abroad. Further, the foundation's tasks include, for example, acquiring exhibits and collections related to emigration, expanding and updating research data in the database and the archives, endorsing conferences and exhibitions dedicated to the scientific study of migration. Furthermore, the foundation sees it as its task to promote student exchange among the countries of Europe and overseas and to award research grants. Every two years since 2015, the Foundation awards the "Kalliope-Preis for Applied Migration Research", which is endowed with 10,000 euro.
> www.stiftung-dah.org

Globalization > Increasing global networking of individuals and business affects economic relations (e.g. company mergers) as well as personal social relations (e.g. Internet). Critics of globalization argue that jobs are being transferred to countries with lower wage levels and that, consequently, major companies based in wealthy countries profit while countries with lesser economic power lose out. Advocates of globalization

maintain that greater economic and social union on multiple levels may result from the coalescence of markets and businesses.

H

Hapag / Hapag-Lloyd > Triggered by the rapidly growing importance of Bremerhaven as a port of emigration, the *Hamburg-Amerikanische Packetfahrt-Actien-Gesellschaft* (Hapag) was formed in 1847 with the aim of participating in the business of emigration by setting up a direct sailing ship route from Hamburg to North America. Whereas **→ North German Lloyd** (NGL) started out with steamship service, it wasn't until 1889 that the Hapag put steamships into service. The shipping line also sold holiday cruises. Hapag opened an emigration village providing accommodation for up to 5,000 in 1901 (see also **→ Veddel**). Hapag and NGL lost their entire fleets as reparation to the Allied forces after both world wars.

The two shipping companies cooperated in rebuilding their fleets and passenger service after 1954 to avoid competition. Hapag merged with NGL in 1970 to become *Hapag-Lloyd AG*. Major Hapag ships include the *Augusta Victoria* (1889) and the *Fuerst Bismarck* (1891), the fastest ship

sailing on the North American route at the time. On her maiden voyage out the *Deutschland* won the **→ Blue Ribbon** in 1900, and the *Imperator* (1913) and *Vaterland* (1914) were both the largest ships of their time.

Home / Homeland > For many people, the term home, homeland or native country is but a mere geographical location to which they feel close, where they feel at home. Thus, home is the direct opposite of anything foreign or a life in exile. Home is often but not always the place where a person was born (adopted country).
The German word *Heimat*—home or homeland—has its roots in romanticism and is a subject of controversy in Germany because of its ethnic and national overtones.

Hyphen-Americans > Numerous ethnic groups living in the U.S.A. still feel deeply connected to their native country despite the fact that they are American citizens, and maintain cultural habits, traditions and customs. Italian-Americans, African-Americans, Polish-Americans and other hyphen-Americans are very loyal U.S. citizens, define their citizenship primarily politically and consider themselves members of the American immigrant society.

I

IMIS—Institute for Migration Research and Intercultural Studies > The Institute for Migration Research and Intercultural Studies is an interdisciplinary and interdepartmental research institute at the University of Osnabrück in Germany focusing on historic and present-day migratory movement as well as the political, social and cultural aspects of migration and integration.
> www.imis.uni-osnabrueck.de

Initiativkreis Deutsches Auswandererhaus e. V. > The commitment of companies and individuals has had a major impact on the history of the German Emigration Center. In 1985, citizens of Bremerhaven founded the "Förderverein Deutsches Auswanderermuseum" (**→ Society of Friends of the German Emigration Center**), in 1988, local companies launched the "Initiativkreis Erlebniswelt Auswanderung" – currently

Sammlung Deutsches Auswandererhaus,
Dauerleihgabe des Initiativkreises Deutsches Auswandererhaus e. V.

Die Registrierungshalle auf der Einwandererstation „Ellis Island" vor New York um 1910, in der jeder Passagier der III. KLasse überprüft wurde. / The registration hall of the immigration station at "Ellis Island" off the coast of New York, around 1910. Every third class and steerage passenger was inspected here.

Ankunft der „Dresden" am Hoboken Pier, der gegenüber von Manhatten in New Jersey lag. Von dort wurden die Auswanderer nach Ellis Island gebracht, um 1930. / Arrival of the *Dresden* at Hoboken Pier, located in New Jersey directly across from Manhattan. The immigrants were taken to Ellis Island from there. Around 1930.

known as "Initiativkreis Deutsches Auswandererhaus e. V." This association was particularly active on a political level and strongly endorsed the construction of the museum. Today it supports the → **German Emigration Center Foundation**, as well as the museum's educational programs for Bremerhaven schools.

Integration → Acculturation / Assimilation

L

Library of German emigration and immigration history at the German Emigration Center > As a result of generous donations and purchases, the German Emigration Center now houses an extensive reference library about European and German migration history in particular. Together with the significant library collection of the Freundeskreis (see Friends of the Museum), containing about 2,000 volumes, it forms the library of German emigration and immigration history at the German Emigration Center. The reference

library is open to the public once a month. For opening hours visit:

> www.dah-bremerhaven.de/bibliothek

M

Meier, Hermann Heinrich > The Bremen businessman and politician (1809–1898) founded the → **North German Lloyd** shipping line in 1857 which soon developed into one of the world's largest shipping lines.

Melting pot / Salad bowl > The U.S.A. was long referred to by sociologists as a melting pot in which immigrants with diverse ethnic backgrounds mixed to create a culture all their own. This perception has been increasingly revised and replaced by the multicultural concept of the salad bowl, a non-homogeneous yet in itself structured and harmonious unit.

Migrant workers > This term refers to people who immigrate to a certain country for a certain

length of time to work. This type of immigration has always had economic reasons.

During the so-called "Economic Miracle" in West Germany in the 1950s there was a shortage of labor. From the late 1950s until 1973, the year when manpower recruitment outside Germany was stopped, an estimated 14 million migrant workers came to Germany from Turkey, Italy and Spain, of which eleven million returned to their home countries while the rest remained in Germany, brought their families to the country, settling there permanently. Albeit to a far lesser degree, foreign laborers were also recruited by the German Democratic Republic, principally from Vietnam.

Migration > The migratory movement of individuals or groups of people connected with a short- or long-term, or permanent change of residence. Migration refers to both emigration and immigration. Domestic migration refers to a change of residence within the same country whereas

Die „Cap Polonio" an den Landungsbrücken im Hamburg, 1920er. / The *Cap Polonio* docked at the Landungsbrücken in Hamburg, 1920s.

transit migration means leaving one country to take up residence in another. The reasons for emigrating and the degree to which this decision is voluntary vary greatly and one distinguishes between → **Emigrants**, → **Displaced Persons**, → **Migrant workers**, and → **Refugee**.

Missler Halls > In order to solve the accommodation problem for emigrants in transit in Bremen awaiting departure from Bremerhaven the *North German Lloyd* shipping line, together with its main agent Friedrich Missler, built emigration halls in Bremen-Findorff in 1906 / 1907. The halls were designed to offer emigrants from Eastern and Southeastern Europe particularly adequate room and board at a very low price. This type of set-up had already proved highly successful in Hamburg-Veddel. The so-called *Missler Halls* – new accommodations with a capacity of over 2,700 persons – were completed in 1907. After Missler's death, → **North German Lloyd** took over the building, renaming it *Lloydheim*, and using it to accommodate its passengers.

N

New Immigrants > Towards the turn of the century an increasing number of South and East Europeans immigrated to America, in particular

Italians and Greeks as well as Catholics and Jews from East Europe. These immigrants outnumbered so-called old immigrants from northern and northwestern European countries for the first time in 1896. Many Americans watched this development with unease as the new immigrants were regarded a threat to American society and hence marginalized. A heated discussion on immigration restrictions ensued, culminating ultimately in the → **Quota Act** of 1921, a law regulating immigration on the basis of a quota system, which was definitely to the disadvantage of East and Southeast European immigrants.

North German Lloyd (NGL) > The *Norddeutscher Lloyd* or *North German Lloyd*—steamship shipping line, formed in Bremen in 1857, was the first shipping company to offer regular service between Germany and New York. During the German Empire (1871–1918), NGL grew into one of the largest shipping companies in the world with routes to the U.S.A., South America and Australia. Whereas the majority of passengers were emigrants, NGL made millions on American and German tourist passages as well.

The company's home port was Bremerhaven where, in 1869, NGL opened the first port waiting hall at *Neuer Hafen* followed by a second one at Kaiserschleuse in 1897. With ships constantly

increasing in size, the Bremerhaven port and lock facilities had become too small so that NGL ships sailed from Nordenham, on the West banks of the Weser River across from Bremerhaven, between 1890 and 1896. From the outset NGL operated its own docks in Bremerhaven for ship maintenance and repair work. This repair yard ultimately became known as *Lloyd Werft Bremerhaven*, still in existence today and one of the foremost shipyards for ship conversion and lengthening. Among the most prominent NGL-owned ships were the four-stacked steamship *Kaiser Wilhelm der Grosse*, the *Columbus*, the *Europa* and the *Bremen*, the latter winning the → **Blue Ribbon** for the fastest transatlantic crossing in 1929. In 1970, the two top shipping competitors, NGL and Hapag, merged to form → **Hapag-Lloyd**.

P

Pilgrim fathers > Persecuted in England for religious separatism the Puritan pilgrim fathers emigrated to America in the seventeenth century and became the first English settlers in New England. The story of the *Mayflower* is legendary: in 1602 the ship set sail for America with 102 passengers—predominantly pilgrims—on board. The ship left Plymouth, England on September 16, arriving in Plymouth, Massachusetts on November 11.

Pogrom > The term *pogrom* (Russian for devastation, destruction, riot) means riots against religious, national or ethnic minorities and has come to stand for violence and looting closely related to anti-Jewish sentiment. In czarist Russia repeated pogroms between 1881 and 1913 led to mass emigration of Russian Jews to the United States and Palestine. In Nazi Germany the anti-Jewish pogroms of November 1938 were government-initiated. The last big pogrom directed against the Jews to take place in Europe was in Kielce, Poland in 1946.

Ports of emigration > The major ports of emigration for German emigrants up through the mid-nineteenth century were Rotterdam, Holland; Antwerp, Belgium; Le Havre, France; and Liverpool and Southampton in England. Emi-

grants from countries in Southern or Southeastern Europe customarily departed from Genoa, Italy. As a result of the **→ Bremen Decree** and the building of an **→ Emigration Center** as well as the internationally successful shipping line **→ North German Lloyd**, Bremerhaven began to develop into Germany's most important port of emigration as of the mid-nineteenth century. Bremerhaven was the home port for the *North German Lloyd* shipping line although its ships sailed under the flag of Bremen, as Bremerhaven is part of the city-state of Bremen. A total of 7.2 million people departed for the New World by way of Bremerhaven between 1830 and 1974. Shiploads of emigrants departed

with the East Coast of the U.S. ranking among those most preferred by European immigrants. While New York was the leading U.S. port of immigration, two million entered through Baltimore, the second-largest port of immigration, and one million through Philadelphia. Other favored destinations were Boston, and New Orleans and Galveston in the South, particularly for immigrants heading for Texas. In contrast to New Orleans, the port of Galveston was sufficiently deep to accept larger ships, thus rendering New Orleans irrelevant after 1855.

By 1900 over 100,000 immigrants had entered the U.S. through Galveston, of which the majority were Germans who had sailed from Bremer-

ports of Quebec or Halifax, the latter evolving into Canada's largest port. An estimated six millions persons entered Canada through these two ports. Australia has also always figured among the major countries of immigration since the beginning of mass migration with several million immigrants entering the fifth continent through the ports of Melbourne and Sydney.

Q

Quota Act > The *Emergency Quota Act* of May 19, 1921 greatly restricted annual immigration levels to the U.S., limiting it to three percent of every nationality living in the U.S. since 1910 and clearly favoring immigrants from Northern and Western Europe. Census data recorded the total number of immigrants at 357,802, of which more than half were from countries in Northern and Western Europe.

The *Quota Act* meant a 75-percent reduction in immigrants from Southern and Eastern Europe as compared to previous years. The quota system based on countries of origin reflects the fear of foreigners that had been rising steadily for decades. The U.S.A. tightened its immigration policy still further with the *National Origins Act* in 1924, limiting immigration to an annual 164,000 and a maximum two percent from every nationality residing in the U.S. since 1890.

R

Raphaels-Werk > This Christian agency, established in 1871 and named after the archangel Raphael, known to protect travelers, has always provided advice and consultation for migrants leaving Germany temporarily or permanently. The church-affiliated *Evangelische Auswandererberatung e.V.* (Protestant Service for Migration Advice), recently renamed Overseas Advice, was an agency offering advice and consultation to migrants.

> www.raphaels-werk.de
> www.ev-auslandsberatung.de

Ratline > A term coined by U.S. intelligence officers describing systems of escape routes for Nazis and other fascists fleeing Europe after World War II. The route went from Germany to Italy,

Sammlung Deutsches Auswandererhaus, Schenkung Christel Schmidt

Bahnsteig auf der Columbuskaje in Bremerhaven : Vor jeder Abfahrt eines Auswandererschiffes spielte eine Kapelle, unter anderem das Lied „Muss I denn, muss I denn", um 1955. / The platform on Columbuskaje in Bremerhaven. Among other songs, "Muss I denn, muss I denn" was always played by a band before a migrant ship departed, around 1955.

from Hamburg on board sailing ships and later steamships, but this was to change by the end of the nineteenth century. Whereas the passenger steamship company **→ Hapag** was located in Hamburg, Hapag ships invariably sailed from Cuxhaven as of 1889 for the simple reason that the latter was more easily accessible. More than five million passengers sailed for the New World on board ships flying the flag of Hamburg.

Ports of immigration > There were a number of major ports of immigration in the New World,

haven. South America attracted numerous immigrants as well, with 6.6 million Europeans immigrating to Argentina between 1850 and 1940, mostly through Buenos Aires. Brazil was also high on the list of preferred countries with people from more than 50 nations immigrating through Rio de Janeiro and Santos between 1819 and 1974, among them Italians, Portuguese, Spanish and Germans. The port of Montevideo in Uruguay, opened in 1868, was South America's most advanced port of transhipment. Immigrants to Canada commonly arrived in the

Southern Italy or Rome, to South America—and, in particular, Argentina. Countless Nazi escaped justice for crimes committed during the National Socialist dictatorship in Germany (1933–1945).

Refugee > In contrast to emigrants, refugees are forced to leave their country for a certain period of time or permanently due to persecution or the threat of persecution. In accordance with the 1951 → **Geneva Convention** refugees are persons, who due to the very real threat of persecution, seek refuge outside their native country or who seek refuge as a stateless person outside their usual country of residence. Reasons of persecution recognized by the *Geneva Convention* are race, religion, nationality, affiliation with a certain social group and political conviction.

Rejected refugees > In the Federal Republic of Germany rejected refugees are called deportees; in so-called "deportation proceedings" they are usually sent by plane back to their country of origin if their asylum application has been expressly rejected.

S

Ship classes > The technical development of ships altered the conditions for transatlantic and other ocean crossings immensely, particularly for steerage-class passengers. Whereas hundreds of emigrants were cramped in the between-deck bunks and suffered catastrophic sanitary conditions for a period of as many as 18 weeks, with many dying en route, sailing time to America dropped to eight to 15 days on board the fast steamers, which also provided adequate sanitary facilities for steerage passengers. Larger ship engines and improved drive technology on board → **North German Lloyd** liners as of 1897 shortened the transatlantic crossing to a mere six days. From 1906, NGL steamers were even equipped with a dining hall for steerage passengers. By the end of the 1920s, shared cabins replaced mass accommodations on board and a tourist class had been introduced.

Society of Friends of the German Emigration Center (Freundeskreis Deutsches Auswandererhaus e.V.) > Society of Friends, established in 2005, originated in the *German Emigration Center Development Association*, founded in 1985. While the Development Association spent 20 years promoting the construction of the Emigration Center in Bremerhaven, Society of Friends focuses on developing and adding on to the program of events offered by the museum since its opening in August 2005 featuring talks and informative events centering on the topic of migration, particularly Bremerhaven and Bremen as ports of emigration.

The extensive library of the Friends of the Museum library contains about 2,000 volumes. As a permanent loan it is now part of the → **library of German emigration and immigration history at the German Emigration Center**.

T

Transit migration > In the late 1900s and during the Weimar Republic large numbers of emigrants from Southern and Eastern Europe traversed the German Empire on their way to Hamburg and Bremerhaven from where they sailed for the New World.

V

Veddel > In order to reroute the steadily growing stream of emigrants past the center of Hamburg, in 1898 the Hamburg-based shipping line → **Hapag** built so-called emigration halls on the Elbe island of Veddel, which separates the North Elbe and the South Elbe Rivers.

Opened in 1901, this accommodation was constantly enlarged, finally totaling a full 55,000 square meters and about 30 individual buildings. The decentralized location and, for that time, unusually good sanitary facilities, were a direct result of the cholera epidemic which had broken out in 1892 and was attributed to Russian emigrants. Upon arrival at Veddel, each immigrant was subjected to a medical examination, and possibly placed in quarantine for 14 days. At the same time, impecunious immigrants were kept at a distance from the center of town.

In addition to dormitories and social facilities the complex included a large dining hall, bathrooms and a disinfecting station. There were a Catholic and Protestant church as well as a Jewish synagogue. Following enlargement in 1906/1907 meals for Jewish and Christian emigrants were prepared in separate kitchens and served in separate dining halls. The emigration halls served as field hospitals during World War I. Reopened for their original purpose the emigration halls were seized by the SS in 1934. Until then, primarily Jewish refugees had departed for America via Hamburg.

Used later as warehouses, the halls were eventually torn down. An emigration museum by the name of *BallinStadt* opened here in July 2007.

Visa > An official permit authorizing a person to pass the border into the country issuing the visa. A visa was and is required for immigration and is a primary element of the migration process.

Volga Germans > This collective term refers to ethnic Germans who lived along the River Volga and the Black Sea. In 1762/1763, Catherine the Great, Empress of Russia, invited Germans and other Europeans to immigrate to Russia and develop the land. By 1864, more than three hundred colonies had been founded. A main reason for their immigration had been special rights granted them for preserving cultural (and linguistic) independence. When, in 1871, these were revoked to a great extent by reforms instituted by Czar Alexander II, a large number decided to emigrate to North and South America.

W

White Star Line > The *Aberdeen White Star Line* was formed in 1845 during the course of the Australian Gold Rush for the purpose of transporting gold and other goods from Australia back to Europe. Its real breakthrough came when it switched from sailing ships to steamships for transatlantic routes. Several ships won the → **Blue Ribbon** (among them the *Adriatic*, 1872; the *Germanic*, 1875, the *Teutonic* and the *Majestic*, both 1891) until a later owner decided to emphasize size and luxury instead of speed. After the loss of its two most prominent vessels, the *Titanic* and its sister ship, the *Britannic*, the *White Star Line* was on the verge of bankruptcy. It merged with the → **Cunard Line** to form the *Cunard White Star Line*.

IMPRESSUM / CREDITS

Impressum Katalog / Credits Catalogue

Herausgeber / Published by
Deutsches Auswandererhaus Bremerhaven
edition DAH

Redaktion / Editorial Staff
Dr. Simone Eick, Julian Herbig

Lektorat / Editor
Ilka Seer, Julian Herbig

Kataloggestaltung / Graphic Design
Andreas Heller Architects & Designers, Hamburg
Alexandra Schäfer, Jutta Strauß

Übersetzung / Translator
Maria Lanman, Julie Penzel-Althoff (†)

Fotos Titel- und Rückseite / Photographs Front Page and Back Page
Kay Riechers (Titel), Werner Huthmacher
Sammlung Deutsches Auswandererhaus / Collection German Emigration Center

Druck / Printed by
Müller Ditzen AG, Bremerhaven

Verlag / Publisher
edition DAH

3., überarbeitete und erweiterte Auflage / 3rd revised and enlarged edition
Bremerhaven 2017

Auflage / Copies printed
6.000

© Deutsches Auswandererhaus / German Emigration Center
Bremerhaven 2017

ISBN 978-3-9817861-1-8

Impressum Deutsches Auswandererhaus
Credits German Emigration Center

Architektur, Konzept, Gestaltung / Architecture, Concept, Design
Andreas Heller Architects & Designers, Hamburg

Betrieben durch Deutsches Auswandererhaus gemeinnützige GmbH
Operated by Deutsches Auswandererhaus gemeinnützige GmbH

Gefördert durch die Stadt Bremerhaven, das Land Bremen und den Bund.
Realized with funds provided by the city of Bremerhaven, the state of
Bremen and the Federal Government.

Wir danken ganz herzlich allen Förderern und Freunden unseres Hauses für
Ihre Unterstützung und allen Schenkungsgebern, die unsere Sammlung
um Objekte ihrer Auswanderergeschichten bereichert haben. / We wish to thank
the supporters and friends of the German Emigration Center for their aid and
assistance as well as all those who have so graciously donated personal objects,
thus enriching our collection with their personal history of emigration.